Reading Pathways, Performance Assessments and Learning Progressions: Grades 3–5

Lucy Calkins with Alexandra Marron
and Colleagues from the Teachers College
Reading and Writing Project

Photography by Peter Cunningham

Illustrations by Elizabeth Franco

HEINEMANN ◆ PORTSMOUTH, NH

Dedicated to Carmen Fariña, Chancellor of the New York City Schools, with thanks for helping thousands of teachers and teacher-educators keep our eyes on what matters most—our children, and their development.

Heinemann
361 Hanover Street
Portsmouth, NH 03801–3912
www.heinemann.com

Offices and agents throughout the world

© 2015 by Lucy Calkins

Cataloging-in-Publication data is on file with the Library of Congress.

ISBN-13: 978-0-325-07742-0

Series editorial team: Anna Gratz Cockerille, Karen Kawaguchi, Tracy Wells, Felicia O'Brien, Debra Doorack, Jean Lawler, Marielle Palombo, and Sue Paro
Production: Elizabeth Valway, David Stirling, and Abigail Heim
Cover and interior designs: Jenny Jensen Greenleaf
Photography: Peter Cunningham
Illustrations: Elizabeth Franco
Composition: Publishers' Design and Production Services, Inc.
Manufacturing: Steve Bernier

Printed in the United States of America on acid-free paper
19 18 17 16   VP   3 4 5

Acknowledgments

HOW PROUD AND GRATEFUL I AM to thank the cadre of people who helped make this book possible. First and foremost, I want to thank Ali Marron, contributing author of *Reading Pathways*. Ali worked on every iteration and every part of this book, bringing her special ability to stand in the shoes of a teacher and of a child and to think, "Is this actually workable? Is it the best it can be?" She has been the one colleague who has joined me on all aspects of this complicated project, helping to pull the entire effort together, and she has done so with enormous finesse. Meanwhile, she's been a terrific writing companion and I thank her.

Ali and I both thank Amy Tondreau who has been at the helm of this project with us, helping to develop, organize, write, research, pilot, and revise the manuscript. Amy brings a scholarly intellect and an attention to detail to everything she does, and wins great accolades from the research team at the Project for her scholarship and her standards.

Kelly Boland Hohne joined me in developing the learning progressions themselves, bringing her usual power and clarity of thought to that effort. The learning progressions have been through scores of revisions, and they stand on the shoulders of years of research. It is impossible to put into words the amount of time, care, and thought that has gone into the progressions, and Kelly has been the lead person in all of that work.

Mary Ehrenworth has a gift for capturing in words the complicated work that readers do—and especially that skilled readers do—and her help on the learning progressions was critical. Mary also is a great advocate for the progressions, seeing beautiful ways in which they can lift the level of teaching and learning, and we thank her for championing them with such power. Janet Steinberg and Mary Ehrenworth both made a great point of studying the new generation of assessments, and helped us to make sure the learning progressions and the performance assessments are aligned to them, and we thank them for this.

Liz Dunford Franco contributed the art that makes these tools so engaging and accessible. We revel in her talent, and are tickled to see the ways in which she makes these tools so much more compelling.

Audra Robb, Emily Butler Smith, and Anna Gratz Cockerille all pitched in to help with the development of the performance assessments that are part of this project, as did the coauthors connected to each performance assessment. In hindsight, the performance assessments may appear rather straightforward and simple, but the process of developing them was mindblowing in its complexity.

Of course, anyone who knows Lucy as a writer knows that I will never stop singing the praises of Kate Montgomery, whose voice lingers in my ear as I write.

We are especially grateful to Ray Pecheone, Executive Director of the Stanford Center for Assessment, Learning, and Equity (SCALE), for his guidance as we developed the performance assessments and particularly for his feedback in the final moments, just before going to press. Ray has been a generous friend to our organization and we've learned from him and from his organization.

When ten people work intensely at the same time on a project that involves as many drafts and melds as many voices as this one does, keeping things and people in order, updated, and accessible requires gigantic coordination efforts, and Sara Johnson is to be thanked for that work.

Finally, we thank the thousands of children who participated in our efforts to pilot the many iterations of the performance assessments. Above all, we thank the teachers who have already and will in the future help to show that yes, indeed, assessment can be a tool for the good.

Contents

PART I

About the Assessment System

Chapter 1

A Toolkit for Reading Assessment

THIS BOOK is an effort to take back assessment and put it squarely into your hands and the hands of your children. I've written this with the knowledge that if your children are going to rise to today's educational challenges, they need the clarity, direction, and resolve that can come from assessing their own growth in reading. The tools within this resource can provide students with clear pathways toward meeting today's exceedingly high expectations, allowing them to answer the question, "How am I doing?" even when it is being asked in relation to the black box of higher-level comprehension. More importantly, this book and the tools that accompany it will help your children answer the question, "How can I improve?"

Reading Pathways aims to take back not only assessment but also *standards-based* assessment. The book has been written to help you understand and support the high levels of reading that are put forward in the Common Core State Standards, International Baccalaureate standards, and in other iterations of global standards. More specifically, *Reading Pathways* helps you understand the ways those standards have been clarified by the arrival of new assessments (including those from the Partnership for Assessment for College and Careers (PARCC), The Smarter Balanced Assessment Consortium (SBAC), and various state assessments that are designed to assess globally benchmarked standards) and to think about the implications that these may have for teachers who also care about young people growing up with a sense of personal efficacy and a deep engagement in reading.

I've come to believe that you need to support your students' development along pathways that were probably not, until recently, foremost in your mind. These global standards may, for instance, require fifth-graders to read a collection of nonfiction texts, noting the authors' different perspectives on a topic and thinking about the vested interests that may inform those perspectives. To help fifth-graders make progress along these lines, you and your colleagues need the tools to help you communicate those literacy goals and pathways to children and to watch their progress along those trajectories. And if fifth-graders are to synthesize the learning from those diverse texts into a well-organized body of knowledge that takes into account different perspectives, then you and your children need to have access to low-stakes assessments that allow you to think about the progress students are (and are not yet) making toward that important work.

I hope that *Reading Pathways* encourages you to hold conversations with colleagues, especially those teaching at your grade level, so that you settle on some shared expectations for how students' entire school experience translates into expectations. For example, at what point are readers expected to realize that even if a nonfiction text is presented as "the truth," it actually is *that author's* truth, seen from that author's perspective? At what point in a child's development are you helping the child become aware of the difference between *her* opinion and *the author's* opinion—and what are the small steps readers can take toward that awareness? And when does the child in your school go from seeing research as gathering up and synthesizing information with no regard to the nature of those sources, to a process that involves assessing the credibility, bias, and perspective of those sources? *Reading Pathways* gives kids clear pathways forward toward meeting those and other ambitious goals.

Providing progressions, rubrics, and exemplars that turn elusive standards into concrete, doable behaviors, allows your children to work with a sense of efficacy—"I can do this, if I work hard." This is nowhere more important than in reading, because all too often, children come to you believing that their abilities as readers are fixed and beyond their control. "I'm a bad reader," a child will say. "My sister is the good reader in my family, but I'm bad at it." "I can read," a child will say, "but I can't get those questions." The progressions and other tools in *Reading Pathways* send an entirely different message. This book challenges the notion that success in reading is hardwired into a child's DNA. Instead, the book makes it crystal clear to kids that when they apply strategies, work hard, revise their first understandings, and get help, their reading will get visibly and dramatically better, right before their eyes.

More than this, *Reading Pathways* provides *you*, as well as your kids, with that same sense of efficacy and power. In this world of ours, when kids are being asked to do things on high-stakes tests that are so ludicrously ambitious that we, as educators, aren't sure that *we* could do those things, it is easy to feel demoralized, overwhelmed, and paralyzed. *Reading Pathways*—and especially the learning progressions within this book—can turn those feelings around by giving you and your colleagues a crystal clear path forward.

A first step is for you to accept the notion that ongoing reading assessment can actually be a potent force for good in your classroom. It is easy to roll your eyes at the way the world has gone data-crazy and to resent how no one talks anymore about the all-important work of helping students develop strong self-concepts as readers and writers or about the need to bring kids together in caring classroom communities. It is easy to be angry about the fact that policy makers who shape the nature of schooling can think of little but data, data, data. But if we're going to talk back to the current obsession with data, it is probably helpful to pause and think about whether there are some parts of that focus that we *can* get behind.

If you pause to consider the logic to the madness, you will see that actually there is a mountain of evidence suggesting that your kids' learning and your teaching can be mobilized and intensified when your classroom becomes more assessment-based in the best sense of that word. John Hattie, author of *Visible Learning* (Routledge, 2008), reviewed studies of more than 20 million learners to understand the factors that maximize achievement. He found that one of the most important ways to accelerate achievement is to provide learners with crystal clear and ambitious goals, as well as frequent feedback that highlights progress toward those goals and provides doable next steps.

So here is where I stand on the topic of reading assessment.

It is clear to me that assessments of reading will inevitably consume an enormous proportion of our teaching lives and our kids' learning lives. I'm convinced that we cannot allow assessment to be part of "The Dark Side." This book aims to *take back* reading assessment. I fully expect you will find that when you do that—when assessment becomes a pathway forward for you and your kids—you'll be both relieved and empowered. Let me explain.

When I wrote *Writing Pathways*, the sister volume to this one, I tried to make the system as kid-friendly and as teacher-friendly as possible, but I knew full well that it still asks a lot of you and of your students. I expected it to be accepted begrudgingly, as a better-than-the-alternatives assessment. I have been floored to see that actually, *Writing Pathways* has been enthusiastically embraced. It has actually received more enthusiastic endorsements than anything else we have ever released. And I think that at least in classrooms where that assessment represents an ambitious ceiling (which is in most grades 3–8 classrooms and some K–2 classrooms), the tool has lifted the level of most students' work. As I have begun to understand the reception that *Writing Pathways* has had, I have come to realize how important it is for us to try to provide students with pathways toward rigorous and important goals for reading.

I think *Writing Pathways* has also been well-received because teachers these days are judged in large measure because everyone who assesses *your* teaching these days wants to know what your goals are, how you use data about your students to determine those goals, and how you will assess students' progress toward the goals. Given that this all-present focus on goal-driven instruction exists, I want you to have tools that make it as easy as possible to keep your finger on the pulse of your students' learning in reading as well as in writing. And I want your assessments to tie in closely with instruction that champions reasons to read, that inculcates a love of reading, and that resonates with authenticity.

I know from the start that when I talk about wanting to give you accessible tools that make assessment doable, you'll skim through the progressions at the back of this book and worry. You'll see that they are not lean. Trust me when I say that we have agonized over this and written literally hundreds of drafts in an effort to make these both as lean and as helpful as possible. In the end, however, we decided that if fifth-graders are expected to talk or write about how one part of a nonfiction text relates to another, and we think the entire enterprise will be new and difficult for kids, we believe it is a good thing if possible answers are embedded in the progression: "Might this paragraph be an example of that point, a case study of the generalization, a cause of the effect, a solution to the problem?"

There are other reasons why this reading assessment is more cumbersome than the writing checklists we developed. First, reading will always be more difficult to assess than writing. While the act of writing itself always produces a product that can be held, saved, and classified, reading is invisible, occurring within the black box of the mind. Any effort to turn reading into a product translates reading into something that is no longer just reading. A child could read a passage very well and yet may not understand the question that has been asked or may not write or talk as well as he reads. Those mitigating factors can skew the portrait that is being painted of the reader. That is, any effort to assess reading will inevitably conflate an assessment of reading with an assessment of writing or talking, of understanding and answering questions. The best you can do is to use multiple tools to assess your readers and their learning, to regard all of your findings as fallible, to keep your conclusions about children as works-in-progress, and to *always* remember that the reason to assess is to empower and support learning.

Then, too, reading assessments are complicated because one can't assess higher-level reading skills unless the reader is working with a text he can decode. If I were asked to do high-level interpretive reading of a text written in German—that is, with a text I couldn't *literally* understand—you might think I am incapable of high-level comprehension skills, when actually what would be at issue is something entirely different.

A SET OF TOOLS

This volume gives you tools for assessing the interpretative and analytical reading skills including and beyond those articulated in the Common Core State Standards in Literature and in Informational Texts and by other globally competitive standards as well. As we write this chapter, the U.S. Congress is voting on The Every Child Achieves Act, which includes within it this statement: "The federal government may not mandate or incentivize states to adopt or maintain any particular set of standards, including Common Core. States will be free to decide what academic standards they will maintain in their states." We are confident, however, that whether a state adopts the CCSS or rewrites standards, many of the reading skills detailed in current versions of globally benchmarked standards will continue to be important goals to meet and surpass. This book and the accompanying digital resources aim to provide you, your students, and their families with a system that makes growth in reading more transparent and therefore more obtainable.

Reading Pathways contains:

- **Tools for collecting data on reading volume and reading habits** and a discussion on how to use these tools to increase students' stamina and engagement in reading.

- **A simple, streamlined system for conducting running records** that allows you to establish the levels of text difficulty your students can handle with ease and with support. This system also tracks each student's progress along this crucial trajectory, noting that progress in relationship to benchmark levels. *Reading Pathways* provides support to bring that system across your school and to use this as a tool to support small-group and one-to-one

Student Reading Log — Name: Isabel

Date	Title of Book	Level	Home or School	Page Started	Page Ended	Minutes Read	Genre
9/2	Rules	R	Home	1	9	6	Fiction
9/2	Rules	R	Home	9	29	8	Fiction
9/3	Rules	R	School	30	69	30	Fiction
9/3	Rules	R	Home	69	116	35	Fiction
9/4	Rules	R	School	116	172	43	Fiction
9/4	Rules	R	Home	172	200	20	Fiction
9/6	Star Girl	✓	Home	1	14	15	Fiction
9/6	Star Girl	✓	Home	14	68	66	Fiction
9/8	Star Girl	✓	School	68	89	23	Fiction
9/8	Star Girl	✓	Home	89	119	35	Fiction
9/9	Star Girl	✓	School	119	137	20	Fiction
9/9	Star Girl	✓	Home	137	183	53	Fiction

Name: Sarah   Class: _____

Date	Title and Author of Book	Time Reading in Class	Pages Read in Class	Time Reading Out of Class	Pages Read Out of Class	Finished or Abandoned	Level
1/5/06	The Spiderwick Chronicles, Vol 1, Diterlizzi	9:30-10:00 Or ½ hour	1-18	4:00-4:30 ½ hour	19-43		
9/8	Felita	9:50-10:10 (20)	13-27 (14)	3:40-4:15 (35)	27-60 (33)		P
9/9	"	start		9:00-9:05 (20) 10:15-10:30	60-83 (23)		
9/10	"	start		10:15-10:30 10:30-10:50	84-105	Finished!	
mon 9/11	That's So Raven	10-10:15 (15) 3:33:20(20)	4-14 15-35	3:40-4:10 (30)	35-65		? P/Q ?
9/12	"	20 min	66-81	10-10:15 7-7:15 car 50	82-105		
9/13	"	30 min 9:30-10:00	106-140	3-3:20 10:50-11:00 50	141-end!!	Finished!!! Q ?	
9/14	Raven II	35 min! 9:25-10:00!	4-44!	½ hr on train 10 min before bed	44-88		
9/15	"	32 min	89-124				

Goal: I need to bring home 2 Ravens this weekend

FIG. 1–1   Students' completed reading logs

instruction. The Teachers College Reading and Writing Project (TCRWP) system for running records has been accepted in many states as research-based for RTI.

- **Learning progressions in reading both narrative and informational texts** that support students' progress along a dozen all-important skill progressions. These progressions are written to communicate expectations to students and to their teachers, so they are written in straightforward, clear language. They help you and your students locate current levels of work and identify the next steps.

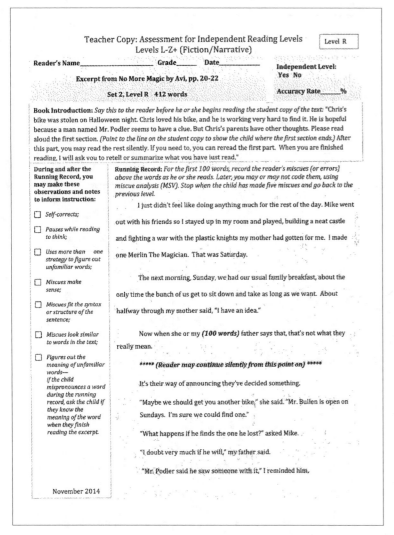

FIG. 1–2 Example of a running record form. The full eight pages of this running record are available in the online resources. ✋

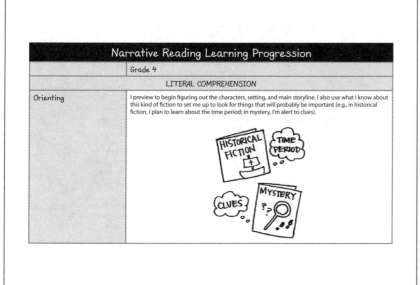

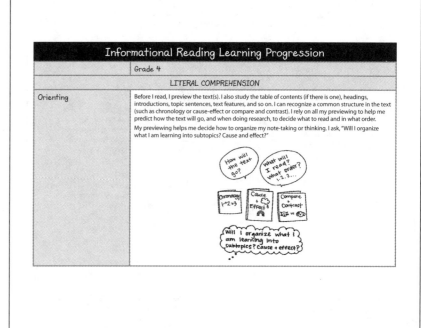

FIG. 1–3   Learning Progressions for Narrative Reading and Informational Reading (Grade 4)

- **Performance assessments that can be used before and after each unit of study** to inform students about key skills they'll need to develop across the unit. These performance assessments are designed to support students' growth in skills that are front and center in twenty-first-century literacy and also on high-stakes assessments. They are designed so they can be scored by either the teacher or student. Either way, their real purpose is instructional. They provide students with pathways along which to improve and goals to strive toward.

- **Simple, illustrated, kid-friendly rubrics, grounded in the learning progressions**, that allow children to self-assess their work on performance assessments, if you make the decision to put scoring into the hands of your children. You can, alternatively, be the person to score your students' work if that is the decision your school makes. Either way, scores can be produced at the start and end of each unit of study if tracking scores is important to you or your students. While these scores

Argument and Advocacy: *Researching Debatable Issues*
Grade 5: Nonfiction, Unit 3

Readers, today you will read three texts about cellphones in schools. Read text 1, then answer questions 1 and 2 on a separate sheet of paper. Then read the rest and finish up.

1. Summarize text 1, "Cell Phones Raise Security Concerns at Schools." When summarizing, remember to: • write about more than one main idea • include carefully selected details to support each main idea • keep your summary brief • write about the ideas in the text, not your own opinions. *Main Idea(s) and Supporting Details/Summary*	2. Read lines 6–8 from text 1, "Cell Phones Raise Security Concerns at Schools." An undercover investigation by police found that at least 24 devices had been stolen over two months at the school, according to nbcphiladelphia.com. Why is this line important to the text? When writing about how one part of the text fits with another, remember to: • explain how the part in question fits into the whole structure of the text and with the main ideas • use academic language: This part explains/ describes/supports/introduces . . . • include evidence or details from the text to support your explanation • write just a few sentences. *Analyzing Parts of a Text in Relation to the Whole*
3. What is the author's point of view in text 3, "Cell Phones Should Be in Schools"? How does your knowledge of the point of view help you think about the text's content? When analyzing point of view, remember to: • name who the author is, as well as his role/ age or the group he belongs to • discuss how the author's points are influenced by the above • write about why the narrator probably thinks or feels the way he does. *Analyzing Perspective*	4. Based on this packet of texts, decide whether cellphones should be banned or allowed in schools. Imagine you are going to write a letter to your mayor and convince him or her that your position makes the most sense. Map out a plan for your persuasive letter to the mayor, making sure you reference the texts. (You do not need to write the actual letter, just your plan.) When synthesizing among texts, remember to: • pull together relevant and important information from different texts (or different parts of a longer text) • organize that information. *Cross-Text(s) Synthesis*

Please remember that including the bullets is a teacher's option. As students become more familiar with these performance assessments, you delete this scaffold. A version without bullets is available on the online resources.

FIG. 1–4   Example of a performance assessment

Text 1

Cell Phones Raise Security Concerns at Schools

Many people think that students having cell phones in school is a great idea. However, cell phones in school can lead to problems. One problem is theft. Cell phones can be stolen. In January 2012, police arrested 13 high school students in Bucks County, Pennsylvania. People accused them of stealing more than $4,000 worth of cell phones and tablets from their classmates. An undercover investigation by police found that at least 24 devices had been stolen over two months at the school, according to nbcphiladelphia.com. Theft is a real concern when cell phones are allowed in schools.

Another problem is cell phone use during emergencies. Many people want students to have cell phones in emergencies. But this might not be safe. The National School Safety and Security Services (NSSSS) says that people in charge should have cell phones during emergencies. But it may cause harm if *students* use their phones in emergencies. If thousands of students make calls at the same time during an emergency, that could slow down the phone system. The NSSSS website says, "The use of cell phones by students could . . . decrease, not increase, school safety during a crisis."

When students use their cell phones during emergencies, another problem can be caused. Students' calls may cause their parents to rush to the school during an emergency. Emergency workers might not want to have tons of parents running to the school. All those parents might get in the way during an emergency. They might make things less safe.

Schools must think about these concerns. They must think carefully about security. Only then should they decide what to do about cell phones.

C. J. Perkins
School safety officer in Walmouth County

are reductive—reducing the complexity of a learner's reading comprehension to numbers, as rubrics always do—they can be used in ways that are helpful for measuring growth across time, noticing patterns that inform whole-class and small-group instruction, and looking at the data from select groups. These rubrics are available in the online resources.

- **A discussion of how to use the data to drive teaching and learning.** Data is worse than worthless if nothing is made of it, so we make a great point to help you turn the data you learn into guidance that can help children, their families, and you. Specifically, you will learn how to use the learning progressions in conjunction with running records and other tools to help you when you are conferring, leading small-group work, writing minilessons, and authoring units of study. Suggestions from district or schoolwide and multiyear data analysis can illuminate patterns and trends and ultimately guide policy.

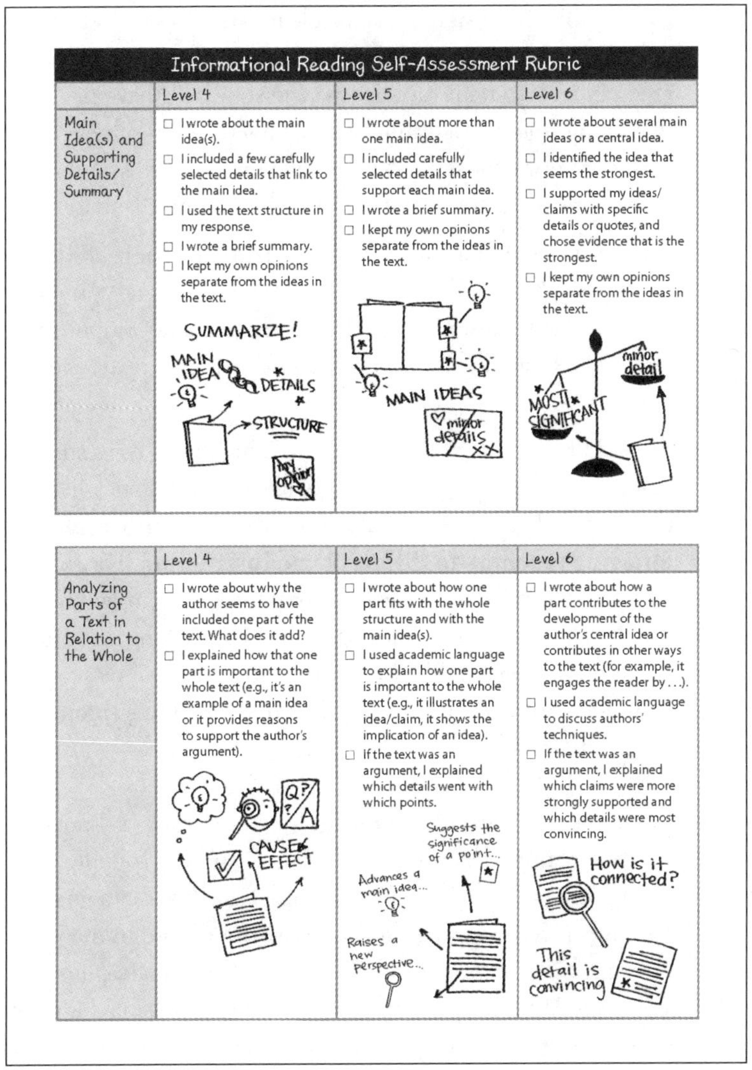

Informational Reading Self-Assessment Rubric

	Level 4	Level 5	Level 6
Main Idea(s) and Supporting Details/ Summary	☐ I wrote about the main idea(s). ☐ I included a few carefully selected details that link to the main idea. ☐ I used the text structure in my response. ☐ I wrote a brief summary. ☐ I kept my own opinions separate from the ideas in the text.	☐ I wrote about more than one main idea. ☐ I included carefully selected details that support each main idea. ☐ I wrote a brief summary. ☐ I kept my own opinions separate from the ideas in the text.	☐ I wrote about several main ideas or a central idea. ☐ I identified the idea that seems the strongest. ☐ I supported my ideas/ claims with specific details or quotes, and chose evidence that is the strongest. ☐ I kept my own opinions separate from the ideas in the text.

	Level 4	Level 5	Level 6
Analyzing Parts of a Text in Relation to the Whole	☐ I wrote about why the author seems to have included one part of the text. What does it add? ☐ I explained how that one part is important to the whole text (e.g., it's an example of a main idea or it provides reasons to support the author's argument).	☐ I wrote about how one part fits with the whole structure and with the main idea(s). ☐ I used academic language to explain how one part is important to the whole text (e.g., it illustrates an idea/claim, it shows the implication of an idea). ☐ If the text was an argument, I explained which details went with which points.	☐ I wrote about how a part contributes to the development of the author's central idea or contributes in other ways to the text (for example, it engages the reader by . . .). ☐ I used academic language to discuss authors' techniques. ☐ If the text was an argument, I explained which claims were more strongly supported and which details were most convincing.

FIG. 1–5 Example of a rubric

WHY THIS ASSESSMENT SYSTEM IS EFFECTIVE

We've built this assessment system to embody the characteristics of effective formative assessments. To do this, we paid attention to the research on factors comprising effective teaching. In the research article "Assessment and Classroom Learning" (*Assessment in Education*, 1998, 5:7–74), Paul Black and Dylan William summarize key findings, suggesting that research indicates that improving learning through assessment depends on five deceptively simple key factors: the provision of effective feedback to pupils, the active involvement of pupils in their own learning, the adjustment of teaching to take into account the results of assessment, a recognition of the profound influence assessment has on the motivation and self-esteem of pupils, both of which are crucial influences on learning, and the need for pupils to be able to assess themselves and understand how to improve.

The approach to assessment in *Reading Pathways* places an emphasis on those priorities:

- **Students can be active agents** of their own reading development, self-assessing their own work on a day-to-day basis, if you support that, and reaching toward next steps. Students can see what is expected of them, clarifying their next steps so they can work with expediency to move forward. They can approach reading a new article or chapter and think, "Wait, what work should I be doing as I read today?" and then work with resolve to achieve those goals.
- The assessment tools are **aligned to global standards but not limited to them**. That is, while the standards tend to be somewhat obscure, leaving teachers and kids thinking, "What? What does

that mean?" this system is crystal clear, providing the Teachers College Reading and Writing Project's knowledgeable interpretation of sometimes unclear expectations. In instances when research on reading development reveals that the standards have neglected key skills and developmental steps in reading—such as entirely overlooking the importance of text orientation, envisioning, prediction, and monitoring for sense—we've filled in those missing pieces. Then, too, when precursor steps to reach later goals are bypassed, this assessment fills in a more detailed progression.

- The assessment tools **help students transfer their skills from one kind of reading to another** by showing how expectations for particular skills are similar, whether one is reading fiction or nonfiction. That is, although the specific nature and components of summary will be different whether one is summarizing in narrative or informational texts, the skills are very similar across the kinds of reading.

- The gridlike design of the assessments highlights ways students engage with skills with more or less complexity, depending on students' level of proficiency. This means that these assessment tools, like the standards themselves, **allow students to move ahead as quickly as possible**, while also **allowing teachers to differentiate instruction**. For example, a teacher can teach the importance of reading for the main idea in nonfiction, keeping in mind that some of her students are still at the third-grade level of learning and will be looking for subheadings and topic sentences that reveal the subtopic being addressed. Other students will be reading texts that do not explicitly name the main idea but leave it up to readers to deduce this through inference and to note not just one but several main ideas.

Expectations have never been higher for young readers—nor for you, as a teacher of reading. By making these expectations clear, understandable, and kid-friendly and by giving you the tools you need to empower students to "own" the expectations, this book can go a long way toward enabling you and your students to meet those soaring expectations. But a word to the wise: this book will be exponentially more potent if your school system also helps you and your colleagues have time to study student work in each other's company. Whereas once upon a time, it was possible for you to close the classroom door and teach in isolation, expectations are high enough now that it is hard to imagine any teacher thinking it wise to attempt to teach without support from colleagues. My colleagues and I have been dazzled by the results when teachers are given opportunities to clarify their shared goals for readers, to norm expectations across grade levels, and to feel confident about providing students with the feedback they need. While you can use these tools on your own, they are most effective when they are used across your grade level and your school, so that neither you nor any teacher needs to teach alone. This system helps you be part of a collaborative system of continuous improvement.

Michael Fullan, one of the foremost authorities on change, points out that the problem in education is not resistance to change but the presence of too many changes, uncoordinated with existing systems and with one another, implemented in superficial or ad hoc ways. The field of education is often characterized by a constant frenzy of efforts to grasp for yet one more magic solve-all—and this is premised on the hope that somewhere, there is a program to buy, to install, that will provide the magic solution.

But the truth is that if there is a magic solution, it is an engagement in a persistent cycle of teaching, observing the results of teaching and then responding thoughtfully to what one sees. What's called for is that you, as a teacher, as well as your colleagues and your students, study student work and develop and adopt curriculum in light of what the evidence shows. In the end, the greatest contribution these tools make is that they help both you and your students self-assess, collaborate with other learners, learn from feedback, and work collectively toward challenging, clear goals. And in the end, if there is a secret to success, it is this process of continuous improvement.

Chapter 2

Assessment Systems as Part of Whole-School "Systemness"

E DUCATIONAL RESEARCHER Michael Fullan has often written and spoken about the significance of "systemness" in achieving a shared vision. He asserts that achieving greatness takes a cultivation of systemness on the part of all. For example, when a school moves from an individualistic culture to a collaborative culture, then teachers think about "our kids," not "my kids." You want that kind of cohesive systemness supporting your reading assessments so that data can be easily passed from one teacher to the next, so that a teacher in fourth grade can get a snapshot of a child's reading history from third grade, so that teachers who work across many classrooms talk the same language as classroom teachers, so that children understand the purpose of being assessed, and most importantly, so that all teachers agree upon what really matters and work in concert.

In the following chapters, you'll get to the nitty-gritty of implementing assessments in ways that allow you and your students to actually benefit from all that time and work collecting the data. For now, let's pull back a bit and think about ways to develop a *system* that creates coherence and community across your school.

DECIDE ON THE KINDS OF ASSESSMENTS TO USE WITH YOUR STUDENTS

Before you launch into assessing readers, you'll want to consider the various assessments that are available and plan and agree with colleagues on which assessments are important. It is helpful for children and teachers if some assessments become systemic and if you think about ways to make those assessments as efficient as possible. When the context for doing these assessments is right, you and your colleagues can lean on each other for help implementing assessments, and the entire staff of the school can be organized to make the assessments as doable as possible. This can minimize the loss of instructional time and maximize the potential influence of those selected assessments. If you and others agree to shared assessments, you can use the results to study growth over time, to monitor progress, and to enliven the professional learning that happens within the walls of your school. When you teach behind a closed door, it's hard to know how your children are really doing. When you teach in an open system, you have transparency and collaboration—all the kids are "our" kids, and problems that arise are "our" difficulties.

To Teach More Wisely, Create Reader Profiles

When you're making choices among assessment options, picture in your mind a child, and then ask yourself, if you wanted a profile of this reader, what would you want to know? Let's say it's a young boy who is making great strides as a reader. I'd want to know how often he is reading and how much he reads in one sitting. I'd be interested in *what* he is tending to read as well. I'd want to know how he processes texts—what does his reading actually sound like? I'd want to know, too, if he actually understands what he is reading and if it made sense for him to progress to more challenging books soon. I'd want to know what kind of thinking he does as he reads. I'd want to know his grasp of high-leverage comprehension skills (especially those I was about to teach), such as reading with an eye to author's craft and thinking about theme.

If I could find all that out, I could teach him more wisely. If I could find that out for every child and be aware of changes over time, all of my instruction would gain more traction. The partnerships I set up among children would be more strategic. My conferring and small-group work would be more informed. I would see the results of my teaching. If all my colleagues knew as much, we'd know exactly how things were going for individual readers, and for reading overall in our school. Reading can feel like invisible work, but with smart assessments, you can know what's really going on with your readers.

Consider Using High-Leverage Reading Assessments

Here are the reading assessments that we consider most high-leverage in upper grades and that we strongly encourage you to consider making a part of your system. If you're unsure, pilot. Make informed decisions.

THE LOGISTICS

When you start the year, it's helpful to lay out your curriculum and your school calendar, and to plan an assessment schedule. This will help you allocate time, match assessments to instruction, and collaborate with colleagues. Mostly, it will allow you and your colleagues to talk about a plan to make the assessments as manageable as possible.

Roland Barth, author of *Improving Schools from Within* (Jossey-Bass, 1991) and many other books on school reform, points out that the health of a school is directly related to the number of elephants in the room. The elephants are the big issues that everyone thinks about and no one talks about openly but that are instead talked about in bathrooms or parking lots. One of those, clearly, will be the challenge to actually get through all the assessments that are expected. Our suggestion is this: talk about it and be practical.

The Assessment	Where To Find It	What You Find Out
Reading Logs	Logs are often kept on paper, but apps are also available. Blank reading logs are also available in our online resources.	Keep track of overall **reading volume**, **book choice**, and **reading rate**. Look across a day, a week, and a month to see what books a child is choosing, how often she is finishing books, and how much time she is putting into reading. Reading logs let children reflect on their volume of reading, asking, "How is reading going for me?"
Running Records	TCRWP Running Records, available online at http://readingandwritingproject.org/resources/assessments/running-records Fountas & Pinnell Set DRA QRI	Find out a child's current **reading level**—the level of text he reads with fluency, accuracy, and comprehension. Gather details about the child's fluency; accuracy; use of cuing systems for word solving; ability to retell, to cumulate the text, to attend to text features, and to answer literal and inferential questions at specific text levels.
Performance Assessments	TCRWP Performance Assessments, available through *Reading Pathways* and http://readingandwritingproject.org/resources/assessments/reading-writing-assessments. Students write responses, assess using rubrics.	Gather evidence of children's **best thinking** on a series of skills, such as comparing and contrasting, thinking between part and whole, and inferring ideas about character. Find out children's abilities to express this thinking in writing. Children can learn to self-assess using student-facing rubrics. Create ladders of exemplars with children.
Auxiliary Performance Assessments (Reading across Texts, Text-Based Opinion/ Arguments)	TCRWP Common Core Aligned Performance Assessments, available online at http://readingandwritingproject.org/resources/assessments/reading-writing-assessments	Measure specific Common Core reading, research, and writing skills such as summarizing information texts, gathering information across texts, and constructing a text-based opinion/argument using evidence from these texts. Using teacher-centered rubrics and annotated exemplars, compare students' skills to normed grade level standard. These are particularly matched to the writing tasks on new Common Core aligned tests.
Records of Conferences, Small Groups, and Observations	Records for each student are often kept on paper in a binder, but apps are also available.	Compile at-a-glance data from readers' periodic and formative assessments. Keep track of dates when children need to be reassessed. Dated record sheets from conferences and small-group work catalog the compliments, teaching points, and next steps recorded for each student, gleaned from ongoing research. Observations of students' reading behaviors—stamina, engagement, independence, partner work, and so on—are also recorded here.

FIG. 2–1   Keep this chart handy when you are thinking about high-leverage reading assessments.

Might it be okay for the most proficient of your readers to read the running record texts silently rather than reading them aloud to you, answering the questions in writing? If you have just recently informally assessed a reader and moved that reader to a new level of text difficulty, and if you know full well he won't be ready to move beyond that level yet, can you use that informal running record in lieu of a more formal one? Can the school bring in some roving substitutes to free teachers up for an hour a day during assessment windows? How can the school's specialist teachers play a support role?

Many schools set assessment windows for running records. For instance, they might say that readers are assessed in September, November, January, March, and June. Those windows play a role—they support a more systematic way to collect cross-class data (see discussion of benchmarks, below), and they ensure that teachers at least do the minimum.

If your school *does* have formal windows for running records, it is helpful to plan systems for securing support during those windows so that they are short-lived and you don't spend your whole year assessing rather than teaching. I address this in more detail in the next chapter.

Establishing Benchmarks that Correlate to Assessment Windows for Running Records

You may want to establish normed benchmarks as targets for each of your assessment windows. In Figure 2–2, you will note the TCRWP benchmarks, based on our data from almost 60,000 children over many years. Our benchmarks come from a correlation between the level of text complexity at which a student can read with fluency, comprehension, and at least 96% accuracy, and that student's scores on high-stakes texts that year, and for younger children, several years later. That is, it was the children who were reading levels D/E in June of kindergarten who scored a 3 on the high-stakes test years later, when they were in third grade. It was the children who were reading level S/T books at the end of fourth grade who scored a 3 on the high-stakes test. The correlation between rising levels of text complexity and rising scores has been extremely strong—so much so that when it is not strong, we know that is a signal that the school is probably misleveling readers and needs intensive help immediately in conducting running records. These correlations also allow administrators, educators, and parents to know when to raise red flags regarding a student's potential achievement, and to do so early enough in the year to actually change students' rate of growth.

There are interesting things to note about this data. First, the correlation between the level of text complexity with which a student read and the scores on high-stakes tests existed despite the fact that the context for collecting these running records was far from ideal. The people doing the assessing were K–6 teachers from New York City's crowded classrooms; during the early years of data collection, many of these teachers had just learned how to conduct running records. And yet levels were still predictive of scores. Problems abounded. And yet there has nevertheless been alignment between the level of text difficulty that readers seemed to able to handle and scores on the standardized tests. We have also found alignment between our benchmarks and other major reading assessment systems' grade level expectations.

Teachers College Reading and Writing Project
Benchmark Reading Levels and Marking Period Assessments

SEPTEMBER	NOVEMBER	JANUARY	MARCH	JUNE
Kindergarten Emergent Story Books Shared Reading	Kindergarten Emergent Story Books Shared Reading A/B (with book intro)	Kindergarten B/C (with book intro)	Kindergarten 1=Early Emergent 2=A/B (with book intro) 3=C (with book intro) 4=D/E	Kindergarten 1=B or below 2=C (with book intro) 3=D/E 4=F or above
Grade 1: 1=B or below 2=C 3=D/E 4=F or above	Grade 1: 1=C or below 2=D/E 3=F/G 4=H or above	Grade 1: 1=D or below 2=E/F 3=G/H 4=I or above	Grade 1: 1=E or below 2=F/G 3=H/I/J 4=K or above	Grade 1: 1=G or below 2=H 3=I/J/K 4=L or above
Grade 2: 1=F or below 2=G/H 3=I/J/K 4=L or above	Grade 2: 1=G or below 2=H/I 3=J/K/L 4=M or above	Grade 2: 1=H or below 2=I/J 3=K/L 4=M or above	Grade 2: 1=I or below 2=J/K 3=L/M 4=N or above	Grade 2: 1=J or below 2=K/L 3=M 4=N or above
Grade 3: 1=K or below (avg. H) 2=L 3=M 4=N or above	Grade 3: 1=K or below (avg. I) 2=L/M (avg. L) 3=N 4=O or above	Grade 3: 1=L or below 2=M/N 3=O 4=P or above	Grade 3: 1=M or below (avg. J) 2=N 3=O 4=P or above	Grade 3: 1=N or below (avg. K) 2=O 3=P 4=Q or above
Grade 4: 1=M or below (avg. J) 2=N/O (avg. N) 3=P/Q (avg. P) 4=R or above	Grade 4: 1=N or below (avg. L) 2=O/P (avg. P) 3=Q/R(avg. Q) 4=S or above	Grade 4: 1=O or below 2=P/Q 3=R/S 4=T or above	Grade 4: 1=O or below (avg. K) 2=P/Q (avg. P) 3=R/S (avg. R) 4=T or above	Grade 4: 1=P or below (avg. L) 2=Q/R (avg. Q) 3=S/T (avg. S) 4=U or above
Grade 5: 1=P or below (avg. M) 2=Q/R (avg. Q) 3=S 4=T or above	Grade 5: 1=P or below (avg. N) 2=Q/R/S (avg. Q) 3=T 4=U or above	Grade 5: 1=Q or below 2=R/S/T 3=U 4=V or above	Grade 5: 1=Q or below (avg. O) 2=R/S/T (avg. R/S)) 3=U 4=V or above	Grade 5: 1=R or below (avg. P) 2=S/T/U (avg. S/T) 3=V 4=W or above
Grade 6: 1=R or below (avg. O) 2=S/T/U (avg. S) 3=V/W (avg. V) 4=X or above	Grade 6: 1=S or below (avg. P) 2=T/U/V (avg. T) 3=W 4=X or above	Grade 6: 1=T or below 2=U/V 3=W/X 4=Y or above	Grade 6: 1=T or below (avg. Q) 2=U/V (avg. U) 3=W/X (avg. W) 4=Y or above	Grade 6: 1=U or below (avg. Q) 2=V/W (avg. V) 3=X 4=Y or above

FIG. 2–2   Benchmark reading levels and marking period assessments

To a remarkable degree, students' reading levels, as measured by their ability to read at a level with accuracy, fluency, and basic comprehension, predicted the scores that they received on high-stakes tests. This suggests that teachers seeking to support students' testing success, among other things, would be wise to work toward moving students up reading levels. Giving book introductions to kick-start students into a new level, getting students into book clubs to practice higher-level comprehension, tracking students' reading growth, and getting children involved in goal-setting—all of these and other ways of fostering reading level growth are likely to prove as powerful as (and certainly more engaging than!) mere test preparation.

You will note that in the paragraphs above, I've written in the past tense. The levels of text complexity *were* predictive of the scores student received; the benchmark levels *came* from correlation between students' levels of text complexity and the high-stakes scores. New York was one of a tiny handful of states to shift to a CCSS-aligned high-stakes test very early on—in 2013—and as predicted, in the first year, two thirds of New York States' students failed that new and alarmingly different test. (The third-grade sample passages that first year included a passage by Tolstoy written at the eighth-grade level!) As this book goes to press in 2015, many districts are reporting a 50% opt-out rate (usually the children from more highly educated parents), so data in the upcoming year will pose unique challenges. During 2013 and 2014, the TCRWP continued to track data from 60,000 students in New York State and to see a correlation between levels of text complexity and scores on the new assessments, but not surprisingly these benchmark levels would only be predictive now if we ratcheted up expectations by another notch at every grade level. That is, for the first two years of implementation of the new Pearson test, to get a 3, the fourth-graders in June tended to be reading levels T/U, not S/T. We did not adjust our benchmarks, because the tests are still changing (it is untenable to have two thirds of New York State's children failing their high-stakes tests as a matter of long-term practice!). Also, raising our benchmarks further would put unreasonable challenges in front of students, and, for this reason, would also put us out of sync with other grade level measuring systems, including the Common Core recommendations.

This, however, is only the tip of the assessment iceberg. Data, schoolwide tracking systems, and their implications are delved into with much greater detail in Chapter 10, "Tap the Power (and Avoid the Harm) of Large-Scale Data."

Parent Letters

It is helpful to prepare letters that can be used to communicate results of assessments to parents and other caregivers. These letters let adults know the level of text difficulty that are "at standard level" for that child's grade level at that time of year and also communicate how the child in their care is doing relative to those expectations. Included in each letter is a list of book recommendations for the child, based on his or her current level. In the online resources, we have provided sample letters that hundreds of schools working closely with the TCRWP have been using (and adapting.) You will see that the collection of letters also informs caregivers about new units of study.

Scheduling Performance Assessments

We recommend that you schedule a performance assessment before and after each of your reading units of study. If the workload inherent in that seems excessive, we encourage you to engage your students in self-assessment. We can also imagine you limiting the total number of performance assessments. What

Dear Caregiver,

When you were young, did you stand ever so still against the doorway of your kitchen while someone—your mom, your grandpa—carefully calibrated your height and made a new mark, complete with the new date, representing your growth? I think one of the ways that I felt cared for was that my parents watched over my growth, cheering for new inches. And of course I watched my growth as well because I was dying to be tall enough to ride the roller coaster at the state fair that came our way every summer.

It is, of course, even more important that we keep track of our sons' and daughters' growth as readers, and this letter will help you make a new mark on your measuring stick as we, at school, have made on ours. Specifically, we want to tell you that when we asked your child to read passages that are leveled according to increasing difficulty and asked your child questions about those passages, we learned the level of text difficulty that your child can handle with lots of success. We're sending that level to you in this letter, and also letting you know the grade level expectations that we maintain.

A few words of caution. First, this assessment is an informal one, done quickly in the class-room. The results don't "go" anywhere except to you and to us. The school system calls this a formative assessment because the point of it is simply to help all of us work in wise ways with your child.

Second, we want you to know that our expectations for the level of difficulty that we hope a child can handle at a grade level are high. One reason we have high expectations is that we always think it is better to aim high. Also, we know that in the year ahead, the entire nation will be bringing in newer and higher standards for children.

Third, the most important thing I can tell you is that you can work with your child to alter these levels. These are the result of the amount of interested, engaged reading that a child does with books that are on the child's level. So if you look at the information and think, "I wish the news were different," then you and your son or daughter need to think about finding ways to support more reading. Limit television and video games, make trips to the library, make sure high-interest books and magazines are everywhere, talk about books together . . . All those things will make a magical difference.

At this time in your child's grade-level, children are "at standards" if they are reading these levels for these grades:

FIG. 2–3   Example of a letter to share assessment results with parents or other caregivers

Kindergarten: Emergent Story Books / Shared Reading
First grade: C/D/E
Second grade: I/J/K
Third grade: L/M/N
Fourth grade: O/P/Q
Fifth grade: R/S/T
Sixth grade: T/U/V
Seventh grade: V/W/X
Eighth grade: X/Y

Your child is in _____ , and is, in fact, reading books at level _____ .
When we are asked to put your child's reading on a scale, the book level that your child can handle suggests that out of a 1–4 scale, your child is at a level of _____ .

1. Needs support
2. Approaches standards
3. Meets standards
4. Exceeds standards

There is one important way for children to progress from the book level they can read to the next level, and it is this: the child must read lots and lots and lots of books at his or her level. The child will do best if he or she can talk about those books with someone who loves reading—and loves the child—and who makes reading into a great pleasure.

Here are a few books at your child's current reading level:

We assess other aspects of reading too, such as your child's understanding of phonics (which relates to spelling) and the speed at which your child reads. Most of all, we assess your child's comprehension, and we do this by listening to your child talk about the books he or she has read. We also assess your child's progress as a writer. Some of those assessments give us numbers on a chart, and some don't. We would be happy to tell you about any of those assessments.

Most of all, we hope that you and the school can work together to make it likely that your child is reading, reading, reading, and that your child knows that you love reading too.

Sincerely,

FIG. 2–3 *(continued)*

we strongly discourage, however, is you deciding to postpone your first performance assessment. Securing baseline start-of-the-year data is important so that you can see growth later. That growth will be much more impressive if the baseline is on the second or third day of school! And it is not a small thing to have evidence to show a child that she has grown.

The good news is that a day in which you conduct performance assessments in reading (like a day for on-demand writing) doesn't have to feel extra stressful to you. You simply assign kids to do some reading work and sit on your hands and tape up your mouth so that you resist the urge to give readers help. The truth is that it is okay if your students don't do well on the start of the year performance assessment. You haven't taught any units yet, and think how dramatic their growth will be when you do! The growth will be especially dramatic because the performance assessments alert students to the goals for the unit—the skills they'll be working to get better at—and this makes it likely that they will work with clarity and purpose on those skills in anticipation of the posttest.

In each of the units, you'll see that we give you the option to score the assessments on your own or to help students score themselves. Either way, we encourage you to get children involved in the process. There's no doubt that the scoring process will be far more accurate if you determine students' scores, even if you do this quickly. At the start of third grade, when students experience their first of these performance assessments, you (or whomever teaches third grade in your school) will probably want to score the students' responses. The important thing will be to do that scoring right away so that during the first bend of the unit, students can get their scores back and can work with partners to study the rubrics to figure out the rationale for the score. That process can be fun for students because they can also be invited to use the rubrics to revise their work immediately, seeing if they can improve their scores.

That is, the initial performance assessments are *not* meant to be an "I caught you! You stink at this!" kind of situation. Quite the opposite! Our hope is that when students are given the opportunity to raise the level of their work, they'll relish the chance to understand the expectations and feel empowered to be able to lift the level of their work in concrete, tangible ways.

By fourth grade, we assume that students who have grown up within units of study will be able to use the student-facing rubrics to score themselves unless the students' school is using the performance assessment as a state-mandated measure of student learning. No matter what the grade level, we suggest that at the start of students' first year using the progressions, you will want to score students' work.

Above all else, we want students to emerge from these initial performance assessments with a clear message: they can *work to improve their reading*; there are doable, accessible ways for them to get stronger as readers.

Conducting the performance assessment requires one fifty- to sixty-minute period, and engaging kids in a self-assessment of their work requires a similar amount of time. We recommend using the "Start with Assessment" piece at the beginning of a unit. Then a few days later, Day Two, Three, or Four of the unit, another day is set aside for students either to engage in "A Day for Assessment"—self-assessment and goal-setting (if they are ready to use the rubrics alone) *or* to study the scores you gave them with a partner, working together to try to raise the level of their responses. We strongly suggest you don't disrupt the unit with more than one day for self-assessment, whether or not those self-assessments are completed on that one day. You'll find that there are plenty of opportunities for self-assessment using strands of the learning progressions throughout the unit itself.

You and your colleagues will also want to decide whether to conduct both pre- and postassessments to every unit, or just to rely on a sequence of preassessments (that is, two fiction preassessments and two nonfiction). We recommend using both the pre- and the postassessments, because children profit from seeing evidence of their growth. With our writing performance assessments, we have found that it is tremendously satisfying for children to "show off" all they've learned in a quick on-demand writing piece at the end of the unit, because that kind of reflection can solidify learning. But you'll need to decide whether you wish to dedicate a day to the postassessments and, if so, add those days to your calendar as well.

Finally, you will also want to consider dates of required state and district assessments—both summative and formative—and put those required assessments into your calendar. Find out which ones are actually required. Many cities and states have used our performance assessments (some we developed for New York State have been on TCRWP's website for a few years), because these assess information reading and text-based opinion/argument writing in a way that is aligned to the global standards. You may find that the new performance assessments for grade level reading skills included here are sufficient. Either way, get all of your assessments onto your calendar.

You will probably want to put dates for parent-teacher conferences and report cards onto this assessment calendar as well, so that you can see how things line up. Once you have done that, stand back with your colleagues to make sure things make sense, and make small shifts as needed.

MAKING DECISIONS ABOUT HOW TO USE PERFORMANCE ASSESSMENT DATA

When you are trying to understand a reader, it is always important to rely on multiple sources of information. Yes, the performance assessments will inform you about the level of work your students are and aren't currently doing. Perhaps even more importantly, once you have given them the learning progression that represents what you hope they can do and shown them that their work needs to go up a notch, it will be really informative to see whether they can make the changes you detail. Say, for example, that a students' summary is a page and a half in length. You point out that the challenge of a summary involves brevity, and with it, selection. You are quite sure the student understands this expectation, yet the student seems unable to distill a brief summary of the text. You'll want to figure out what the student can do, and to try to understand the hard part. All of this will be fascinating—and helpful. And the one performance assessment might also reveal the reader's ability to compare and contrast, to grow ideas about a text, and so forth.

However, the performance assessment won't reveal a student's abilities to monitor for sense, to read with fluency, or to orient himself to a text before reading. Those skills will be revealed more through the running record. It will be important, then, to collect data from a variety of sources.

You and your colleagues will also need to decide on the relationship between your various reading performance assessments and report card grades, and then communicate this information to parents.

Our advice on this is complicated. The late Marie Clay, one of the world's most renowned literacy experts, has pointed out that when one asks a child a few questions about a text, the child's ability to answer those questions shows as much about the child's grasp of the syntax and assumption behind the questions as it does about the child's comprehension of the passage itself. And when children are asked to write their responses to the questions, the assessment also reflects the child's ability to write. This is why Clay recommends that assessment involve a conversation, not a battery of written questions. We agree with this argument yet know it is not practical to suggest you conduct thirty pre- and postunit conversations! Then, too, we know that, at least in the United States, children's comprehension will continue to be assessed based on their abilities to write or select answers to questions.

The performance assessments that are included in this series are primarily aimed at making children's best thinking visible so that children themselves can self-assess and improve their work, with your intensive help. Could you record a number for each child, for each skill, and track those numbers over time? Yes, if you need or want to use this data as formal performance assessment data, probably in lieu of a bad or expensive assessment your children would otherwise be required to take, you could decide to score and track the level of proficiency that each child demonstrates for each skill. If you are expected to conduct semi-high-stakes performance assessments and to track measures of student learning, the good news is these assessments are aligned to curriculum. Also, using these will mean you won't need to add yet another layer of assessments.

Yet there are downsides to deciding to do this. We are absolutely confident that these performance assessments have a tremendous teaching power when they are used as tools within the curriculum. Yet if these assessments become high stakes, if children's (and even your) self-images and sense of well-being are at stake around these assessments, their power can become toxic. Then, too, we are not in a position to show you large-scale data that correlates the results of these performance assessments with other high-stakes assessments, or even to tell you the percentage of students who will achieve this or that result on these assessments. We have piloted the assessments with hundreds of children but do not have high-stakes assessments for those same children from the same year. What we can ask is that if your district does use these assessments in high-stakes ways, you let us know so that we can gather the data (and adjust the assessments) so that in time, they can be used with increasing confidence.

We're honestly not sure that it's worth the effort for you to record data from these performance assessments. The primary goal of assessment is to tailor instruction and increase achievement. Presumably, the level at which the child first works will change over a week or even over one class period, so spending time assessing each child's work does not seem very productive. Often when children self-assess, especially when they have good student-facing rubrics and exemplars, they can then fix up some of their work right in the moment, usually because they could have done what the rubric suggested; they just didn't realize (or remember) they were supposed to!

ORGANIZING ASSESSMENT MATERIALS

Once you've made a plan for the assessments you'll give, and when to give them, you'll need to assemble materials. In many schools, parents volunteer to help with this task, because your time is better spent elsewhere than huddled over that copy machine. In brief, you'll need:

- **A binder or folder with the teacher copies of the running record forms, and some folders with the student copies.** The students don't write on their copy of the running record text (usually), so you won't need so many of those. You will write on your copy, so you will need a new one for each student. Remember that you'll need enough space to record the child's retell and responses to the comprehension questions. You can, of course, go paperless. It is hard to keep notes on their meaning, structure, and visual cues without writing on the document itself, but there are remedies. Some teachers use a PDF writer such as Adobe or Nitro Pro to record digitally right on the form. Others use Evernote or Notability or the Confer app to jot their notes. In the near future, we'll surely be keeping records in new ways. And yet sometimes, that pencil on paper can be really efficient.

- **Copies of the performance assessments.** This is very simple, because children only need a copy of the texts and then a piece of paper with the questions, and then half-sheets of paper for their responses, so they can sort them, make ladders of exemplars, put them in their notebooks, and so on.

- **Versions of the student-facing rubrics for the performance assessments.** You have options for how to print these and put them in children's hands. You might have a large version printed or projected while kids are self-assessing. You might have baskets of rubrics available.

- **Copies of the strands of the learning progressions that pertain to the performance assessment.** Students will use these, more than the rubrics, to guide their future work. Encourage students to tape these into reader's notebooks or to laminate them and keep them close at hand.

- **A system for recording classwide data.** Many teachers have found it helpful to maintain a spreadsheet that includes students' assessment scores. This allows them to easily color-code the data and notice patterns. These patterns can help you plan for small groups, as well as shape your whole-class teaching.

CREATING LEVELED LIBRARIES FOR YOUR CLASSROOM

If you have not already leveled your classroom library, you'll probably want to do so. This will allow students to use those levels to locate books that are within reach for them. Children benefit from opportunities to engage in lots and lots of high-success reading, and developing a system of leveling books supports those opportunities. On the ski mountain, I'm glad to know that the green circles are trails for me to ski when I have young kids with me, the blue squares indicate trails that I can glide along, and the black diamonds require me to ski with a friend and to be up for a challenge. Levels on a book's spine work in similar ways.

Instituting a leveled library and a schoolwide assessment system is no easy task. Trying to do so in the midst of the school year can feel a bit like trying to change the tires on your car as you hurtle down the highway. The relentless press of twenty-some kids, of today's and tomorrow's teaching, can consume so much time and attention that it is not easy to rethink or rebuild. You will find yourself looking with jealousy at the duplicating machines with their little illuminated buttons that say, "not ready," "not ready."

Right from the start, then, let me say that if you and your school are starting with the very first steps—leveling books, helping teachers to begin taking running records, starting schoolwide measures to track student progress, communicating information about children's evolution as readers with parents and other caregivers—then you'd be well off to bring on some extra hands to help with the behind the scenes work. It is amazing how enabling it can be to staff this effort with a few college students as interns (even just during May through August) or some paraprofessionals as literacy support staff, or even some high school kids who work after school or over the summer. In any case, everyone needs to be ready to forgive some chaos and approximation and to be candid and forthright about the challenges.

FIG. 2–4   An example of a classroom leveled library

If classroom libraries in your school are not already leveled, start by making sure that you decide on a system. Think of your leveling system as a currency system that will be shared across the building, even if every teacher isn't participating in the project right now. Most educational publishers and distributors sell books that have been preleveled, although not all leveling is equally valid. Schools using the Fountas and Pinnell system can use *Leveled Books K–8: Matching Texts to Readers for Effective Teaching* (Heinemann, 2006) and the Fountas and Pinnell website as resources (www.fountasandpinnellleveledbooks.com). Systems should be in place so that someone does the clerical work of finding a title on the Fountas and Pinnell website. Locating a book's level of text difficulty is not rocket science; parent volunteers, teacher aides, high school and college interns, publishers, and even kids themselves (after school) can be recruited to help research the level and then affix a dot with that level to the spine of a book. All efforts to level are fallible, and any level should be adjusted if the book proves to be easier or harder than its label.

If your classroom library has already been leveled, try to find an opportunity to check that things are in good working order. Chances are that your library is overdue some attention. Books are often wildly mislabeled. It is important for teachers (and/or for teachers and kids) to look across the books bearing a certain label—say, level S books—and make sure these texts all feel as if they are in the same ballpark of text difficulty.

The other job is to make sure that the books that are available to students in a classroom match the actual reading levels of the students. Oftentimes schools purchase books that are leveled as "third grade," and those books are probably appropriate for the children in that class who are reading approximately at benchmark level. But chances are great that a fair proportion of the readers are not reading at that "high-average" level—and if readers are working in more accessible books, they read more of those shorter books in a day a week, and therefore need especially large numbers of those easier books. Once libraries are leveled, the next step is often to consider shifting books from one classroom to another so that the classroom libraries are ready for the children they'll be supporting.

Finally, let me put out on the table, from the start, that there are schools in which teachers do none of this. Instead they simply lay out an array of books and invite kids to choose those that appeal to them, hoping and trusting that kids will choose well and will progress toward increasing levels of text complexity over time. The arguments *against* leveling books claim that a reader's prior background and motivation to read a book play a role in determining whether a book is or is not within reach for that particular reader. That is, a reader who is a sci-fi fanatic will be able to read sci-fi books that are much more challenging than will a reader who is totally new to the genre. A reader who has grown up trout fishing and knows the names of every rod, bait, and fish will be able to read a magazine on trout fishing that is far beyond that student's ascribed level of text complexity.

Those observations about reading are true—but they can be the arguments for a cautious use of leveled libraries or an argument against having such a library in the first place.

If your school does not do running records to track students' growth or level its class libraries and what is in place is working for your students, I do not mean to insinuate that the approach is wrong. Long ago, Marie Clay, founder of Reading Recovery, pointed out to me that *any* approach to teaching reading has its costs and its benefits; one of the most important things we can do is to be aware of those. And certainly the effort to match readers to books and to track their progress, as described in this chapter and the next, has its own costs as well as benefits.

Still, if I were a school principal, I'd want to have a system in place that helped me and others to stay attuned to whether our kids were progressing. I'd also want to be able to give an early heads up to caregivers and to kids themselves if kids were in just a bit of trouble as readers, which would give everyone a chance to alter the course. I'd worry that if teachers across the school simply laid out an array of books and invited kids to go at it, teachers would not have a way to know patterns that were derailing kids. Once a system is in place and consistency of expectations has been established, the flexibility to consider the background and motivation of a particular student for a particular text can be done in a more thoughtful, purposeful way—but these are the exceptions rather than the rule.

NORMING HOW YOU ASSESS

You'll need to gather colleagues to norm how you assess, so that your data will be meaningful to each other, to children, and to parents. You'll want to do this for running records and for performance assessments. Even if the performance assessments will be primarily made by the children themselves, it is important that teachers across a grade level agree on the work you expect students to be able to do. I caution you to remember that selecting schoolwide tools for assessing readers will not mean that your school community's assessments are in alignment. This requires shared conversations about assessments.

For teachers to develop assessment systems that are aligned, it is crucial for people to be willing to engage in hard conversations. If the fifth-grade teacher received records indicating that in fourth grade

Randall read at level T, and the teacher thinks that at the start of fifth grade, he instead is reading at level O (some summer regression is expected but not that much!), then this requires a conversation. The fifth-grade teacher in this instance needs to talk with her colleague, saying, "I know you thought Randall was reading at level T, but I don't know how you came to that conclusion because I'm assessing him as reading at level O." And if the fifth-grade teacher sees a pattern, with a number of kids from that one fourth-grade class entering fifth grade with what seem to be exaggerated levels, there may need to be a way for some other professional to help adjudicate this and provide the extra professional development or extra collaborative conversations that are needed for children to progress more seamlessly from one year the next. We don't do kids any favors if, in the name of collegiality, we circumvent the hard conversations that are necessary. It is also hard on children and on their parents if during one school year, the child is reading level T books, and the next year, the child is directed to level O books!

One actually needn't wait for students to pass from one grade to another before spotting telltale signs that suggest a particular teacher might need help reading the data available in running records. A system of checks and balances is readily available. That is, if a student's scores on last year's standardized reading test were extremely low, and yet the child had been assessed as able to read texts at grade level, then this disparity should function as a blinking yellow light, signaling, "Proceed with care." It may well be that the child was actually not able to read those challenging texts.

For running records, you might want to bring a child into a faculty meeting (with parental permission, of course), and ask all the teachers in the school to record running records of the child's reading while one teacher works with this child in a fishbowl situation. The important part of this will be for each teacher to analyze the running records separately. Then time should be allotted to compare and contrast conclusions as part of an effort to norm expectations and to align methods for analyzing running records and assessing retellings and answers to comprehension questions. What constitutes a just-right retelling or an acceptable answer to recall questions? You'll discover dramatic differences in judgment, and you'll need to come to a place of consensus. It's also interesting to assess a few children who read at the same level. Listening to a second-grade reader who reads at level O, for instance, will be quite different than listening to a fifth-grade level O reader. That kind of pairing helps teachers pay attention not just to the level, but to what you find out about the reader.

You will also want to practice whichever notation system you decide to use with colleagues. Marie Clay's system, in her book, *Running Records for Classroom Teachers* (Heinemann, 2000), or Peter Johnson's, shown below from his book *Running Records: A Self-Tutoring Guide* (Stenhouse, 2000), are two options used in many of the schools we work with. Whichever notation system you decide to use, the written record of your running records needs to be sufficient so that others can use the notations to reconstruct exactly what the reader did as he read. This way, people can retrieve the running records from an earlier time and, if necessary, reconsider the conclusions that were drawn based on those running records. This means not only norming the coding system, but also recording each reader's answer to each comprehension question. It is not enough for the assessing teacher to deem a child's answer acceptable and to record just a check mark. Experience shows that the only way for a school to actually develop this sort of shared practice is for teachers to share their actual running records, not just the scores gleaned from those records, and to have time to discuss differences.

Even if you are not formally recording your performance assessment data, you'll want to have shared expectations for what represents grade level work around theme, for instance. You can norm your reading performance assessments much as you did your writing performance assessments. That is, put a student response (without the name) in the center of the table and compare it to the exemplars. Once you agree on which exemplar it is mostly like, see what grade level that is. Then consider the rubric as well—does the student's work fit, more or less, what's on the rubric? The rubrics are meant to be reminders, which is why you'll want to use exemplars as well. They'll give you a richer picture of what grade level thinking might sound like. Remember that the point is not to get all children to think and write exactly like the exemplars. It's to establish shared expectations.

The good news is that once a school truly has shared systems for assessing readers and matching books to readers, then all of a sudden the system itself can empower teachers in ways that make a world of difference. When a teacher receives her roster for an incoming class, the teacher can receive the levels of text difficulty at which each child can read, as well as a record of the child's progress over the past few years. For example, there may be eight readers in an incoming fourth-grade class that at the end of third grade are still reading level M books. The fourth-grade teacher will absolutely want to look backward and see each reader's trajectory of progress. Some may have been stuck at level M since the end of second grade, when they were doing just fine, and the problem is that they have not progressed since then. Some of them may have entered the school just a year ago and may actually have moved steadily up for the whole second half of last year, making fairly dramatic progress. Those readers may not have had opportunities to do a lot of reading until arriving at this school and may be on a good course toward catching up. Of course, all this means that when one teacher communicates a child's reading levels with the following year's teacher, it is important that not just the final, end-of-the-year levels be communicated, but instead, the child's progress across the previous year(s).

FIG. 2–5 This notation chart shows conventions for marking running records.

ASSESSING YOUR READING WORKSHOP(S)

For your system to be complete, you need some ways not only to assess children, but to self-assess. How well is your reading workshop going? How is reading going in your class, in your grade, and in the school? Your data will give you a lot of information, but it may not tell you about kids' attitudes toward reading, about their sense of agency and independence. It may not tell you about teachers' stress levels or sustainability. You can assess these things, too. Essentially, you can give yourself a lens and then use that lens to look at your classroom or school. Educational leadership author Doug Reeves, when he was speaking about assessment to principals at Teachers College, reminded us that it's important to assess what you value. He chided schools for being at the mercy of their state test because they didn't assess in other ways as well. One school, for instance, was a school where virtually every child spoke a second language. Rather than lamenting how their ELL status would affect their test scores, Doug suggested they visibly demonstrate how their children were continuing to grow in their command of multiple languages. Another school had just taught the social issues book club unit. They value how books teach us how to live. After Doug's speech, children in that school began to keep tallies of how often they applied lessons learned from their books. They literally had tally sheets for standing up to bullies.

One decision you can make, then, is to decide what you value and figure out some ways to assess that quality in your workshop. You can also assess how deeply you are implementing workshop. Doug Reeves notes that the growth associated with any initiative is directly related to the depth of its implementation. His research led us to create a quick guide to assessing, which we include here, called "Bottom Lines: What to Look for in the Teaching of Reading, Grades 3–8."

This is a document we developed because sometimes it seemed to us that it was all too easy to lose sight of the forest for the trees. Yes, it is important to differentiate during the active engagement portion of a minilesson. But really, is it more key for a teacher to orchestrate every child's work during that three-minute interval so that no child is left unsure how to proceed for those three minutes, or is it more important to note whether kids are actually engaged in reading texts they can read during the bulk of the reading workshop? The document tries to highlight goals that matter most in the teaching of reading. Of course, the important thing is for you to revise the document so that it reflects the values that you and your colleagues hold dear. And above all, the document should be a source of feedback you value to so that it helps you and your colleagues work in a system of continuous improvement.

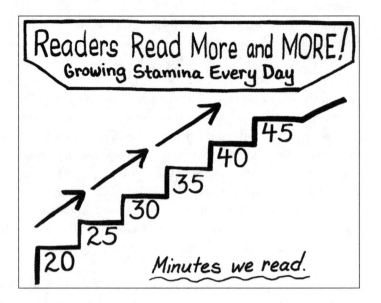

BOTTOM LINES
What to Look for in the Teaching of Reading, Grades 3–8

Readers Read a Lot: Teachers Track Volume and Progress up Levels

- Every student has a book baggie/bin, holding roughly a week's worth of books. For a reader working with level L books, the baggie may contain ten books. For level W baggies, it may contain two or three books. The levels of books reflect the assessed level—with some departures. If, for example, the reader was assessed at level R a month earlier, the bin may contain a level Q book, a few level R books, and a level S book. The reader is perhaps planning to read the latter in a same-book partnership, and the teacher may read the first chapter or two aloud or give a book introduction to keep tabs on work in this book.

- Students read (eyes on print) every day for thirty-five to forty-five minutes in the reading workshop. Teachers expect them each to read at least twenty-five pages in that time (strugglers are in easier books, so this is applicable to them as well). If they are reading J/K leveled books, they should be finishing a book approximately every ten minutes. Students read an equal amount at home each day. Volume is vigilantly watched. If it dips, the teacher self-reflects on whether her teaching is denying kids time to read. If that is not the case, the teacher works with individual students to devise solutions, including consequences if needed. During book clubs, volume is especially important and critical so more reading may be done at home. Some book clubs need to be brief.

- Students keep reading logs in which they record the number of minutes and pages read in school and at home. These are always on hand during reading time so teachers are able to refer to them in conferences. There is a lot of hype about these logs as scientific records, requiring precision and accuracy. Readers who record forty minutes each night are challenged to be more precise: was last night thirty minutes? The night before fifty? Those who record that they did not read one day are supported for recording accurate data. Teachers, readers, and partners mine the logs for patterns and developments, yielding goals.

- Readers are matched to books with 96% accuracy, fluency, and inferential comprehension. Teachers reassess (often with informal running records) in independent reading novels. Most schools ask for more formal running records least four or five times a year. Teachers should expect on-level grade 3–5 readers to move up approximately three levels a year, and below-level readers to progress more quickly. Readers who are transitioning to new levels will have books from both easier and harder levels in their baggies and will read the harder books in same-book partnerships or with a book introduction or support from a group. If teachers are in doubt about a book level, they can support the reader in a brief, harder trade book and watch. It is important to note disparities between reading and writing levels. If a strong writer has been assessed as a weak reader, reassess.

Units of Study Teach Readers to Approach Texts Ready to Do New Work—Partnerships and Writing about Reading Hold Readers to Goals and Allow Teachers to Track and Support Progress

- If one goal is that readers read a high volume, a second and equally important goal is that readers are explicitly taught the skills and strategies they need to move toward increasingly proficient work. Post-its® and notebook entries are a good window into the work readers are doing. One should be able to look at these across the grade levels in a school, and see, for example, first- and second-graders pause on particular pages to think about character feelings and find evidence of these. Then, by third grade, readers develop larger theories about the kinds of people their characters are, their traits, and are able to read through the lens of those theories. By fourth grade, readers note how a character acts differently in different roles, relationships, and settings. By sixth grade, readers' Post-its will be more apt to note ways characters carry the texts' theme.

FIG. 2–6 ❋ *(continues)*

- Once a teacher is teaching strong units of study, then it is a natural next step for the teacher and student to review their work (their Post-its and notebook entries) to make sure their work reflects the new teaching, as evidenced on charts. If students are not yet doing the new work that is on the charts, teachers can point this out: "Character traits—you've done this since second grade. It is important, yes, but what *new* work are you doing?" Teachers can rally them to do some now: "Try some NW: new work! Mark an *NW* on the Post-it so I pay attention to it."

- Every student has a reading partner and knows who this partner is. Partners are matched by level because relationships often involve "swap-book" and sometimes "same-book" work. Partners generally work together in the minilesson and meet sometimes during mid-workshop teaching and usually for the share session for the workshop, providing an audience for each others' writing about reading. Book clubs are generally comprised of two partnerships. Struggling readers usually work in same-book partnerships and progress in sync through books.

- Students use Post-its or very quick jottings to capture the thinking work that they are doing as they read. Units of study and whole-class instruction set readers up to approach texts with specific lenses or questions or theories in hand, which are sometimes tweaked in conferences and small groups. Readers are expected to have goals for the work they are doing as they read. The reading work a reader does will reflect the whole-class unit of study (e.g., instruction in interpretation will lead readers to ask, "What is this text mostly about?" and "How does this author decision fit with the text's main meaning?"), but the text, and the reader's own thinking and skill needs, will also influence the work the reader is doing. One should be able to look across the trail of writing a reader has done and see two or three lines of thinking that have been initiated, developed, coached, extended, and developed.

- Teachers and students are often prompted to try their reading work again, ramping up the level of it. "Look at your predictions and those of your partner. Have you been predicting not only what will happen next, but also how it will happen? Have you drawn on prior knowledge from earlier in the text? Go back and revise your predictions to make sure your work shows the best predicting work you can do. Put a mentor prediction in front of you and read on, pushing yourself to continue doing that level of work."

- It is helpful for the reader to approach the page with the intention to do particular kinds of work and for the reader to make note as he reads of places where his thinking has developed. The important thing is that the reader intends to do some work and carries that self-assignment as he reads. Simply jotting page numbers or leaving blank Post-its when one does related work as one reads, returning to these later, is probably sufficient for some readers. But generally it is not advisable for readers to think about writing only after they have completed the reading, because chances are not good that such writing will ramp up thinking during reading.

- Post-its and writing in a reading notebook show the work of the unit. One can look at the chart of skills and strategies for a unit and say to readers, "Which of these have you been doing? Can you show me the evidence of that work? Let's look at how that sort of work has changed over time as you've gotten better at it."

Record Keeping Helps Teachers Use Long-Term Goals to Power the Class's Progress

- A teacher's record-keeping system should reflect the whole-class goals that are embedded in the unit, so the records show the teacher's efforts to track each reader's (and small clusters of readers') progress along the trajectory of the unit's goals. What have these readers begun doing effectively, and what is still around the bend? What about for those other readers? The teacher will also have a skill or two that he is working on with particular readers (or groups of readers), and the records will also reflect continued efforts to scaffold and track progress toward those goals.

FIG. 2–6 *(continued)*

- A teacher is aware of readers' progress, not only as they do or do not move up the ladder of text difficulty, but also as they develop their abilities with particular skills and clusters of skills. The teacher does every possible kind of teaching to move readers along the pathways to more skilled reading. Small-group work, then, is usually compelled by an urgent need to push readers into doing the work they need to do, and once they are doing that work, the small-group work provides feedback on what is and is not working and lifts them to next steps. The teacher's knowledge of what kids need next also leads to whole-class voiceovers, mid-workshop teaching points, the development and temporary use of new tools, suggestions for partnership work, and new content in minilessons and read-aloud work.

- In minilessons, small-group work, and conferences, teachers will often use either the ongoing class read-aloud, a prior read-aloud, or a very short new text to demonstrate the step-by-step work that they do (and recommend students try) when working on a skill. Teachers demonstrate and talk about the sequence of steps that the reader takes, starting usually with reading along, then incorporating whatever it is that signals the reader to initiate the strategy use, then the first step in using the strategy, the next, and so on in ways that are transferable to another text, another day. These strategies are then listed on charts, with the goal being to *capture* the steps, not just overview the work. Teachers typically carry the present and past read-aloud books as they move among students, because they often demonstrate within these books in their small-group work and one-to-one conferences.

Read-Aloud

- The teacher reads aloud daily, usually for fifteen to twenty minutes. Usually the teacher will weave a short (or easy) text or two as well as a chapter book through a reading unit of study. Because minilessons are brief, it isn't usual for a teacher to read more than a page in a minilesson. Because reading work that the teacher is demonstrating can't be done on just any page of the read-aloud, the teacher first reads the read-aloud, noting when the text especially compels readers to do particular kinds of work. The teacher may make plans to read pages 4–6 in the first minilesson of the unit and then pages 17–18 in the third minilesson. In this instance, the teacher will gauge the amount of reading aloud she does outside the reading workshop so that between those two minilessons, she reads pages 6–17 aloud to the class. That is, teachers do not read aloud in every minilesson, and the book is also read aloud outside the unit of study. The teacher plans her progress through the read-aloud with an eye toward bringing particular portions of the text into minilessons.

- The teacher generally prepares for a read-aloud by reading the text and noting the main work that it asks readers to do, thinking, "Which of that work do my students need to do?" The teacher then plans instances in which he will show readers some work and therefore bring them along in it, and also plans to slow reading work down at certain places to demonstrate as one might in a minilesson. The teacher also plans to set kids up to do some work by stopping and jotting or turning and talking. Usually these interludes do not lead to whole-class conversations, but sometimes the teacher will support a brief whole-class conversation before reading on. Approximately twice a week, after reading for fifteen minutes, the teacher supports a ten- to twenty-minute long whole-class conversation, working to be sure students talk back to each other's ideas, cite the text where appropriate, follow lines of thinking, and use all the class has learned.

- The books that a class has shared become a resource that is dipped into continually all year. So if the teacher wants to demonstrate the way readers compare and contrast characters, she might compare the main character from the current read-aloud with characters from earlier read-alouds. The teacher might suggest students keep copies of previous read-alouds out on their desk and often compare and contrast the new insight that a reader has formed in a current book with ways that idea lives inside previous read-alouds.

(continues)

- Teachers read aloud a variety of books, including nonfiction books. These may relate to any part of the curriculum. The read-aloud work that readers do can be similar, whether the book is fiction or nonfiction.

Room Environment and Library

- Each reading level has its own basket, clearly labeled, and the books in any particular basket are all aligned to each other by level. The array of leveled books in a classroom reflects the readers in that room. That is, if most readers are reading levels L/M/N, then the majority of books in that classroom library will be in those levels. The baskets that are prominent in a classroom also reflect the current unit of study.

- Books that are not leveled are organized by topic or genre. Sometimes these are kept in baskets or on shelves with labels such as "light sports stories."

- Charts are placed front and center in the meeting area of a classroom. There are about four charts being developed or used at any one time in a reading workshop, and approximately the same number in a writing workshop. Charts have titles that reflect the overarching goal, such as "Nonfiction Readers Figure Out the Main Ideas and Supporting Details of a Text," and then cite specific strategies—procedures—readers might draw upon to do that work. For example, one item in such a chart might say, "At the end of a chunk of text, readers ask, 'What was that section mostly about?'" and then write what amounts to a little subheading for that section. The bullets on a chart usually support readers taking a sequence of steps to do some reading work.

FIG. 2–6   *(continued)*

Chapter 3

Implementing Running Records

Running records will help you and your children know how they are processing texts and comprehending at various levels. This will help you track their progress, get the right books into their hands immediately, and make intelligent reading plans together. Some may critique these assessments as reductive—and of course, describing a reader by identifying the level of text difficulty that child can independently handle is not a sufficiently rich description of that child's reading. But as one component of a complex system of reading assessment and instruction, I think it does provide schools, teachers, and caregivers a leg up as they work to identify needs and ensure success for each student. If you ask a child to read up a ladder of increasingly difficult texts or if you work with a child as she reads a text at a particular level of text complexity, you can, in just a few minutes, get a snapshot of that child's fluency and rate, accuracy, and literal and inferential comprehension. You will see these indicators change as the reader tackles increasingly difficult texts. You can never get an exact picture of what's happening in that child's mind, but running records provide a way to note the reading behaviors and decision making of a reader. You can analyze this information about a child's reading and use it to guide teaching decisions. It's such a simple tool, and it gives you a whole profile of a reader. I can't imagine anyone not wanting that information.

GETTING STARTED WITH RUNNING RECORDS
Selecting the Right Tools

There are a variety of tools you can use for conducting running records. Fountas and Pinnell have produced a boxed set. Your school may have versions of DRA and QRI available. The TCWRP website offers running records that you can download (although for your level A–L readers, you'll need to purchase one set of books from the publisher, because you can't assess those readers well from a printed-out text). Our tools aren't better; they're just shorter and free of charge. Teachers can access them instantly and put every possible penny toward purchasing books. Of course, there are downsides: you or your school system would need to duplicate the sheets and to devise a system for keeping the forms organized.

In the end, all of these systems essentially accomplish the same task. If texts have been leveled A–Z (or 1–40), then the assessment tool essentially extracts snippets of those leveled texts or provides you with briefer texts, putting these passages onto forms so a child can hold one form and you another. The teacher's form needs to be written in such a manner that you can record on it exactly what the child does when he reads the passage. This allows you and other teachers to later reconstruct the child's reading of the passage to ascertain if a text at this level of difficulty represents the child's independent reading level and to begin to develop some tentative theories about what it is that falls apart for the child at levels that are a bit too hard.

The payoff for conducting running records becomes apparent when you can use the information to channel students toward books that they can handle. To do this, you and the other teachers in your school need at least a quick introductory course on giving running records.

Giving Running Records

Marie Clay, the founder of Reading Recovery and the person who developed the term *running record*, wrote a short, accessible book on this topic, *Running Records for Classroom Teachers* (Heinemann, 2000). That is a good place to start if you do not already know how to conduct running records. If you don't have an assessment tool that guides you through this process, I suggest that you learn to conduct running records from the master herself by referring to this book.

For those of you who have established some familiarity, though, here's a quick review of the process in a nutshell. You give a leveled text to a child, providing a quick book introduction, and then ask him to read about 100 words aloud. Meanwhile, you hold a form that reproduces a portion of that leveled text. On this form, you note exactly what the child says and does as he reads the text. You note the words the child reads correctly with a check mark, as well as if he corrects himself or substitutes words to take the place of the words in the text. After the child finishes reading the text silently, you ask him to retell the text, considering how well he can hold onto the key details in the text. Then you ask a few simple questions about it, assessing both literal and inferential comprehension. Using a set of criteria, you'll determine if the child has understood the story well enough that you can ask him to try the same process again with an even harder leveled text.

Using records from the previous year or some quick questions and observations, you should be able to start the process with a text that is slightly too easy for the child to ensure that she will have great success and be at ease for the assessment. It is important, though, not to stop the assessment of a child once you find the first level at which she reads with 96% accuracy and adequate comprehension. To find a reader's just-right text level, you need to continue assessing her reading as she works with increasingly difficult texts until her comprehension of the text begins to break down—in other words, until her "ceiling level" is established. You also cannot chop off or even cut short the part of the assessment where you assess understanding. Reading is not reading if a child does not understand the passage enough to retell it and to answer a few literal and simple inferential questions.

Once you've figured out the text level that is just right for the child, you can show him how to find books at that level in the classroom, or you can offer him a stack of books to choose from. The child will then be able to keep a short stack on hand, perhaps in a bin or baggie, to read for the coming weeks.

WHAT INFORMATION WILL RUNNING RECORDS GIVE YOU?

Of course, the data gleaned from a running record reaches beyond matching the child to a level. It is a tool that is especially suited to telling you what it is that readers do and do not rely upon when reading. Look through students' running records carefully, not so much for the accuracy level—though it is important to keep this in mind—but more for the processing students are doing in their reading. As children are reading, they need to practice using all available sources of information in an integrated, reciprocal way: the meaning (semantic), structure (syntactic), and visual (graphophonic) cueing systems. If a child neglects to use or overuses one source of information, the teacher needs to teach the child to integrate her cueing systems more effectively.

As you look over a child's running records, you'll want to think about the patterns of reading behaviors you notice. For example, does the child lean mostly just on the visual information—the print—when solving an unfamiliar word, or does she draw also on context clues? Does she attend to punctuation cues to read in fluent phrases? Does she monitor for meaning, pausing or rereading to clarify when, for example, her intonation and phrasing are wrong and therefore the meaning is disrupted? Does she pause or reread to solve new vocabulary?

The best source for insight is the child's ceiling level, which is the level at which the child's reading runs into big trouble. For upper-grade readers, self-correction often "goes underground," and we suppose that the reader is correcting his errors before saying them. However, when presented with a more challenging text, fix-up strategies and self-correction behaviors often reappear. It is only when the child begins to miscue or when comprehension breaks down that you'll be able to see what a particular reader does and does not rely upon. Therefore, you will need to study what children do when they are faced with a challenge, having them read at instructional level—or even a frustration level—to discover this information. A running record without miscues leaves you nothing to study!

As you analyze the miscues in your student's reading, approach the work with a sense of curiosity. Unlike writing, where we can study what a child has put on the page, reading is an invisible process; the child's thinking is tucked inside his mind and out of reach. Analyzing a running record or listening to a child read aloud allows you to make this process visible, to peek inside his mind and try to figure out how he is making sense of one of the most complex things children will ever learn to do.

As you read running records, ask yourself:

1. What are my students doing when they encounter trouble?
2. Do they make attempts?
3. Do they check their attempts?
4. Do they make multiple attempts?
5. What sources of information do they use?
6. Do they use meaning, structure, and visual information equally, or do they lean more heavily on one information source?
7. How effectively do they use sources of information?

For example, imagine that you notice the child mumbling past hard words. If this happens more than once, you'll probably have a pretty good clue that this is what this particular reader does when encountering unfamiliar words. That is an important thing to know because it suggests this is not a child who is apt to learn vocabulary words from reading. And when reading social studies and science texts, the child's lack of attention to unfamiliar words will probably end up creating some serious issues.

Then too, say this is a child who substitutes a word for the word on the page. Imagine that the substitute only works when the child adds -ing to it. The child does that and continues reading. You will have just been given an important window into this child's attentiveness to syntax.

Perhaps another child seems to regularly stumble on question marks at the ends of sentences. You hear her suddenly pitch her voice high, trying to make a hasty accommodation to the presence of that question mark, but you are aware that other children reading the same level of text see ahead, noticing the upcoming punctuation. You begin to wonder if this reader proceeds through texts as if with blinders on, seeing only the immediate text that is before her. That will compromise her ability to synthesize and to predict.

Another student might read quickly, making a series of miscues that all seem to make sense in the context of the story but don't match the text. He seems to understand the text, and you imagine he's predicting the words that likely come next. Though miscues that draw on all three cueing systems appropriately can be insignificant, a pattern of this behavior can be problematic. These miscues can affect shades of meaning or academic vocabulary important to a topic. Slowing down and drawing this child's attention to the visual information on the page will help him avoid plowing right past miscues that *will* change the meaning by reinforcing the self-correction of miscues and support more sophisticated skills such as vocabulary acquisition and noticing author's craft and intention.

Of course, you'll be noting patterns in a student's comprehension, as well. A student may be able to read a text accurately and fluently but is simply word-calling, not understanding the text she is reading. Another student might accurately respond to all of the literal comprehension questions but struggles to discuss the inferential aspects of the text. The discussion after reading the text will help you to detect when this is happening.

Until you have collected running records of the child's work with a too-hard text, there is no possibility of analyzing patterns in that reader's struggles. Once you've identified these patterns, though, you can use this information to prioritize goals for individual students, as well as to form flexible small groups that you'll want to support across the next few weeks. You'll also want to study the data for patterns across your whole class and use that information to shape your whole-class teaching. Running records will be an invaluable source of information as you work to teach in a way that is responsive to your students' needs.

As you do this work, remember to work from a strength-based model, notice what each child *can* do, and then think about what their next steps might be. Often we are so eager to decide what to teach next that we skip right over what it is children are already doing. Take time to notice their strengths, and use this as a jumping-off point for your next teaching. This work is just as critical for our upper-elementary students—especially those who struggle. Literacy learning is an ongoing process, not something that's mastered and left behind in the primary grades.

Example: A Running Record at the Beginning of the Year

Here is an example of a running record a teacher conducted at the very beginning of her school year. You'll see that she abbreviates the analysis of the details of the reader's miscues and instead looks for wider patterns in Meghan's reading. Is this text level comfortable yet still challenging enough for her?

Leveled Text Excerpt and Meghan's Reading and Retelling

The teacher uses forms she downloaded from the Teachers College Reading and Writing Project website, and you could do this too if you are not already using another assessment system. Or you can simply make a photocopy of the leveled text you are about to give the child so that you can have something on which to mark the child's reading as a record of your assessment.

Drawing Conclusions Based on Meghan's Running Record

As we can see from the teacher's records, Meghan read this passage with only three miscues that she didn't correct, and all of her miscues made sense in the passage. This is a high accuracy rate for her at this level—97% in fact. We can see she had one miscue that she self-corrected immediately. She reread to make sure it made sense, looked right, and sounded right by rereading. She slowed down to process the information, confirmed that it was right, and picked her pace back up, sounding phrased and fluent through the next sentence.

Meghan demonstrates that she continues to use all sources of information to help her solve unknown words by using what she knows. For example, notice how she attempts to solve the word *familiar*. She initially breaks the word up into meaningful chunks (*fam-il*) and, using meaning and structure—what would make sense and what would sound right—correctly solves the word *familiar*. Again, she slows down to process, and then quickly picks her pace back up, reading fluently.

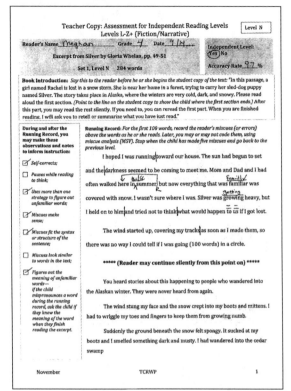

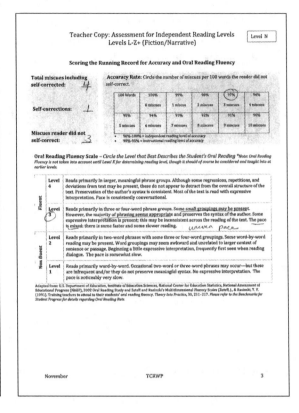

FIG. 3–1A   Meghan's assessment for independent reading levels (L–Z)

We can also see that Meghan miscues, reading *getting* for *growing*. This miscue shows that Meghan is drawing on all three of her cueing systems, because the miscue looks visually similar, sounds right, and make sense in the context of the sentence. Meghan also omits two words—"to us"—an error that, again, sounds right and makes sense in context. These errors indicate that Meghan is drawing on all three cueing systems but might indicate that she could use a reminder to pay closer attention to visual information.

Meghan's reading, however, did not always sound smooth. We can see from her teacher's notes that Meghan paused fairly often, making her phrasing somewhat inconsistent. To support students as they work with increasingly challenging texts, you will want to continue to push them to read with fluent phrasing and expression. It's important to remember that noting what the reader sounds like while she reads is just as important as recording her miscues during a running record. It's a common mistake to keep notes of the child's accuracy rate and neglect paying attention to and keeping anecdotal notes on how the reading *sounds*. A child can, for example, score at a high level, such as 97% accuracy, while scoring a level 2 on the Oral Fluency Scale on the same running record. When we move children up levels without considering the

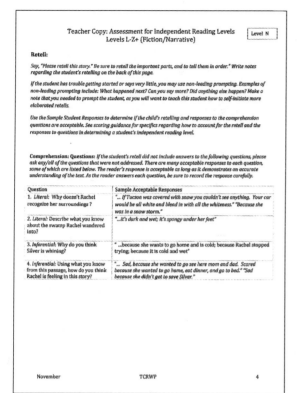

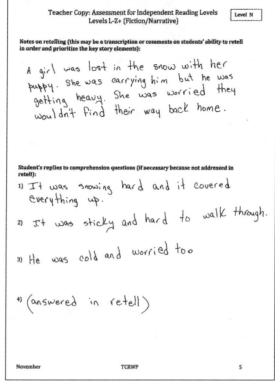

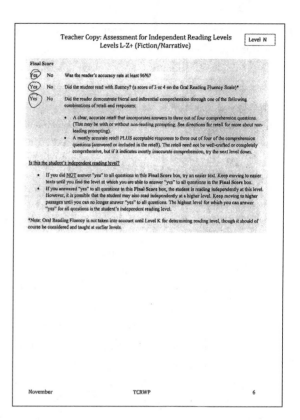

FIG. 3–1B   Meghan's assessment for independent reading levels (L–Z) *(continued)*

support they need to build their fluency, they end up working in higher-level texts with more challenges, rather than developing the fluency skills they need.

Looking at Meghan's retell, we can see that she has a deep understanding of what is happening in the story. For further information on what she understands, when asked the inferential questions, she answered them successfully, demonstrating her understanding of the question and the story. Additionally, we see evidence of her using meaning to help her solve an unfamiliar text, which is what we encourage our readers to do as they work in increasingly complex texts.

As we analyze Meghan's running record, we can see that she is doing a lot of things successfully. She integrates all sources of information efficiently and uses what she knows to solve unfamiliar words, though she might benefit from an emphasis on sampling more visual information. She slows down to process and regains her momentum quickly, though her fluency is a bit inconsistent.

Taking all of this into account and following the formula applied to running records, this text level, level N, could be Meghan's independent reading level for the time being. However, it would be appropriate to provide her with a more challenging text to establish her ceiling. Meghan's teacher gave her an excerpt to read from text level O, and her running record showed that to be her instructional level. As we work with a reader like Meghan, we need to pay close attention to how the reading sounds and how she solves when she gets to unfamiliar text, and ensure that she maintains flexibility with her solving.

It's important to remember that the point of running records is not that you open a notebook or a computer and record "level N." It's that you and the child find out what's next for that child—what reading work is needed for level O. The point is also not to gatekeep—to keep children *out* of levels. It's to get them *into* levels, with a better understanding of what work they need to attend to at that level.

FREQUENTLY ASKED QUESTIONS ABOUT RUNNING RECORDS

How can I streamline assessment at the beginning of the year?

Running records can feel overwhelming. At the beginning of the year, the goal of assessing all your students in the first few weeks can make you feel like there isn't possibly enough time to get to each and every one of your students. The effort to assess each child carefully and to create impeccable records could easily consume most of your time and energy. You are well aware that this is also an important time to establish a productive work environment in the classroom, develop individual relationships with children, create a culture of excellence even in places where that has not been the norm, and launch the learning life of the community. It is possible, however, to develop systems for streamlining running records—and doing so will make the rest of your reading instruction easier at the start of the year.

For example, you can prepare your materials in bulk, so that you've got a long-lasting supply of forms at each level, to avoid a time-consuming interruption if you run out. In your classroom, create a station at a table or desk for conducting running records, where all your materials are organized and easy to find: copies of forms organized by level, benchmark books, teacher guides and resources, extra paper for recording student comprehension responses, binders or files for completed running records.

Many schools also find it is enormously helpful if, at the end of a school year, every teacher goes to the classrooms that will become the new homes for the children they are sending on, and creates a baggie of books for each child to read at the start of the year. The year-ending classroom teacher works with the child, filling the baggie with an old favorite or two and with a whole batch of new books that promise to be just-right or easy (remembering that for children who do not read during the summer, there is always a slide backward) and that promise to be as enticing as possible. That teacher can even coach children to plan their progress through one or two of the selected books, using Post-its to mark reading for Day One and Day Two, using page-number patterns from the year that is ending to project progress through books in the year that is approaching. This system allows a teacher in September, who is assessing her incoming class, to watch those kids working with books that her colleague believed would be just right (allowing that incoming teacher to align herself with the previous teacher's judgments). Meanwhile, this process allows the teacher's running records to be informed by informal observations of children reading books that at least *someone* judged to be roughly just right. More important, it means that every child can get started from Day One, reading books that have been carefully selected by the child and a teacher who knows the child well.

If that can't be done, hopefully last year's teachers will at least send along the levels of text difficulty for those kids at year-end. And if even that can't be done, fourth- and fifth-grade teachers will be able to access scores on high-stakes tests, which can give them a general guess as to the levels of text difficulty for incoming students. Another way you can accomplish this is to do a quick running record or the independent running record sheet that is on TCRWP's website.

In any case, once you have your new class and the children are reading texts that someone believes are just right for them, you can quickly eyeball to see if youngsters seem actually to be able to read those levels. Did they slip over the summer (in which case it may take just a very short while to get summer rust worn off and to be back to the levels at which they left off). To help you scan your new class to get an approximate sense for reading levels (which then makes the process of giving running records more efficient), you may want to group children so that those who seem to be reading at similar levels are sitting together, allowing you to watch them reading in relation to each other. You can observe the scene as these readers read a bin of similarly leveled books, looking for signs of engagement or disengagement. This will let you know whether the book any one child is holding is at least roughly appropriate. If, for example, a child has been reading *Sarah, Plain and Tall* with engagement, then you'll use your knowledge of that book to decide that you might begin your running records at level R or S.

Professionals other than the classroom teacher can participate in conducting running records and matching readers to books. Many schools hire a reading specialist or others with special training in reading assessment to work with children during summer school or during the final two weeks of summer, conducting assessments and matching books to children. Some schools ask that these professionals conduct all the assessments for those who are particularly at-risk, thereby making it especially likely that these youngsters' time in school will be maximized, with every moment spent doing work that has been tailored to the child, and that their assessments will be as informed as possible.

Sometimes schools ask that summer assessments be given to a random sampling of children from every classroom, because having a few already-assessed children dotting a teacher's roster provides another way for classroom teachers to align their assessments with a schoolwide standard. In this situation, the teacher will have standards of measurement right there before her eyes. She can think, "If Kelci has been assessed as someone who can handle R books, then Zoey can't be an R as well, because her reading is considerably less strong." Even if a school is not able to use professionals to help during the summer, it is likely that at the very start of the year, some of the specialist teachers will not yet have their full caseload in place. Those teachers, then, can be brought into the work of assessing readers.

I also recommend that you and all your colleagues become accustomed to assessing students in groups, not in a one-by-one fashion. That is, when you conduct assessments, bring a cluster of children to the area in which you do assessments. Then explain what you'll be doing just once to that whole cluster of children, asking them to sit near you and start their independent reading while you assess one child after another. You'll find that this increases the efficiency of your running records.

During the running record process, a child reads aloud a leveled passage as you mark his reading. Then the child continues reading that passage silently. While one child is silently reading the rest of the assessment passage, try asking a second child to begin his reading aloud. Then, as the second child shifts into reading the second half of the passage silently, you can turn back to the first child to assess comprehension.

In these first weeks of school, our top priority must be matching each child with a book—a stack of books really—that she can read. This is not the time to dive into conducting any one assessment in depth, discovering every detail of that reader's strengths, preferences, and needs. For now, it is more critical that you buzz through the whole class, conducting quick assessments that allow you to launch all students into reading just-right books—and, better yet, reading with a partner at about the same text level. If you get every child roughly assessed within the first two weeks of the school year, there will be plenty of time later to conduct more detailed, rigorous assessments and to follow up on all the questions that your initial assessments provoke.

What do running records look like across the year?

Your school will probably also want to establish that teachers conduct more formal running records at regular intervals across the year. As mentioned earlier, most schools we work with give running records at predetermined times at least four times a year for all readers—RTI requires five—and much more often for lower-level readers and children who read below grade level. Formal windows for conducting running records are quite common and have their advantages, but they also are problematic because it is common for teachers to only assess during those windows, and children often need to progress to new levels far more often than those four windows allow. For example, assuming you assess at the start of the year, you'll find that within a month, the summer rust will have worn off for many readers and they'll be able to progress to higher levels. It is imperative, then, that assessing readers becomes no big deal.

If you know the level of the book the child is reading, you can give running records on-the-run constantly, using any scrap of paper to record words correct and miscues in any book. You can ask the child to read a little bit aloud to you, retell, and answer some literal and inferential questions. Hopefully, if you have just moved a child to a new level a week or two before the dates for the window for more formal running records, your school will accept the informal running record and your judgment that there's no need to reassess.

When you first start taking running records, especially on-the-run, they have the potential to be intimidating. You might feel paralyzed by the thought that you have to catch *every* thing the child does. This anxiety may distract you from the main purpose of the running record, which is to get a quick snapshot of how the child is processing text. In the beginning, you will miss some of what the child did. But your accuracy and efficiency in taking a running record will improve over time.

Remember that you only need to study what a child is doing on a portion of the text (usually 100–150 words). Try starting a conference with a quick running record, or begin a small group with students rereading for a bit while you take a record on one student at a time. Remind yourself that imperfect data is better than nothing, and pull up beside your readers for on-the-run running records whenever you can.

What about assessing children's nonfiction reading levels?

Your initial running records will use fiction texts and will give you a baseline for children's reading levels, as well as a wealth of information about each reader. Now you're asking, what about their nonfiction levels?

If you have lots of time for assessment, and plenty to spend on assessment tools, it could be very interesting to assess kids as fiction and as nonfiction readers, using parallel running record assessments. (The Fountas and Pinnell boxed set for assessing fiction and nonfiction springs to mind.) You could even assess children using both assessments at the same time, which would let you know which children read nonfiction at lower levels than fiction, which read at the same level, and so on. You might find that their patterns of fluency and accuracy are not always similar or that their ability to do inferential thinking is or isn't similar. I have to say that we would love to be in a study like that, and if your school is doing that kind of deeply calibrated, parallel assessment, let us know, because we'd love to study the data to see if patterns emerge.

However, all of that requires an enormous amount of time, and therein lies the rub.

You only have so much time with the children, and it can start to feel as if you are spending time on assessment that needs to be spent on instruction. Then, too, it can seem like you spend so much time collecting data that you have no time to teach in response to it, to apply it. It is also not good if you have time to give running records but no time left for performance assessments of higher-level thinking skills.

Ultimately, we decided it was good enough to assess children's fiction levels and then start with those as their most-likely/nearly-right/good-enough-to-start-with levels for nonfiction, with the intention to observe kids and move them down a level in nonfiction if they seem to struggle, which happens fairly often, because children's nonfiction levels often lag a bit behind their fiction levels. Hopefully, you'd then be able to move readers back up so they are reading the same level in nonfiction as in fiction after they have been studying nonfiction for a while. That's our best advice to you.

If you do have a deep assessment budget and time to do assessments in both fiction and nonfiction, you will note that we do not include a tool for leveling nonfiction texts on TCRWP's website. You'll have to look elsewhere for that tool. We found it difficult to level nonfiction with high degrees of reliability because, for one thing, there are so many different ways that nonfiction might get harder. The topic might become more nuanced. The text features might begin to add complexity rather than illuminate meaning. The vocabulary might become more technical, or the explanations of vocabulary might become more technical. The structure might become hybrid or confusing. It simply becomes very difficult to compare one authentic level P nonfiction text to another level P, let alone be sure that this N and this O and this P text really do demonstrate a cohesive ladder of difficulty or are the same level of difficulty as a fiction text at levels N, O, and P. But the more important reason we found it difficult to level nonfiction texts with reliability is that the difficulty a child experiences reading a nonfiction text relates directly to the knowledge the child brings to that text.

Granted, this is partly true for fiction texts too: knowing something about mystery or fantasy will help a reader with a mystery or fantasy story. But the importance of background knowledge is not nearly as significant a leg up when children are reading fiction as when they are reading nonfiction. Knowing a lot about dinosaurs dramatically helps a child read about *Tyrannosaurus rex*. The fact that the child comes to that text already knowing the concepts of carnivores and herbivores; scavengers and predators; Mesozoic, Jurassic, and Cretaceous eras; and that he already knows a lot about tyrannosaurus too, makes a huge difference! So the level at which a child reads nonfiction on highly familiar topics won't represent the level at which that child reads nonfiction texts on totally unfamiliar topics.

What should I consider when assessing students below benchmark?

As I write this, I know that you and your school will already have a plan for assessing students who are reading considerably below benchmark. Clearly, these students cannot wait until you have other things in place. Although I cannot do justice in this section to this critically important topic, let me lay out some nonnegotiable bottom lines around which research is crystal clear.

First and most importantly, any child who is reading considerably below benchmark needs instruction that is particularly assessment-based. This means that adopting a one-size-fits-all approach for readers who worry you will never be a viable solution. Think of these readers as children who are sitting on three legged stools that are each missing one leg. Some of those stools are missing the leg of word solving, others of comprehension, still others, of fluency. Whereas readers who are successful tend to be somewhat alike—they can do the essentials in ways that work—readers who struggle will be especially unlike each other. If these students are reading at levels M (Magic Tree House) or below, you will want to assess them as beginning/transitional readers. After all, that is what they are, which means that you need not only to conduct running records to establish their independent and instructional reading levels, but you also need to code those running records carefully so that you know what sources of meaning those readers do and do not yet draw upon when reading. If one of these children reads the sentence "I got on my horse and rode away" as "I got on my *house* and rode away," and that child doesn't see that as a problem and self-correct, you'll be able to adjust your instruction to support meaning. With these children, it will be essential for you to administer a full battery of assessments, including those for fluency, letter-sound knowledge, and high-frequency words, to gain a full picture of them as readers. You might consult *A Guide to the Reading Workshop, Intermediate Grades* for more information on these assessments and the characteristics of readers below level J.

Children who are reading well below benchmark profit from one-to-one support or, at most, one-to-three support, and they benefit from support that is as frequent as possible. This means that if you have

FIG. 3–2   This chart shows some of the challenges of reading complex nonfiction.

a choice between an hour of instruction with a group of six children or half an hour with a group of three children, go for the latter. And if you have a choice between twice a week support for an hour and four times a week support for half an hour, go for the latter. Our organization works with paraprofessionals, parents, and volunteers in a huge number of schools—sometimes as many as thirty people in a school—to help those adults learn to provide highly structured, half-hour, one-to-one sessions several times a week with first- and second-graders who are reading well below benchmark. That work, known as Reading Rescue, is guided by staff developers who assess the readers, channel appropriate books to the tutors, and coach the tutors. The results of this one-to-one work are astonishing, with students progressing an average of six to eight levels over a semester of support—and with the tutors coming to new levels of competence and self-confidence. Of course, this sort of one-to-one support needs to be in addition to and not instead of class time (no student should ever be taken from a reading workshop to receive help in reading) and in addition to RTI, Tier 2 supports children receiving help from knowledgeable teachers.

I strongly suggest that teachers working with readers who are reading below benchmark levels use Richard Allington's *What Really Matters for Struggling Readers* (Pearson, 2011) as a resource. I also suggest that upper-grade teachers who are teaching students whose reading resembles that done by younger students in the school be given time to observe K–2 reading teachers and to participate in staff development led by those teachers to learn theories of reading development and methods, such as leading small-group shared reading, interactive writing, word study, and the like.

How can I make sure children have ways to define themselves as readers that are not related to levels?

Your first job at the start of the year is to fall in love with each and every child—right away. That is not always easy when you are still mourning the loss of last year's kids, but the truth is that your students know when they are surrounded by positive regard. For them to learn, they need to be in a place where they can take risks, reveal vulnerabilities, and aspire toward big goals—and your methods of assessing readers play a big part in helping readers know they are in such a place.

At the start of the year, I recommend that every teacher across a school find ways—straightaway—to invite students to teach you who they are and what they care about as people and as readers and writers. During those first days of the school year, when no one is yet accustomed to sitting at a desk all day anyhow, it is important to set children up to represent their strengths and interests and quirks and habits as readers and writers. Perhaps you'll ask children to draw pictures of one time in their lives when reading was the best it could ever be and one time when reading was the worst it could ever be or to create a timeline of their reading lives. The important thing won't be the pictures alone but the stories that children swap about their reading histories as they share those pictures. Perhaps you'll want to give each child a square of the bulletin board, and ask them to bring in stuff that shows their histories as readers. That's a more powerful idea than you might think: imagine if you were asked to fill a square of the bulletin board with things that show *you* as a reader. Which books, of all that you have ever read in your whole life, would you choose to put into that square? What ways of responding to reading would go there? It's not lightweight work to take the time to construct images of who we are as readers and to put those out into the world.

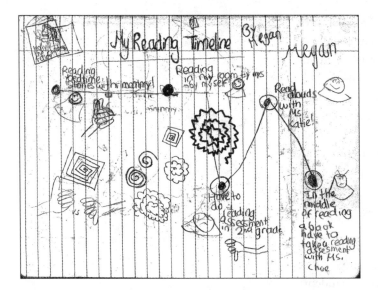
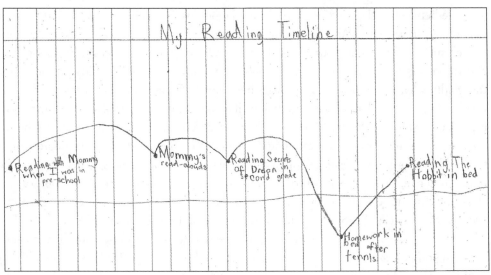

FIG. 3–3   Students create timelines of their reading lives.

Perhaps you and other teachers across your school will ask each child to read something—a poem or a picture book—and to leave a Post-it that shows what that child was thinking, and then you can teach children to conduct reader studies, noticing the different kinds of thinking that each tends to do.

All of this work will allow you to begin to develop some language about how each of your readers is different from other readers. To one child, you might say, "You've got this way of reading and asking questions that gets right to the heart of everything. It's such a special thing because you take us into really deep conversations with those questions. I hope over the year, you teach us all about how you do that." The important thing to realize is that that child might be reading books that are the least complex of any books being read in the class, and yet the child is not just a reader who is working with that level of text. She is also an inquirer and a teacher of inquiry to the class.

My point is that you can temper the emphasis on a ladderlike progression of reading development if you highlight the many ways your students have composed reading lives for themselves. Each student is a complex combination of habits, aspirations, talents, preferences, and worries—far more than just a text level. Once you match kids to books, chances are good there will be talk such as, "I'm an N reader." You'll want to have the goods to broaden and balance that. "You are also our class expert on the sports page, aren't you? I can't believe that you actually read it every single day—and do that before you even come to school! You are going to have to teach the rest of us how to read statistics, 'cause I think most of us just ignore them. But you don't, do you?"

Teachers have extraordinary power to make each child feel seen and respected—or to feel just the opposite.

Chapter 4

Understanding Bands of Text Complexity and Using Them to Move Readers up Levels

ONCE YOU HAVE CALCULATED the level of text difficulty that each of your students can handle, you can steer each child toward books that are apt to be supportive—and you can also steer your teaching toward skills that are apt to be required by those books. When you pull a chair alongside a youngster to talk about the text he is reading, even if you do not know that specific text, you can draw on your knowledge of books within that text's general place along the gradient of text difficulty to ascertain the work the reader is apt to be doing.

WHY RELY ON BANDS INSTEAD OF SINGLE TEXT LEVELS?

There is some debate over whether each and every text level will be informative or whether it's the "band of text levels" that can inform your teaching. My colleagues and I believe it's the latter, although we've considered both positions carefully. We ordered 100 books for each level, J–Z, and looked across all those books to determine if we found it convincing to say there are specific features for each discrete text level. We came from this work believing that although there is validity to saying that books can be categorized according to ascending levels of difficulty, there is less merit to saying that all books at a particular level are at that level for the same reasons. That is, there are lots of ways for a book to be hard: one book may include foreign language words, another, a sea of characters, and in yet another, the passage of time may be especially complex. There is no one way for a book to be hard—or easy (although it's true that the books in levels A–K are vastly more amenable to being differentiated by precise level). Look at a collection of books at any level above K, and you'll quickly see that books ascribed to that level are not easily characterized by a precise list of traits.

Having said that, my colleagues and I have found that it is not only possible, but extraordinarily helpful to describe some of the main ways books within a *band* of text difficulty, a clump of several text levels, tend to pose new challenges for readers. To cluster text levels into these bands, we studied data from 60,000 students and found, as mentioned earlier, that kids tend to move fairly easily between some levels and to get stuck at the transition to other levels, suggesting that those places where kids are prone to get stuck might involve larger steps up. For this reason, and others, we have come to think of upper-grade text levels as falling within these bands:

Band K/L/M

Band N/O/P/Q

Band R/S/T

Band U/V/W

Band X/Y/Z (These texts are complicated to talk about because many texts have been categorized as Z not because of text complexity but because of adult content.)

WHAT KINDS OF READING WORK ARE CALLED FOR AT EACH BAND?

For each band of text difficulty, it is helpful to ask, "For readers who are working with books in this band, what is the new work that they will be expected to do?" If you, as teachers, have a sense for the new work that readers will need to do, then you can draw on this knowledge when you help a reader move into one of these bands. For example, you can provide book introductions and strategy lessons that help readers do this new work. You can also keep an eye on readers' progress by paying attention to their abilities to do the new work required in their specific band of texts. In addition, you can think about whether your minilessons and small-group work are supporting the skills that your readers are expected to use.

It is possible to catalog a huge list of all the work that readers are apt to do when working in a band of text difficulty, but the longer and more detailed the list, the less broadly applicable it will be. More importantly, the reason to talk and think about bands of text difficulty is that this knowledge can inform your teaching. The reason that it helps to describe the new work readers are apt to need to do within a band of text difficulty is this: when you draw a chair alongside a reader and ask, "How's it going?" you'll have some hunches about the challenges the reader is likely to be facing. The main goal of this work, then, is for it to be portable. The teacher should be able to look at a book that a child is reading (a book the teacher may or may not know) and draw on her internalized knowledge about a gradient of text difficulty to predict the challenges that book is likely to be posing. My colleagues and I, then, have worked hard to develop the shortest possible list of characteristics for any one band of text difficulty and to talk about the work readers are required to do in language that does not require a PhD in reading instruction to be understood.

Bands of text complexity

	kim Lower End: Nate the Great Higher End: Freckle Juice	**nopq** Lower End: Amber Brown Higher End: Fudge-a-Mania	**RSt** Lower End: Because of Winn Dixie Higher End: Bridge to Terabithia	**UVW** Lower End: Loser Higher End: Walk Two Moons
STRUCTURE/PLOT	• One clear, central problem and solution • OR one clear, central problem and resolution	• Characters encounter not just one concrete problem, but a blend of pressures, or a multidimensional problem. • Between the character's motivation and the story's resolution there will be a few subplots	• Stories are layered with meaning • Only part of the problem is labeled and discussed; the other parts of the problem have to be extracted • Problems are too big and too layered for all to be solved	• Multiple plotlines
CHARACTERS	• A lot of dialogue between several main characters which isn't always tagged • Characters are static • Characters have a few dominant characteristics which are explicitly and repeatedly labeled • Feelings change over the course of the story, but traits are fairly consistent (and these are usually related to the main problem)	• Characters are conflicted and therefore more ambivalent. • What characters want is usually more complex or complicated • Character traits change from beginning to end • Narrator or character will tell the reader about the character's complexities. Reader can pay attention to what characters do, say and think to get a full understanding of the character	• Character traits are not explicitly stated • Characters encounter problems and work to respond to those problems, changing and learning in the process • Characters are gray; good and bad; more than one way as a result of complex internal emotions (which the characters or the narrator does not come right out and say as in the preceding band) • Minor characters become important. Reader has to pay attention to how the minor characters influence and teach the reader about the main character	• Characters continue to become more complex and nuanced • Characters are increasingly teenagers CAUTION: If the reader isn't a teenager it can be hard to empathize with the characters and therefore can miss out on a huge part of the story • The point-of-view of each character

Bands of text complexity

tricky parts	• Tricky words (number of 2 syllable words increases dramatically, a few 3 syllable words, irregular spelling patters, picture support can be useful) • More and more words in these books that are not used conversationally and many are subject specific	• Now, there are also tricky phrases and passages • Figurative language that sometimes matters; impt. to teach readers how to handle this language because eventually it is important to understand in later bands • Readers need to be able to self-correct inaccurate interpretations if later details disprove their theories.	• Now, there are also tricky chapters (Readers need to expect that at times books are hard on purpose. Readers are not supposed to entirely get what is going on. Instead, readers read and say, "Huh?" Then, they read on, expecting things will become clearer in the end.	• Shifts in time: Backstory is increasingly prevalent. Backstory is revealed through the text. Usually not a flashback, but instead a character telling or discovering some background information. • Shifts in voice (sometimes there is a new narrator at the start of a new chapter signaling a new plot line unfolding.)
OTHER THINGS TO CONSIDER...	• Reader has to hold onto the problem for a longer period of time because the text is longer • Because books preceding this band of difficulty were episodic, readers now need to work on synthesis and determining importance	• Less picture support than the preceding band • Synthesis • Thinking about why characters do what they do (looking for multiple reasons, not just one) • Determining importance • Being a flexible reader: While progressing through a story, readers should expect the need to refine their sense of the problem that holds the whole story together	• Setting plays an important role; can be considered a character – setting influences the characters and the plot • Reader must be willing to learn content • When reading HF, readers need to extract the timeline of historical events as well as of the protagonist's events, and synthesis the intersection of these two timelines • Setting evolves across a story and is just as important as the characters' evolutions • Prediction - subplots and minor characters who may seem inconsequential in the end usually fit into the story • Readers realize things about characters that the characters themselves do not know	• Symbolism is important (Theme is important) • Stories in this band are statements about the world and life and the social issues both carry • Think whether the setting could be a symbol for a theme or issue in the lives of the character • Think about changes in the setting. For example, when readers find in Walk Two Moons that Sal says, "The hot air pressed against my face and the air was like a hot heavy blanket draped on my neck and back," the heat has become a metaphor for the weight of Sal's journey and also a warning signal that previews the snakebite in the chapter.

FIG. 4–1 Bands of Text Complexity "cheat sheet" shows the characteristics of text bands.

What kind of work is called for in band K/L/M?

(Nate the Great to *The Paint Brush Kid)*

Structure

When readers move into books within this band of text difficulty, they are apt to find that instead of reading episodic chapter books, where each chapter is essentially a self-contained story involving the same characters, they are now reading books in which a single storyline tends to span the entire book. At the lower end of this band, that might mean the story is told across *pages* without chapters but that the story has parts to it (such as *Nate the Great*), and at the higher end, that might mean the story is told across *chapters* (such as in the Magic Tree House series). This means readers are required to carry a lot of content across a broader swath of text, so synthesis and determining importance are important skills. Readers profit from understanding how stories tend to go because when reading fiction at these levels, most of it fits neatly into the traditional story structure of a character who has traits and motivations, runs into problems, and somehow resolves those problems.

The good news is that books at this level tend to provide youngsters with a lot of support. Both the books and the chapters (when there are chapters) tend to be short. The title of the book (and sometimes of the chapters) and the blurb on the back cover help readers grasp the main through-line in the story (as is the case for the book *Horrible Harry and the Ant Invasion*).

Characters

The characters in these books have a few dominant characteristics, and these are explicitly labeled, repeatedly. Horrible Harry is horrible! The characters tend to be relatively static. They change their feelings over the course of the story, but their traits remain fairly consistent throughout the book. Often these traits help the character solve the problem (such as in the Cam Jansen series, where Cam has to figure out the mystery, and her amazing memory helps her), and sometimes the traits are related to the main problem. In *Horrible Harry and The Ant Invasion*, Harry likes creepy things, so when the teacher asks, "Would you like to be the ant monitor?" story elements coalesce around this character trait.

In these stories, the character often wants something concrete—to take care of creepy creatures, to win the prize, to get the shoes that popular kids wear. In the books at the high end of the band, it fairly often happens that the character ends up getting not the concrete thing he wanted, but rather, satisfying the deeper motivation that made the character want that concrete object in the first place. The boy does not get the shoes that the popular kids all wear, but he does get a friend and a chance to feel popular.

There is a lot of dialogue in these books, often between several main characters. It is not always tagged and is sometimes interrupted, as in this example: "'I'm going,' Mark said, getting up to walk out. 'I won't ever come back.'" Dialogue also reveals emotions in many cases, such as this one, and often readers can infer how characters are feeling by studying the dialogue. The settings in these texts are fairly consistent.

The settings may shift as scenes shift (Cam and Eric were at her house, now they are at the movies, for example), but the settings act as backdrops for the main action, which is between the characters.

Vocabulary and Syntax

Readers of books in the K/L/M band of difficulty will find themselves required to tackle an increasing number of two- and three-syllable words. They will find more and more words that are not words they use conversationally—and many of them will be subject-specific. A story about soccer will include *opponent*, *cleat*, *faceguard*, and *positions*, for example.

What kind of work is called for in band N/O/P/Q?

(*The Chocolate Touch* and A to Z Mysteries to *Fudge-a-mania*)

Structure

Before this band, the narratives that children tended to read fell neatly into a traditional story structure in which a single main character has a big motivation. He wants something and gets stymied, but like *The Little Engine that Could*, the character tries, tries, tries and eventually makes it over the top of the story mountain.

Once readers are working with texts in the N/O/P/Q band of text difficulty, the texts will be more structurally complex. The narrative frame is still present, but the character encounters not just one concrete problem but a blend of pressures, or a multidimensional problem. In *Amber Brown Is Not a Crayon*, the big problem is that Amber's best friend Justin is moving away, but because Justin puts the best face on this, Amber feels that he doesn't share her agony over the impending separation, and consequently they have problems in their relationship. Then, too, there are smaller problems that pop up. Will they be able to convince the family that is considering buying Justin's home that it's not at all the house they want? When reading texts in this band of text difficulty, a fair amount of abstraction is required for readers to extract the one overarching storyline that provides the bearing walls for the story. In addition, the narrative structure is not always as simple. There is sometimes a flashback or a dream sequence in the text, particularly in texts that are higher in this band.

This means, of course, that the work readers were doing earlier in synthesis and determining importance is all the more necessary now, and the question "What seems to be the central problem in this story?" is both important and challenging. Readers should expect that quite a bit of thought is required to respond to that question and that the answer often has several parts to it. Problems will start to be a bit multidimensional, and between the character's motivation and the story's resolution, there will be a few subplots. These subplots will also come about through the minor characters, who come to be more important in these levels.

When working with readers in this band of text difficulty, then, it is helpful to show them that readers work to keep focused on the central storyline. It helps if readers understand that the question "What *now* does this text seem to be mostly about?" will produce an answer that evolves over time. As they read more deeply into a book and as more information is provided, readers should expect they'll refine their sense of the overarching problem (the one that holds the whole story together). A reader might read about a point of contention between two important characters and think this will be central to the story and then be shown that actually that one conflict was only a small part of the main storyline. The important thing is that the reader be willing to let go of her first expectation to fashion one that is more grounded in the text as it actually unrolls.

Characters

One way to help readers who are working in this band of text difficulty synthesize the text is to help them think about *why* characters do what they do, ascribing more than one cause to an effect, using phrases such as "Another reason is . . . ," "Another part of this is . . . ," and "And another part is . . ." To talk about cause and effect, readers need to link earlier parts of a book to later parts, uncovering the through lines ("Because of . . ." "Additionally, this happened because . . ." "As a result of . . .").

It's not only the storyline in these books that is more complicated; the main character, or protagonist, will tend to be complicated as well. The character is often conflicted. Amber wants to be a little kid and wants to be a teenager at the same time. She is thirteen years old, but also nine. She both likes her mother's new boyfriend and resents the way he has replaced her father. She both adores her pal Justin and is furious at him for moving away. Feelings tend to be ambivalent, and at least some of the trouble in the story is internal, related to these ambivalent feelings. You may notice that these descriptions match many of the students in front of you and their own emotional development. Their feelings and relationships, too, are becoming more nuanced and complicated—and that is reflected in the books they're holding.

Usually, however, readers do not need to deduce these characteristics. The characters are complex, but readers are told about this complexity. Usually, it will not be subtle. Someone—the character or the narrator—will come right out and tell the reader the traits of the main characters. Readers need only pay attention to these descriptors and then carry them so that when the character later acts accordingly, the reader is able to think, "Yep, there she goes again, acting . . ." When readers do need to infer traits, characters' feelings will tend to relate to traits. Students can study what characters do and feel and begin to infer, "Oh, I saw how she reacted here and here. That tells me she is the type of person who . . ."

As the storyline becomes a bit more complicated and subplots begin to emerge, these can relate to minor characters. In books at these levels, in particular at the higher levels, there may be minor characters who have problems as well, and these can connect to the major character's problem. For example, Ramona's father has lost his job and Ramona is thinking of ways to make money for the family. But meanwhile, each member of the family is dealing with the job loss, as well.

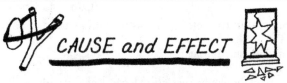

CAUSE and EFFECT

S-t-r-e-t-c-h your thinking by considering more than one cause.

- Another reason is...

- Another part of this is...

- And another part is...

LINK earlier parts to later parts.

- Because of...

- Additionally, this happened because...

- As a result of...

In books at these levels, in particular at the higher levels in the band, the setting is also starting to become more important, especially in historical fiction or fantasy books.

Vocabulary and Syntax

Earlier, I suggested that readers who are working in the K/L/M band of text difficulty need to be prepared to work with tricky words, because they will begin encountering many more multisyllabic words, and this trend will continue. There are two things to note as readers move into level N/O/P/Q books.

First, readers will encounter many words that live in the world of written language and are rarely part of a child's spoken language. A teacher may not, at first, think of *unique* as a tricky word. After all, it is not a term like *ambivalent* or *morose*—but how often might a child use the word *unique* over terms like *special* or *different*? It is helpful, then, for teachers to realize that reading is now taking children into a world of academic language, and there are far more unfamiliar or vaguely familiar words in that world than a teacher might realize.

But my main point is that at this band of text difficulty, readers encounter not just tricky *words*, but tricky *phrases* and tricky *passages*. Usually these are tricky because they include a play on language, perhaps a pun or a metaphor or a figure of speech. So at these levels, students will start to encounter figurative language and, especially, nonliteral language. The title of the book *Amber Brown Is Not a Crayon* is a perfect example. The reader who knows there is a character named Amber, surname Brown, and who has never had one of those boxes of 300 crayons, including one bearing the title "amber brown," might well miss the entire point of that book's title. Another example is in *Forever Amber Brown*. Readers know that the mother's boyfriend and Amber both like to bowl. At one point, Amber is discussing whether her parents might get reunited, and she says that the chances are about as great as that of her scoring 300 in bowling. There are a few challenges in these tricky parts of books. One is that often some world knowledge is required to grasp the point: readers need to know that 300 is a perfect (and therefore unlikely) score in bowling. The other problem, though, is that passages such as these could lead readers astray. A reader might misread Amber's comment about her parents getting back together and somehow get the idea that the characters are now going bowling. As the language in texts becomes more complex, it is almost inevitable that readers will misinterpret in ways that could lead them astray. The important thing is that readers need to be able to revise inaccurate interpretations if, as they read on, they are not borne out.

What kind of work is called for in band R/S/T?

(*Because of Winn-Dixie* to *The Tiger Rising* and *Bridge to Terabithia*)

Structure

In this band, there is a trend toward stories becoming layered with meaning. It is as if the characters and the events, too, are like icebergs—with the part that shows, which is labeled and discussed, being only part of what's really going on. The problem may seem to be the relationship between these two characters, but really, deep down, the problem is a bigger sense of loneliness (or other big issue). The problems are big enough and layered enough that they are not all solved. In fact the storyline is less about a character who encounters a problem and rises to the challenge, solving the problem, and more about characters who encounter problems and work to respond to those problems, changing and learning in the process. Particularly in the higher levels of this band, readers will need to consider more complex social issues such as homelessness or coming to terms with the death of a parent—and figure out what the story is saying about them.

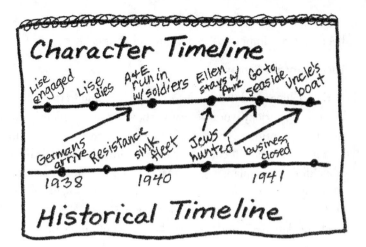

It is especially notable that in this band of text difficulty, readers need to follow the evolving plot line—and also the evolving setting. The setting becomes a force in the story, influencing characters and the plot, just as, say, an antagonist might. The setting sets the tone and mood and could relate to the characters' problems and motivations. In historical fiction, for example, readers need to construct two timelines—one for historical events and one for the protagonist's events—and then see how the two timelines intersect.

In most well-written novels within this band, the setting evolves across the story and plays a role in the story. There is an evolution to Terabithia and to Narnia, for example. Settings change because characters relate to them differently across the story. Readers are expected to accumulate a growing understanding of the setting, just as we accumulate a growing understanding of main characters.

As more important elements emerge in these more complex texts, readers need to hold more parts of the book in mind. In particular, there are subplots and minor characters in books in this band of text difficulty that might seem to be inconsequential but in the end fit into a synthesized whole. Readers, then, are expected to keep some of these in mind as they read, predicting, for example, that the sister who was mentioned in passing at the start of the book may return to play a role at the end of the book.

Character

In the preceding band of text difficulty, the main character was often ambivalent, and the problem often had several parts (as in Amber being upset with Justin for moving away and also upset because he was not feeling crushed about their looming separation). The trend toward complexity increases in this band, and increasingly the characters are characterized by complex internal, emotional lives. Jesse, in *Bridge to Terabithia*, is full of anxiety, self-esteem issues, and self-doubt. Rob, in *The Tiger Rising*, is equally conflicted. In level N/O/P/Q texts, the characters or the narrator often came straight out and labeled the character's emotional life, but now readers are left to infer what the character is feeling. In fact, readers of the R/S/T band often realize things about the character that the character herself does not know. In particular at the higher levels in the band, the title may relate to the main character's issue, such as in *The Tiger Rising*. At these higher levels and beyond, readers will need to ask themselves, "Why might the author have made the character feel this way? How does that fit with the rest of the story?" There also may be minor characters who do not play large roles, who are there just to populate the story. Readers will have to figure out which of these minor characters merits attention.

Vocabulary and Syntax

Whereas the previous band contained tricky sentences—usually figurative language—books in this band of text difficulty often contain tricky chapters. A teacher might say to these readers, "Before, if you came to a tricky chapter and were totally confused, you might think the book was too hard for you. Now, at this level, you need to expect that sometimes books are hard on purpose, and you are not supposed to entirely get what is going on. You can say, 'Huh?' and read on, expecting things will become clearer as you go."

In addition, sentence structures at these levels are beginning to be more complex. Authors will play with commas, ellipses, and so on, perhaps making it harder for readers to read a sentence to get the phrasing. Students may need to reread to get the phrasing or the mood of a part. There also may tend to be more academic vocabulary in these texts. And particularly in historical fiction texts, there may be domain-specific vocabulary, specific to a time period and or a place.

What kind of work is called for in band U/V/W?

(*Loser* to *Walk Two Moons*)

Books in this band of text difficulty exacerbate most of the challenges described in band R/S/T. A few elements of story are apt to become especially complex at this level, and one is the passage of time. These stories still tend usually to unfold somewhat chronologically, often in a relatively straightforward structure, yet there is often some big event that occurred before the novel begins, and we have to read on to learn about that event and to find its significance. Backstory, then, becomes increasingly prevalent, and a reader can be two-thirds of the way through a book and still be learning more about the backstory. Usually the backstory is not an action-packed flashback, in which the character actually relives the event, but instead involves a character telling or discovering some background information.

Sometimes these texts have multiple plotlines. Readers will be apt to discover this first when they are reading along and find that as a new chapter begins, there is a new narrator, or a character has been left behind. Usually when this happens readers are not utterly mystified—it's usually easy to see the connection between the different fragments of the story. In *The Thief Lord*, by Cornelia Funke, for example, one chapter tells the story of two boys who are runaways in Venice. In the next chapter, however, we are following the detective who is pursuing the boys.

The characters and setting at this level start becoming more symbolic of bigger themes. It pays off for readers to think whether the setting could be a symbol of a theme or an issue in the lives of the characters. Readers should also think about changes in the setting (especially times when the setting becomes oppressive), such as perhaps foreshadowing developments that are not exclusive to the setting alone. For example, in *Walk Two Moons*, Sal says, "The hot air pressed against my face and the air was like a hot heavy blanket draped on my neck and back." Here, the heat has become a metaphor for the weight of Sal's journey and also a warning signal that previews the snakebite in that chapter.

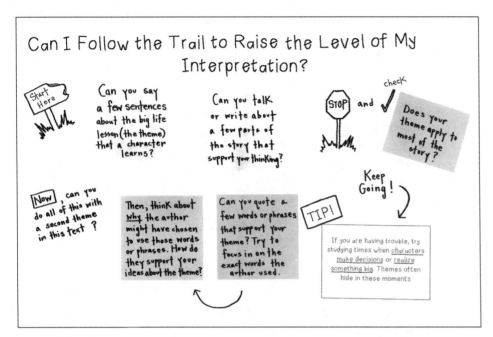

Can I Follow the Trail to Raise the Level of My Interpretation?

Start Here

Can you say a few sentences about the big life lesson (the theme) that a character learns?

Can you talk or write about a few parts of the story that support your thinking?

STOP and ✓ check

Does your theme apply to most of the story?

Now, can you do all of this with a second theme in this text?

Then, think about <u>why</u> the author might have chosen to use those words or phrases. How do they support your ideas about the theme?

Can you quote a few words or phrases that support your theme? Try to focus in on the exact words the author used.

TIP!

Keep Going!

If you are having trouble, try studying times when <u>characters make decisions</u> or <u>realize something big</u>. Themes often hide in these moments

FIG. 4–2 Theme game

Structure

In this band, there are many more complex structures in the books. A story may start with a flashback or a prologue in italics and then back up to start the main story. Readers have to figure out why that beginning part was included and how it relates to the story and the themes. As mentioned, there usually tends to be something important that happened before the story started that influences the story as it unfolds (Naomi's mother leaving, the death of Harry Potter's parents). There can also be more jumps in time within the story. There may be more foreshadowing of events to come—a later action, a new character coming.

Not surprisingly, the characters continue to become more complex and nuanced—but something else begins to happen at this level. Increasingly, the characters are teenagers.

If the reader herself is not yet a teenager, she can sometimes have a hard time empathizing with the characters. When the main character in *Things Not Seen*, by Andrew Clements, wakes up one morning and finds that he has turned invisible, that invisibility becomes a metaphor for the feeling teenagers often have in adolescence that their parents don't see them for who they truly are. Readers who see this as simply a story about a boy who wakes up invisible miss a huge part of the story.

Also, in this band, the point of view starts to become even more multidimensional. It starts to be not just interesting but necessary to consider the perspectives of characters other than the protagonist. An unreliable narrator can come into play, as well. It is not so much that the narrator can't be trusted, but that the narrator's point of view is incomplete. He is often figuring out the past and the present of the story as it unfolds, along with the reader, and there are apt to be many times when a reader feels as if she sees more of the big picture than the character whose point of view is presented. Often books at this level require readers to hold on to large casts of characters. Some of the characters who turn out to be hugely important might be adults, so the reader must bring more of an understanding of the complexities of the adult world.

Increasingly, the story is not only a story, but also a statement about the world and life. Very often, the story makes a statement about major social issues such as oppression, injustice, and social norms.

What kind of work is called for in band X/Y/Z?

(*Homecoming* to *Monster*)

Books in this band of text difficulty are notably more complex. First, many of them employ a postmodern structure in which multiple genres are included and multiple voices are heard. Perspectives overlap but also conflict. Whole chapters, not just short passages, jump back in time. The texts take risks with form and genre, usually using this complex structure to convey ideas. Often, these texts include the idea that our lives and the world defy any attempt to be pigeonholed and the idea that it is not easy to communicate or to understand one another. For example, the narrator is often unreliable and will proclaim things that the reader is expected to realize are not true (or not completely true). The unreliability of the narrator reinforces the theme that it is impossible for anyone to be all-knowing, even when talking about oneself. Or, conversely, the narrator may be more truthful with the reader about all of the events that are occurring and may provide a contrasting perspective to those events so that the reader identifies more with the narrator as he reads. Readers who are working with texts at this band, then, need to fully engage in figuring things out as they read.

However, the expectations on readers go way beyond that. Readers of texts at this level are expected to have and to draw upon a lot of knowledge about the world and other books. In this band of text difficulty, many references are left unexplained. For example, in fantasy books, the reader needs to bring a wealth of knowledge, often carried over from reading mythology, fables, and other fantasy texts to understand the author's references. There is an assumption that readers who are working with these texts are reading (or have read) related texts and are aware of other sources of information. While reading one book, readers are invited into the canon of literature. These literary references are not essential to understanding the characters and the themes but greatly enhance that reading experience if they are recognized and understood. For example, the epigraph to *Criss Cross*, by Lynne Rae Perkins, is a quote from Shakespeare's *A Midsummer Night's Dream*, and there are references to that play throughout. A reader unfamiliar with the play can still read *Criss Cross* thoughtfully, but knowing the treatment of the difficulties of love in *A Midsummer Night's Dream* would enhance understanding of the characters in *Criss Cross* and their struggles with identity and relationships.

Information about science and history may also be part of these texts, and the reader must understand that information to understand the story. *Criss Cross*, for example, contains references to Einstein's theory of relativity. One of the characters is struggling to make sense of it. If the reader has no specific knowledge of this complex theory, this is not going to interrupt the story. However, if there is *no* understanding of the basic concept of atomic science—that the universe is constructed of microscopic atoms—then the reader will not be able to appreciate one of the more significant threads in the book. In these books the reader will tend to be offered multiple perspectives on issues and content and need to come up with his own perspective on that content. The reader will need to begin to make deeper connections to present life, considering things like, "Could this really happen? What would that mean for life today?"

Readers at this level are assumed to be the kind of readers who like challenging books and don't want things spelled out for them. In fact, it seems like many books at this level are set up like puzzles. Even dialogue, which was an aspect of narratives that readers found easiest to follow in the lower bands, can become tricky as characters begin to speak in the vernacular and use vocabulary from another time and place.

What comes before the bands?

While the bands span the benchmark levels of your students, we know that some of your students may fall below benchmark. So your knowledge of readers' development can't just begin at level J. There are critical things for you to know about how readers develop at lower levels. This knowledge will empower you to meet your below-benchmark readers at their level and to help accelerate their progress up the ladder of text complexity. For detailed information and advice for working with students below level J, you can refer to Chapter 4, "A Knowledge of Reading Development Can Power Your Teaching" in *A Guide to the Reading Workshop: Primary Grades*, from the K–2 series.

INSTRUCTION SHAPED BY BANDS

Understanding the progression along these bands of text complexity will inform your teaching in countless ways. Once you understand how the texts your students are reading increase in complexity in a manageable way, you can use your knowledge of the work readers are likely to encounter in their books to help them take their next steps. While the teaching implications outlined below are by no means an exhaustive list, they have proven to be effective and powerful ways to shape instruction and foster student growth.

Using the Bands of Text Complexity in Conferring and Small-Group Work

You will, of course, want to carry information that sums up the bands of text complexity with you as you confer and lead small groups, referring to your crib sheet often until you have an in-your-bones sense of the work of each band. This will help you to pay attention to whether or not kids are doing the work of the band in which they're reading. Often, kids are reading their N/O/P/Q or even their R/S/T books as

FIG. 4–3 To understand fantasy books, readers use knowledge from other sources.

though they are K/L/M books—tracking the main problem and solution, cataloging the character's dominant characteristics—and not shifting their thinking work to do the work that is called for by the more layered and nuanced books. They're reading as plot junkies, plowing through the text without pausing to notice craft or complexity. If this is the case, you can use the Bands of Text Complexity document (see Figure 4–1), to determine the work required by bands that are relevant to your students and ensure kids do some of that work with their books. Or, if students are doing the work of the band, you can use this document to identify what work is likely to be called for next and to prepare students for what to expect as their texts begin to change.

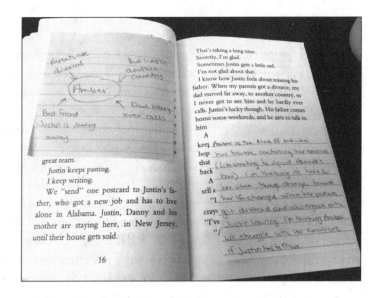

Teachers often find it helpful to identify an anchor text for each band their students are reading in, one that exemplifies the type of work that a reader is asked to do at each new level. *Amber Brown Is Not a Crayon*, for example, exhibits many of the characteristics we ask readers in the N/O/P/Q band to consider. As we pointed out previously in this chapter, Amber is a complicated character (who wants to be both a teenager and a kid) who faces a blend of pressures (her best friend moving, her parents' divorce). There are tricky parts of the text, including figurative language and word play, and readers are expected to track several subplots in addition to thinking about Amber's motivations and how she changes. Similarly, *Because of Winn-Dixie*, by Kate DiCamillo, provides an example of the R/S/T band's work, and *Number the Stars*, by Lois Lowry, provides an anchor for the U/V/W band. *The Egypt Game*, by Zilpha Keatley Snyder, can anchor the X/Y/Z band. Of course, you can alter these titles. The important thing is that you select books or short stories that you know and your students know as well.

Once you've selected your anchor titles, you can read carefully, with the lens of the band, and annotate the texts. Placing Post-its in the books to guide you to important teaching points that you know will come up over and over again will set you up for success in your conferences. You might even want to keep a running list on the anchor title's inside front cover of all the teaching points and their page numbers for each well-loved text. As you prepare for conferences or small-group instruction to move readers up the levels of text complexity, consider ways to use the texts you annotated to anchor your teaching. If you choose to teach using demonstration, you might scan your annotated texts quickly, looking for a place you marked to teach a strategy needed by your readers. After sharing your teaching point with students, you might say, "Watch me as I . . ." and demonstrate how you try the strategy on a chunk of annotated text.

Or you might decide to teach using explanation and example, particularly if you are revisiting a text the students know well. Rather than having students watch as you demonstrate the entire process, you'd simply explain what you hope to accomplish, for example, to notice how setting influences the character and the plot. Then you would show them, for example, the scene from *Number the Stars* when the Nazi soldiers stop Annemarie, Ellen, and Kirsti in the street. You'd then help students to notice the setting in their own books, coaching them to consider the ways the setting can almost be considered a character. Your students will get more out of this teaching if they are familiar with the text, so you might select anchor texts that you have used as read-alouds or one that many students have read in a previous unit or book club.

Level Introductions

When students are ready to move to a new band, it's important to alert them to the new work that they should expect to do. Calling students to move into a band together for a small group can serve not just as *a book* introduction, but as *a level* introduction. This can be a high-leverage move that will set your students up for success across multiple texts. "You are marking a major milestone in your reading lives," you might tell this group. "You are starting to read more complicated and sophisticated books, and you are ready to do the more exciting thinking that these books ask you to do. As you read your new level N books, and even through O/P/Q books, you're going to notice that your characters are complicated, and they change across your books. Before, you were reading books where the author clearly told you your character's traits, but now, you need to use the clues the author gives you to try to figure those traits out yourself." You might name—or recruit students to name—examples students will be familiar with. "Now, you'll want to pay attention to what the characters do, say, and think to get a full understanding of the characters and how the characters change." You can set students up to pay attention to this in their own books, to jot Post-its about it, and to talk with their partners or clubs later about the new things they've noticed about their characters.

You might then channel students to begin reading a book at their new level, which you may have marked with Post-its in places that call for the reader to do the new, more challenging work. Students could jot, preparing to talk to their partners about these new features. The book club could work together to support one another, meeting with you periodically, to stay alert to the features of the new level.

Transferable Prompts by Band

Of course, there are other ways you can use the bands of text complexity to drive conferences and small-group work. For example, we have found it to be helpful to use band-specific prompts to coach students in ways that provide them with transferable cues. If Marisol is reading books at the R/S/T band of text difficulty, we know some of the demands those books place on her. In other words, we can deduce from her text difficulty band some of the work she will need to do to understand texts at this level. For example, you'll recall that in the text difficulty band before R/S/T, many stories contain conflicted, complex characters (such as Rob in *The Tiger Rising*, who is conflicted over whether or not he can open up and share his feelings), and the texts at these earlier levels tend to state, outright, the nature of that conflict or complexity. In that band, readers needed to carry and apply this information about the character, but they did not need to infer it. Now, at the R/S/T band, however, readers are often left to infer a character's complicated mix of traits. The reader is given windows through which to observe the character, but it is the reader's job to generate implicit traits and figure out the character's complex nature. Ideally, readers will generate ideas about a character and then think more deeply, refining those ideas. You may need to support Marisol in making that leap in her character work.

> Level Intro: Number the Stars
> Level U
>
> You've all been reading historical fiction, and you've gotten quite good @ thinking about the time period, looking for the details the author has included to educate the reader about what was happening as the story took place.
>
> You're going to begin a new book — this book is the next level up. It's a level U. As you read books like Number the Stars, it's important that you look @ the small things, the details that would be easy to pass over and think "What do these represent?" Often in books @ this level, the author puts in symbols but doesn't repeat them — so you have to look closely for them. Almost everything could be a symbol.
>
> So, like your other books, this one takes place during the Holocaust. At the beginning, we meet Annemarie and Ellen. They are best friends running home from school in Nazi Germany.

FIG. 4–4

You might, then, carry with you some prompts and cues to help you coach Marisol to think a bit differently than she has about character. Specifically, here are some examples that might be helpful for character work in the R/S/T band:

Developing Theories about Characters

We have made the talk and thought prompts below available on our online resources, as well additional prompts for levels N to Z.

R/S/T Text Difficulty Band ✦

Talk and Thought Prompts Readers Can Use to Understand Characters in R/S/T Texts

- Even though the book doesn't come right out and say this,
  I think [character] _____ is [some traits] _____ . There are hints that show this. For example: _____ . Another example is _____ .

- At first I thought [character] _____ was [some traits] _____ , but as I get to know him/her more, I'm coming to think that deep down, he/she's really [some traits] _____ .

- Sometimes the main character acts and talks one way but really is feeling a whole other way. For example, one time he/she acted this way _____ and said _____ , but actually he/she was feeling _____ .

- One way the author helps us know a character is the author gives that character objects or ways of acting and talking that are meant to represent something about the character. I think it's perhaps significant that the author gave this character [objects or ways of acting and talking] _____ . To me, this might show _____ .

- The main character has different sides to him/her. When he's/she's _____ , he's/she's _____ . Then when he's/she's _____ , he's/she's _____ .

You may be perplexed. "What do I do with those blanks?" you might ask. "Do I fill in what the child says?" The answer is "No." The prompts are written like this to help you say them in such a way that children can use them as conversational prompts (I want to add on . . . , I agree because . . . , I disagree because . . .). And the concept is not that you'll ever run down this whole list, flooding the child with an excess of good ideas. But if Marisol looks up from *The Tiger Rising* and says, "Rob is sort of a soft person," you might glance at the last item on your list and say, "Can I give you a tip? You are reading books where the characters will have different sides to them. Could you think, 'When Rob is doing this one thing, he's soft—yet when Rob is doing this other thing he's . . . what?'" You could leave that reader with a Post-it with this prompt on it, suggesting the reader try thinking this way about more characters than just Rob.

Of course, you will have students in your class whose comprehension skills are not as strong as Marisol's. You may think, "I don't think they are ready for this work that I think of as suited to readers of R/S/T books." In this case, you may look over their Post-its and entries they've already been keeping, thinking, "Is the work that this student is doing now more like what I envision readers of K/L/M doing, or is it more like I envision readers of N/O/P/Q doing?"

Looking between the prompts listed below and the earlier descriptions of the work that readers tend to do when working at different bands of text difficulty, we can suggest the following prompts.

K/L/M Text Difficulty Band

Talk and Thought Prompts Readers Can Use to Understand Characters in K/L/M Texts

- [Character] _____ is [some traits] _____ because _____ .

- She's/He's doing or saying _____ . This shows me she's/he's _____ .

- In this book, the main character's feelings change. First, she's/he's _____ because _____ . Then later, she's/he's _____ because _____ .

- She/He could have done this _____ but instead she/he did this _____ . This makes me think that she's/he's _____ .

N/O/P/Q Text Difficulty Band

Talk and Thought Prompts Readers Can Use to Understand Characters in N/O/P/Q Texts

- Sometimes my character is _____ . For example, _____ . But other times, she/he _____ . For example, _____ . This makes me think _____ .

- In the beginning, my character was _____ , but as the story continues, I think my character could be changing. By the end, she/he _____ .

- Sometimes the book comes right out and tells readers about the character's personality/ feelings. For example, it says _____ . Then there are places in the story where it doesn't say this, but it shows this. For example, _____ .

When conferring with Kody, who is reading in the K/L/M band (*Frog and Toad Are Friends*, by Arnold Lobel), you might say, "In the books that you're reading now, the character's feelings often change over the course of the story. Can you think about how Toad's feelings change? You might say, 'First, he has *one feeling* because . . .' and then, later he has *another feeling* because . . .'"

But pulling up next to Devon, an N/O/P/Q reader, you might instead prompt him to pay attention to the way a character changes across a story. You can begin by alerting him to the new work that the band is asking him to do. "Before, the books you were reading came right out and told you what a character was like, and that character generally stayed the same across the whole book. Nate the Great is usually clever. And Horrible Harry is mostly horrible, right? But now, the characters in your book are more complex. They might be one way in one situation—or with one person—and another way in another situation. Usually, they will experience something that prompts them to change in an important way by the end of the story. So you might think, 'In the beginning, my character was . . . , but as the story progresses, I think she might be changing. By the end, she . . .' Be on the lookout for how your character changes, and why."

Then, too, you may have readers in the upper bands of text complexity who are ready for the kind of sophisticated thinking these bands demand. You might use the prompts below to confer with readers in the U/V/W and X/Y/Z bands, pushing them to consider the characters in their books in even more complex ways.

Text Difficulty Band U/V/W

Talk and Thought Prompts Readers Can Use to Understand Characters in U/V/W Texts

Sometimes the author writes a story to address an issue or convey an idea. The author creates characters who'll carry (or represent) part of the idea. You might say:

- In this book, the author uses _____ to convey _____. Evidence for this includes _____ .

- On the other hand, it could be that the author uses _____ to convey _____.

In a complex book, the author sometimes adds seemingly inconsequential people, traveling on what seems for a time to be a side track from the main storyline. But in the end, some of these people turn out to be essential to the story's resolution. You might think about:

- These minor characters are in here because _____ .

In complex books, readers need to read, realizing that some of what a character says is actually not trustworthy—that some of what the character says is meant to reveal that character's perspectives and readers are supposed to know, all along, that this is just one, biased perspective—that there are other ways to see things. You might say:

- For example, in this book, when _____ said _____, I didn't entirely trust her/him. I sensed this could mostly reveal that he/she _____.

Text Difficulty Band X/Y/Z

Talk and Thought Prompts Readers Can Use to Understand Characters in X/Y/Z Texts

Often characters in these kinds of stories are revealed slowly. The reader sees more and more, including conflicting sides of characters. You might, therefore, think about:

- This character often seems _____ . For example, _____ . At other times, though, he or she seems _____ . For example, _____ .

Characters also reveal social issues and themes that have implications beyond the character's experience. You might think about:

- This character _____ suffers or reveals _____ . For example, _____ .

Characters' motivations in these kinds of stories will be complex and related to events earlier in the narrative. You might think about:

- Why is the character acting this way? What forces or pressures are being exerted on this character? What flaws or strengths does he or she show?

For example, you might confer with Sophia about *Walk Two Moons*, a level W text. Ask her to think more deeply about Phoebe. What issue or idea might the author, Sharon Creech, be conveying through this character? You might prompt Sophia to consider more than one possibility and challenge her to collect evidence for each one. You might leave her with the following prompts on a Post-it to remind her of this work at the conclusion of the conference: In this book, the author uses _____ to convey _____ . Evidence for this includes _____ . On the other hand, it could be that the author uses _____ to convey _____ .

With Zack, an X/Y/Z reader, on the other hand, you might highlight the powerful themes or issues that arise in these complicated texts. Support him to think through their implications, both for the characters in the story and, beyond the text, for the reader and the wider world. In *Out of the Dust*, a level X novel, Zack might consider the many tragedies that Billie Jo suffers: so much loss and disappointment. Zack might then ponder how the novel allows for thinking about the wider implications, in the form of multiple themes—perhaps the power of the human spirit to overcome adversity or the power of family working together to endure a challenging environment. You might, then, leave Zack to consider the prompt: This character _____ suffers or reveals _____ . This leads the reader to think that in the world, _____ but also _____ . For example, _____ .

You'll want to make these prompts easily accessible and portable, so you can refer to them as you're conferring with different readers. You might, for example, select one skill that you are working on with a student and create a prompt that can help the reader work with that particular skill in ways that fit into the particular band. Or you might select several skills, some emphasized by the unit you're teaching and some individualized goals, and create a page with prompts for each skill in a quadrant of the page. Steadily, you'll accumulate a set of prompt sheets for yourself, containing prompts and cues for these four skills for each band of text difficulty.

One possibility is to print the prompts out on labels. If the prompts for every stage of the development of every skill you want to focus on are printed out on a ready-made stack of stickers, you can easily adjust a prompt sheet for one child by grabbing the right sticker and attach it to a blank sheet of paper, creating an individualized prompt sheet for the child with whom you are working. That will be your decision to make, according to what works for you, your experience level, and your teaching situation.

After you've taught students some of these features, you could then turn them into cue cards or bookmarks like the ones below to nudge your readers to immerse themselves in the work of the new level. Readers can make a plan for the books they'll read at their new level, tackling the characteristics of the band.

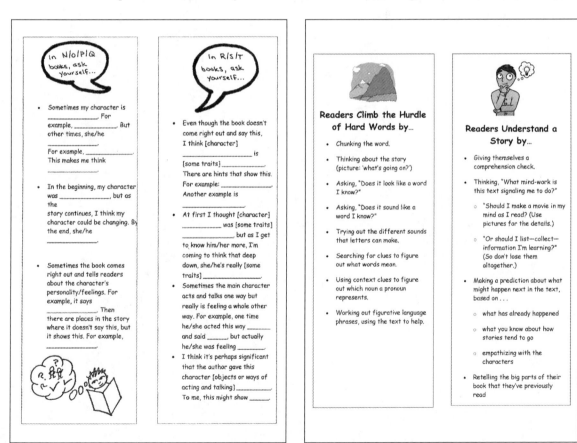

FIG. 4–5 These bookmarks tell readers what to expect in a new text band.

PROMPTS AND RECORD KEEPING

You'll wonder about the record-keeping portion of these prompts. You may be thinking, "Should I check off what readers can do?" And you may wonder, "Can I turn this into a checklist of some sort?" I encourage you to experiment. Sometimes, I think we busy ourselves recording all sorts of stuff that we never use at all. Instead of creating a checklist, maybe the most important thing we could do would be to collect Post-its from time to time that illustrate each reader's ability to grow theories about a character or to consider story structure or anything else.

Perhaps the most important thing is that these records allow us to "read" what a child is *already* doing, understanding that work so that we can place that child somewhere on a developmental trajectory, to meet him where he is and take him to the next step. It's also important to keep in mind that our records should allow us to be agile, responding to whichever curveball the reader throws our way. "You are noticing story structure? Let me help you do that even better." "You are growing ideas about characters? Great, let's work on that." However you choose to organize these records, we know that they will help your teaching to be more targeted and supportive for all of your students, no matter what band they're reading in.

Chapter 5

Understanding Strands of Nonfiction Text Complexity and Using Them to Support Readers

D AY BY DAY, the seventy staff developers at the Teachers College Reading and Writing Project disperse to schools across the planet, and always, we aim to help reading and writing instruction. Over all these years, across all these schools, my colleagues and I have from time to time found ourselves bringing a method or a tool that teachers found particularly helpful. This chapter aims to bring one such tool to you.

A SYSTEM FOR LEVELING NONFICTION TEXTS: STRANDS, NOT BANDS

The story behind this tool begins as most stories do—with characters (my colleagues and me) who had motivations (we wanted to find a way to level nonfiction books, to match nonfiction readers to books, as we'd done with fiction) and who encountered problems. When we began trying to master the leveling system that undergirds the ladder of text complexity in nonfiction, we sometimes—fairly frequently—would spread out four or five texts that had each been assigned the same level of text difficulty, and our eyes would grow big. We'd gape at each other. "How could anyone think these texts are equivalent in difficulty?" we'd ask.

For us, coming up with descriptors to level nonfiction texts with validity and confidence seemed nigh on impossible. We weren't sure if this undermined our confidence in existing systems of leveling nonfiction books (and in the whole prospect of leveling nonfiction books). We just knew that we couldn't be authorities on this topic. With so many textual, structural, and content differences between texts, coming up with characteristics of different levels of text complexity seemed problematic.

The hundreds of hours we spent studying texts to understand systems for ascribing levels of text complexity did yield insights, however. Although we are not able to describe *bands* of nonfiction text difficulty, as we have done in fiction, we *do* think that one can see evidence of *strands* of nonfiction text difficulty. That is, there are some threads (or strands) along which expository nonfiction texts tend to progress, from less to more complex.

Example of Ascending Strands of Nonfiction Text Complexity

To illustrate how nonfiction texts get more complex, we have revised a nonfiction article about the octopus to show ascending strands of text complexity. These examples show the same text becoming more complex. Once you understand these strands in nonfiction texts, you can assess what your readers are able to do and plan the next step of instruction.

"The Amazing Octopus"		
Level 2	**Level 3**	**Level 4**
Octopus Bodies The octopus has a body that is different from any other animal. Its body, called a mantle, is soft and shaped like a bag. The octopus can squeeze into very small spaces because it has no bones in its body. The octopus has eight rubbery arms that attach to its head near its mouth. The octopus's arms are covered in suckers. The suckers help the octopus grab and taste things. The octopus hunts by grabbing its prey with its arms. Then, the octopus bites its food with its tough beak and injects, or shoots, poison so the animal can't move. The octopus eats a diet of snails, fish, turtles, and even other octopuses!	**Bodies Like No Other** The octopus has a body unlike any other animal. Its body, called a mantle, is soft and shaped like a bag. The octopus can squeeze into very small spaces because it has no bones in its body. Its eight rubbery arms are attached to its head near its mouth. The octopus's arms are covered with suckers. The suckers help the octopus grab and taste things. The octopus can see very far distances, but it cannot hear anything at all. The octopus's body is amazing on the inside, too. The octopus has three hearts. Two of its hearts send its blood, which is light blue, to its gills. Its gills are organs for breathing, and they're located on two of the octopus's arms. The third heart sends blood to the rest of the octopus's body.	The octopus has a body unlike any other animal. Its body, called a mantle, is soft and shaped like a bag. The octopus can squeeze into very small spaces because it has no bones in its body. Its eight rubbery arms are attached to its head near its mouth. The octopus's arms are covered with suckers, which help the octopus grab and taste things. The octopus can see very far distances, but it cannot hear anything at all. The octopus's body is amazing on the inside, too. Along with its stomach and other organs, the octopus has three hearts. Two of its hearts send blood, which is light blue, to its organs for breathing, called gills, on two of its arms. The third heart sends blood to the rest of its body. When the octopus breathes out, water comes out of the tube called the siphon.

FIG. 5–1   This chart shows the first section of levels 2, 3, and 4 of "The Amazing Octopus."

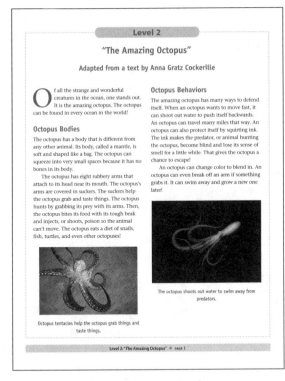

Level 2

"The Amazing Octopus"

Adapted from a text by Anna Gratz Cockerille

Of all the strange and wonderful creatures in the ocean, one stands out. It is the amazing octopus. The octopus can be found in every ocean in the world!

Octopus Bodies

The octopus has a body that is different from any other animal. Its body, called a mantle, is soft and shaped like a bag. The octopus can squeeze into very small spaces because it has no bones in its body.

The octopus has eight rubbery arms that attach to its head near its mouth. The octopus's arms are covered in suckers. The suckers help the octopus grab and taste things. The octopus hunts by grabbing its prey with its arms. Then, the octopus bites its food with its tough beak and injects, or shoots, poison so the animal can't move. The octopus eats a diet of snails, fish, turtles, and even other octopuses!

Octopus Behaviors

The amazing octopus has many ways to defend itself. When an octopus wants to move fast, it can shoot out water to push itself backwards. An octopus can travel many miles that way. An octopus can also protect itself by squirting ink. The ink makes the predator, or animal hunting the octopus, become blind and lose its sense of smell for a little while. That gives the octopus a chance to escape!

An octopus can change color to blend in. An octopus can even break off an arm if something grabs it. It can swim away and grow a new one later!

The octopus shoots out water to swim away from predators.

Octopus tentacles help the octopus grab things and taste things.

Level 2: "The Amazing Octopus" ◆ PAGE 1

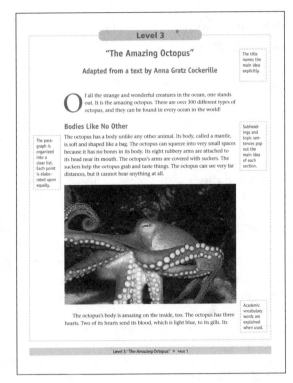

Level 3

"The Amazing Octopus"

Adapted from a text by Anna Gratz Cockerille

The title names the main idea explicitly.

Of all the strange and wonderful creatures in the ocean, one stands out. It is the amazing octopus. There are over 300 different types of octopus, and they can be found in every ocean in the world!

Bodies Like No Other

The octopus has a body unlike any other animal. Its body, called a mantle, is soft and shaped like a bag. The octopus can squeeze into very small spaces because it has no bones in its body. Its eight rubbery arms are attached to its head near its mouth. The octopus's arms are covered with suckers. The suckers help the octopus grab and taste things. The octopus can see very far distances, but it cannot hear anything at all.

The paragraph is organized into a clear list. Each point is elaborated upon equally.

Subheadings and topic sentences pop out the main idea of each section.

The octopus's body is amazing on the inside, too. The octopus has three hearts. Two of its hearts send its blood, which is light blue, to its gills. Its

Academic vocabulary words are explained when used.

Level 3: "The Amazing Octopus" ◆ PAGE 1

Level 4

"An Animal Like No Other"

Adapted from a text by Anna Gratz Cockerille

Of all the strange and wonderful creatures that live in the ocean, one stands out above the rest. It is the amazing octopus. There are over 300 different types of octopus, and they can be found in every ocean in the world!

The octopus has a body unlike any other animal. Its body, called a mantle, is soft and shaped like a bag. The octopus can squeeze into very small spaces because it has no bones in its body. Its eight rubbery arms are attached to its head near its mouth. The octopus's arms are covered with suckers, which help the octopus grab and taste things. The octopus can see very far distances, but it cannot hear anything at all.

The octopus's body is amazing on the inside, too. Along with its stomach and other organs, the octopus has three hearts. Two of its hearts send blood, which is light blue, to its organs for breathing, called gills, on two of its arms. The third heart sends blood to the rest of its body. When the octopus breathes out, water comes out of the tube called the siphon.

The octopus has many amazing ways to defend itself from predators. When an octopus wants to move quickly to escape a predator, it can shoot water out of its siphon and push itself backwards. This is called jet propulsion. Using this technique, octopuses can travel many miles. An octopus can also protect itself by

Image © Juniors Bildarchiv/Alamy/HIP

Level 4: "An Animal Like No Other" ◆ PAGE 1

FIG. 5–2 "The Amazing Octopus"

To begin orienting yourself to this process, you can examine the first section of levels 2, 3, and 4 of "The Amazing Octopus." You might take a moment right now, before reading on, to read those paragraphs and name what you notice about what makes each level more complex than the one that came before.

Among the first things that might jump out at you are the text features and the level of support they give the reader. In the level 2 article, the heading clearly identifies the topic the section will be about, "Octopus Bodies," while in the level 3 article, the heading, "Bodies Like No Other," is less direct and clear. In the level 4 article, the headings disappear, leaving the work of sectioning the article and noting when the topic shifts to the reader. In a similar way, the photographs and captions become less supportive and connected to the text as the levels increase.

You might also notice the increasingly challenging vocabulary. The level 2 article introduces a few domain-specific words, such as *mantle* and *injects*, but it provides the definition or a synonym right next to the word. In the level 3 text, the word *gills* is introduced and then explained in the following sentence. By the level 4 text, the density of academic vocabulary has increased, though support is still provided to help readers learn new vocabulary such as *mantle*, *gills*, and *siphon*.

More subtle differences occur in the structure of the article. In the level 2 text, an explanation of the octopus's hunting behaviors is provided as part of the discussion of the octopus's arms. In the higher-level

What Challenges Do Readers Face as Nonfiction Texts Increase in Difficulty?	
Strands of Text Complexity	**Some Ways Each Strand Becomes Progressively More Complex**
The Explicitness and Complexity of Meaning/ Central Ideas/ and/or Author's Purpose	The two main ways that nonfiction texts will get harder in terms of meaning are in: • The number of ideas the text forwards • The explicitness or implicitness of those ideas **At the easier end of the spectrum** are texts that are organized around one main idea, and that idea is stated obviously, often in the heading or in a topic sentence that opens a paragraph or part. **Texts where the main idea is not so clearly stated** challenge the reader more. The main idea may be explicit but embedded in the paragraph(s). The reader must think about and decide what a section of text is mostly about. These texts will have no headings, or the headings don't clarify the most important ideas. Some have more than one main idea. The reader will need to use author's hints to help them understand the main idea. For example, repeated words, pop-out sentences, or text features can provide clues to help the reader determine the main idea. **In the hardest texts, there are often multiple main or central (or overarching) ideas**, few of which are explicitly stated. The reader is expected to make inferences to determine these main/central ideas. Perhaps the text provides specifics and the reader is expected to infer the generalizations. It is also important for the reader to create relationships between the ideas (and the supporting details) to understand the text as a whole. These texts not only suggest overarching ideas but also make related points in a hierarchical fashion (such as an outline with A heading, B heading, and C heading). These texts are not always organized in a way to make those ideas immediately obvious to the reader. The multiple main or central ideas are often not brought together in the text, but in the illustrations or guides that are written alongside.
Language/Vocabulary	There are two main ways that the language or vocabulary of nonfiction texts gets harder: • The level of challenge in the words themselves • The degree of support the text provides to readers How easy is it for the reader to determine the meaning of the words from the text? Some texts include hard words but explain them with simple terms and clear examples. Other texts include domain-specific or technical vocabulary and explain that vocabulary with other domain-specific or technical vocabulary. Words themselves get harder when they are unfamiliar, technical (such as *photosynthesis*), or when the meaning of a term is the secondary meaning (such as *solution* referring to a liquid). The degree of support a text provides often decreases as texts become more complex.

FIG. 5–3

Language/Vocabulary *(continued)*	**Easier texts often explain new vocabulary immediately**, often through a text feature and/or an example. In harder texts, the support is often less close in proximity to the word or less obvious. Still, readers can figure out the meaning of tricky words by looking for parenthetical explanations or clarifying examples. **Still harder texts demand that readers come to the text with a knowledge of expert vocabulary or are willing to learn** that vocabulary from sources outside the text. At this level, using morphology to figure out the word may pay off more than context clues.
Structure (Including Text Features)	• Texts that have conventional, easy-to-follow structures are easier than texts that have hybrid or unconventional structures. • **In easier nonfiction texts, the structure is easy to see**, and the text features help the reader follow that structure. The entire text often has a single structure. For example, if the text follows a "question and answer" structure, each section may start with a question followed by an explanation. A chronological structure may start each section with a date or may use terms in prominent places that indicate the passing of time. **Texts that are somewhat harder often have multiple structures** across the book or article. These may still be highlighted by the presence of a new chapter, a new section, or a text feature, indicating that the structure has changed, but the changes in text structure are lightly signaled. **In the hardest texts, new text structures exist throughout a text.** It is left to the reader to discern when the author has switched from, say, a chronological retelling of a life cycle to a paragraph about the effects certain factors have had on that animal. Text structures might shift even from paragraph to paragraph. Text features may become even more indispensable to understanding, or they may be absent altogether. In these harder texts, text structure is at times exceptionally difficult to discern or disappears entirely. **Ascertaining the structure of a text is difficult work.** Some texts might be poorly written. Other times, the author is expecting a lot of the reader and has taken big detours or included parentheticals or examples that might go on for a page or more. In the end, to learn from a text, readers must be able to construct an infrastructure that helps them hold onto what they are learning. This might be based on the reader's purpose.
Knowledge Demands	• There are several interrelated ways that knowledge demands become more complex: • The amount of prior knowledge a text expects a reader to bring • The degree of support a text provides to a reader to learn • The sheer amount of information a reader is expected to absorb. **The amount of prior knowledge a reader is expected to bring relates to text difficulty.** Easier texts will teach the reader the vocabulary, concepts, and knowledge of the topic as if all of this is new and unfamiliar. Harder texts assume some knowledge of the subject, including basic technical vocabulary, essential concepts, and perhaps some historical or scientific background.

FIG. 5–3

(continues)

Knowledge Demands (continued)	**Texts are also easier or harder depending on whether they are written in ways that support readers in learning the information.** Easier texts provide more support for readers to learn about an unfamiliar concept. Often comparisons and examples are used to make an unfamiliar subject more accessible. As texts get harder, they might be less accessible in parts. Some concepts might be explained in more depth with examples, while other concepts are not, and it might feel as if the author assumes a concept is already known to the reader. As texts become even more demanding, the text might feel as if it is written to an audience that already has in-depth knowledge of much of the content and offers little support for the reader to learn that content.
	Texts at higher levels of complexity often have information that is extraneous. This information may come in the form of an illustration or a text feature that contrasts the information being given or seems to go on a tangent relative to the main text. It's often challenging for the reader to determine its purpose.
	Another way that texts can be easier or harder relates to **the sheer volume of information a reader is expected to absorb**. Easier texts are light on the amount of information they expect readers to hold onto. When there are a lot of little details, the reader may get the feeling those details are there as examples only (and the whole part is easy to sum up in a sentence). More demanding texts ask readers to learn a lot of information but provide footholds for them to know what matters most and to help them hold onto the information. In the most demanding texts, the reader often gets the feeling that he can't let go of a detail or a critical piece will be lost. Information and ideas are layered more densely, and these texts often make allusions to (or citations of) other texts, events, or ideas. Information at these levels is also often inferential, and it is left up to the reader to decide what the text is saying and the reason the particular information is included.
	No matter what, the reader will need to see what information should be taken in, what perspective this information is being presented from, and what (if anything) might be let go.

FIG. 5–3 (continued)

texts, these topics are separated, with the author expecting the reader to carry the information from the earlier section to synthesize with the later section on hunting. In the level 3 text, the paragraph is structured into a clear list, with each point elaborated upon equally. In the fourth-grade text, however, some points receive more elaboration than others. Sentences are combined and phrases are added, which serves to slightly obscure the list-like structure.

   The amount of information the reader is expected to learn from the article also increases as the levels ascend. The second-grade text teaches the reader about three body parts of the octopus—the mantle, arms, and suckers. The third-grade article adds information about the octopus's sight and hearing, as well as its gills and three hearts. The level 4 text adds references to its stomach and other organs and teaches about the octopus's siphon. Across the three levels, it becomes more challenging for the reader to determine what information is most important to hold on to and what information can be let go.

Challenges: Strands of Text Complexity for Nonfiction

These and other challenges, outlined below, comprise the strands of what makes nonfiction texts more difficult. Discerning these challenges can be tricky, but it is important work. If we can notice and discuss the ways these texts become more complex, our teaching of nonfiction becomes much more powerful. In targeting the new work that students can do in each of these strands, we can help our students tackle more difficult texts successfully.

STRANDS OF NONFICTION TEXT DIFFICULTY

A Strand of Difficulty: The Explicitness and Complexity of Meaning/Central Ideas and Author's Purpose

We have discovered two main ways that nonfiction texts get harder in terms of meaning. One is the number of ideas that a text forwards, and the other is the explicitness or implicitness of those ideas.

Explicit Main Idea

In simpler texts, the text is typically organized around one main idea. This main idea is usually explicitly stated in either a heading, a subheading, or a clear topic sentence, set in a dominant place. For example, level 4 of the octopus text has a paragraph that goes like this:

> The octopus has a body unlike any other animal. Its body, called a mantle, is soft and shaped like a bag. The octopus can squeeze into very small spaces because it has no bones in its body. Its eight rubbery arms are attached to its head near its mouth. The octopus's arms are covered with suckers, which help the octopus grab and taste things.

Even simpler texts might have a subheading that carries the main idea of the section. In level 2 of the octopus article, the heading reads "Octopus Bodies," and then the passage states that the octopus has a body that is different from any other animal and goes on to describe the unique body parts, such as the mantle, eight arms, and suckers.

Implicit Main Idea

As texts become more difficult, the main idea is not as easily spotted. In more complex texts, the idea may be conveyed through several sentences, not just one, and those sentences might be embedded in the middle of a paragraph. The level 6 text about the octopus, for example, includes this paragraph:

> There are over 300 different types of octopus, and they can be found in every ocean in the world. This cephalopod's unique body, called a mantle, is soft and shaped like a bag. Boneless, the octopus can

squeeze into impossibly small cracks and crevices. Its eight rubbery arms are attached to its bulbous head near its mouth.

The reader is expected to make inferences and decisions to determine what a section is mostly about. Headings are often absent or fail to clarify the most important ideas. Then, too, some texts contain more than one idea. Even more complex texts may not explicitly state the idea that readers are meant to construct. On one of New York State's tests, for example, readers encountered this passage in a text about Frederick Olmstead:

> In 1850, he ended up in charge of creating Central Park in New York City. Olmstead and a partner entered a design contest for a new park and won with a design patterned after gardens and natural sights that Olmstead had admired around the world. To create the new park, they shifted nearly 5 million cubic feet of dirt, blasted rock with 260 tons of gunpowder, and planted 270,000 trees and shrubs.

The reader is left to synthesize all that information, constructing her own idea from the list. Some readers might try to record and learn all the little facts, but a reader who can handle this level of text will hopefully be able to synthesize that paragraph in such a way as to almost write an abstract overview sentence like this:

> Olmstead used an unbelievable amount of stuff to make Central Park—nothing was going to stand in his way.

That is, in more complex texts, sometimes the big idea is left implicit, with the reader needing to almost write that idea as he reads. In the hardest texts, there are often multiple central (or overarching) ideas, most of which are implicit. These texts not only suggest overarching ideas, but also make points related to each of them in a hierarchical fashion (you might be reminded of a classic outline with headings for A, B, and C). Even more complicated, these texts are not always organized in a way that makes this hierarchy clear to the reader.

More Details with Less Relevance

The task of constructing the main idea becomes more challenging when the text forwards information that is tangential and not particularly relevant, as well as containing specifics that go together to make a larger point. The level 6 octopus article mentioned above, "Lessons from the Deep," is an example of a nonfiction text that requires students to synthesize information about the octopus's body, behaviors, and intelligence. In addition, like many higher-level nonfiction texts, this article *also* requires readers to rank and analyze information to differentiate what's important in terms of the main idea, as opposed that what's tangential and unimportant.

More complex expository texts sometimes contain subordinate information which does not directly pertain to the main idea, posing an additional challenge for readers. The level U article, "What a Ride," is about Sally Ride, the first woman astronaut to travel in space. The article begins by summarizing Sally Ride's career and the fact that she is celebrating the twenty-fifth anniversary of her first ride in space. Then the article jumps to a subordinate segment about Therese Peltier, the first woman to take a ride in an airplane, then returns to Sally Ride's career and to details on how she was trained. Even within the information about her career, there is a flashback to her relationship with her father while she was in school and how he encouraged her to do her best. That reference, again, is a subordinate one; it is not a new subject, but a parenthetical aside. The article returns back to Sally Ride, this time to tell about her life today. But meanwhile, many readers unfamiliar with this kind of reading challenge will have gotten lost in the back and forth and interesting but tangential information about Peltier. In other words, more complex texts tend to contain subordinate points, asides, and parenthetical comments that can sometimes take a reader off course.

More Complex, Interlocking Main Ideas

Of course, the most complex texts leave the main ideas to readers to create out of the precise information—and also expect readers to develop not just a single big abstract idea, but an interlocking web of such ideas. "The Honorary Vertebrate," the level 8 octopus article, expects students to consider the implications of intelligence on an animal's treatment, how the media depicts the octopus, and the uncertainty of scientific findings, in addition to learning the most important information about the animal.

A Strand of Difficulty: Language and Vocabulary

As texts become more difficult, they contain longer, more uncommon, and discipline-specific words that may be difficult to decode. Tricky words are less apt to be defined in the text.

It is absolutely the case that as a reader progresses toward more challenging nonfiction texts, she can expect to encounter an increasing number of challenging words. For example, in a hundred-word passage in a level N nonfiction book about wild animals, there were nineteen two-syllable words (e.g., *blooded*), nine three-syllable words (e.g., *family*), one four-syllable word (e.g., *scientific*), and one compound word. On the other hand, think about the words listed here as exemplars, and you'll see that many of these words could be sight words for students reading level N books (e.g., *family*, *blood*).

By contrast, in a hundred-word passage in a level U book about Albert Einstein there were again nineteen two-syllable words (this time, they tended to be words such as *captured* and *announced*), sixteen three-syllable words (e.g., *universe*), four four-syllable words (e.g., *expeditions*), and three compound words. The number of complex words will increase even more as a student progresses to even harder texts. The words themselves get harder both because they are unfamiliar or technical (e.g., *parallelogram*, *monarchy*)

There are several big/central ideas

and when the meaning of a term is the secondary meaning (e.g., *grave* meaning *serious*, or *cabinet* as a governing body).

This fact occasions us to make another set of generalizations about books at higher levels. Most of the two- to four-syllable words that students have difficulty reading in books at higher levels are unlikely to be sight words for most readers. Also, the challenging words in these higher-level texts often contain unusual spelling features that make the words difficult to decode, and they often contain affixes (*con-*, *-tion*) and inflectional endings (*-ed*, *-er*, *-est*). This means it would be helpful for students to understand how these parts of a word affect the word's meaning. Then, too, in these complex nonfiction texts, the challenging academic vocabulary is usually essential to the passage's meaning, and miscues could completely change the meaning of the passage. In an article about endangered animals at level N, a student read this sentence, "By 1986, this ferret species was nearly extinct, or totally wiped out" as follows: "By 1986, this ferret species was nearly *extended*, or totally wiped out."

More Challenging Words, Less Support for Figuring Them Out

Of course, the challenge here is not only to pronounce the word, but also to figure out its meaning. In the easier texts, the hard words are followed by a synonym, and there may also be a text feature or an example as support for the word. Readers can be taught to "read around" the word in question, and when they do this, they often find, right nearby, other words they can use instead of the hard word. A line from "The Amazing Octopus," level 3, illustrates this:

> The octopus has a body unlike any other animal. Its body, called a **mantle**, is soft and shaped like a bag. The octopus can squeeze into very small spaces because it has no bones in its body.

Then, too, in easier texts, the reader encounters a word more than once while still being given support. For example, "The Amazing Octopus," the level 3 text contains the lines:

> Two of its hearts send its blood, which is light blue, to its **gills**. Its gills are organs for breathing, and they're located on two of the octopus's arms.

Notice that the tricky word is bolded and then explicitly defined in a sentence that exists for solely for that purpose. On the whole, in the harder texts, the tricky words are left for the reader to figure out, and the reader needs to rely on a broad understanding of the text, not just the surrounding words, to ascertain what the word probably means. At these higher levels of complexity, a vocabulary word might be defined by other technical vocabulary or referred to through different synonyms. Readers read about the octopus shooting out water, then about using its *siphon*, then *jet propulsion*—and are expected to understand that these are all restatements of the same concept.

The vocabulary is hard and technical, and it's explained by other hard technical words

Chemoreceptors serve as natural biosensors.

Let's look, in contrast, at the Seymour Simon text, *Earthquakes*. Scanning the book, you can certainly see lots of technical words introduced, and Simon does not go so far as to write a whole-sentence definition for each new word. But Simon does tuck definitions into some parts of his writing, while in other instances he leaves technical vocabulary to the reader.

Cracks in the rocks, called faults, run through the crust. The rocks on one side of a fault push against the rocks on the other side, causing energy to build up. For years, friction will hold the rocks in place. But finally like a stretched rubber band, the rocks suddenly snap against each other. The place where this happen is called the focus of the earthquake.

In the above passage, *friction* is never explicitly defined, although the passage absolutely describes what the term means in this context. The *focus of the earthquake* is defined, as are the *faults*. Still harder texts expect that readers come to a text with a knowledge of expert vocabulary on a topic or are willing to seek out and learn that vocabulary from external sources. In these texts, context clues are rarely present, so using morphology will pay off in bigger ways.

More and More Various Connective Words

It's interesting (and not surprising) to notice that as texts become more elaborate, they involve more linking words, or conjunctions. In more complex texts, one is much more apt to encounter additives such as:

- Furthermore
- Thus
- In the same way

We're also more likely to encounter adversative connectives:

- Yet
- But
- However
- On the other hand
- In any case

Then, too, in more complex texts, one is more apt to encounter causal connectives:

- So
- Because

- It follows
- As a result

We're also likely to find temporal connectives:

- Finally
- Meanwhile
- To sum up

When readers have a sense for the way words such as these tie a text together, this can help them build relationships between one part of a text and another. As soon as a reader sees the word *but*, that reader needs to begin thinking, "Get ready, this author is going to say something that is an exception to the first part of the sentence."

More Complex Pronoun Referents

In addition to understanding the words and phrases writers use to tuck in subordinate points and elaborate on their ideas, readers of more complex texts will also need to have finesse with understanding pronoun referents. In the article "Lessons from the Deep," level 6 of the octopus text, notice the mental gymnastics a student must execute to hold on to the information about the octopus's methods of defense.

An octopus can also protect itself by squirting ink at a predator, obscuring its view, and causing it to lose its sense of smell temporarily. This makes the fleeing octopus difficult to track. And if a predator manages to grab an octopus by the arm, the octopus has one more trick up its sleeve. This escape artist can break off its arm, swim away, and then grow a new one later with no permanent damage.

In the first sentence notice that the pronoun *it* has different forms and different meanings—the octopus and the predator. The next sentence also contains the demonstrative *this*—meaning the predator's temporary impairment of smell and sight.

Try reading a piece of text without using any of the forms of reference given above. For example, you would read the above text:

An octopus can also protect *the octopus (itself)* by squirting ink at a predator, obscuring *the predator's (its)* view and causing *the predator (it)* to lose *the predator's (its)* sense of smell temporarily. *The temporary impairment of sight and smell (this)* makes the fleeing octopus difficult to track. And if a predator manages to grab an octopus by the arm, the octopus has one more trick up *the octopus's (its)* sleeve. *The octopus (This)* escape artist can break off *the octopus's (its)* arm, swim away, and then grow a new one later with no permanent damage.

Continue reading the remainder of the article with this lens. When you try to read a text this way, you experience the kind of thinking students must do to truly comprehend text.

A Strand of Difficulty: Structure (Including Text Features)

In easier nonfiction texts, the structure is clear and easy to determine. The entire text often has a single structure. For example, in the level 2 text, "The Amazing Octopus," each section is structured with a clear main idea and supporting details.

> The amazing octopus has many ways to defend itself. When an octopus wants to move fast, it can shoot out water to push itself backwards. An octopus can travel many miles that way. An octopus can also protect itself by squirting ink.

As texts become harder, students are often faced with multiple structures across a book or an article. These might be highlighted by a new section or chapter, or even by a text feature, but the changes in structure are only lightly signaled.

For example, a subtle difference between the level 3 and 4 texts of "The Amazing Octopus" comes in the paragraph about the octopus's methods of defending itself. In level 3, the paragraph is structured as a clear list, which ends:

> The octopus can also escape a predator by breaking off its arm, swimming away, and then growing a new one later!

However, the level 4 paragraph ends with a twist on the list structure, which serves to contrast all the ways the octopus tries not to get caught with its technique once it does get caught:

> But, if a predator does manage to grab an octopus by the arm, the octopus has one more trick up its sleeve. It can break off its arm, swim away, and then grow a new one later!

In the hardest texts, text structures might shift from section to section or even paragraph to paragraph. The reader is left to discern these shifts from, for example, a cause-and-effect paragraph about the influence of an animal's habitat on the animal's life to a chronological account of the animal's hibernation pattern throughout the year. The reader is expected to develop her own infrastructure to help organize and hold on to the information the article is teaching. Strong readers take into account the author's purpose—to raise awareness of an endangered animal, or to highlight how misunderstood a seemingly "scary" animal might be—to construct their infrastructure.

However, it is important to acknowledge that this is truly challenging work for our students. Deciphering text structures can be tricky and becomes even harder when a text is poorly written. Authors might assume a lot of background knowledge on the part of the reader and jump around a topic, leaving few supportive

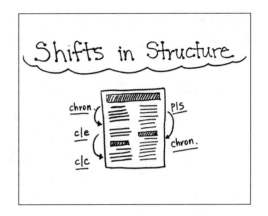

clues to transition from one part to the next. Others might take grand detours, highlighting fascinating, but irrelevant, examples and information. In complex texts, the reader is asked to weed through all of this to find or build the solid, structural bones underneath the surface of the text.

Text Features

In easier texts, we've found that text features tend to be explicitly aligned to the main idea; in the harder texts, this connection tends to be less explicit. The features may actually convince readers to give more significance to particular details than they deserve.

Surprisingly, we've found that in more challenging texts, the text features are not as helpful to readers wanting to ascertain what the text is mainly about. Instead, they're more apt to serve the purpose of seducing readers to read the passage. Instead of a subtitle such as "Octopus Behaviors," these books will have titles such as "Talents Like No Other." The pictures, too, are less apt to be aligned to the text and more likely to be attention-grabbers to draw readers in without a laserlike focus on the topic at hand. They might match just a part of the text, rather than the whole or offer a different perspective.

In very accessible expository texts, the title will often provide readers with a synopsis of the text's main idea. An article might be called, "Snowstorms Cause Massive Cancellations, Disrupting Travel across the East." The content of that article won't be a big surprise! If this is an accessible article, the accompanying pictures will tend to support the meaning of the article—perhaps showing the Arrivals and Departures board at the airport, with row upon row containing the word *cancelled*.

Meanwhile, in the level 5 article "Lessons from the Deep," the title is not explicit, though the graphics do match the main ideas. The graphics in this article illustrate the features of the octopus's body and its use of jet propulsion to move through the ocean. This is information that is directly related to the content of the article and supports a reader's understanding of the movement of these creatures through their environment.

In contrast, in the difficult level U article, "What a Ride!," the title is a play on astronaut Sally Ride's last name to lure the reader into finding out what kind of "ride" they are talking about. It gives no hint about the main idea of the article. A reader studying the photographs in the article might easily assume it was about a new space ride at an amusement park! Then, too, this article has a side bar extending from 1922 through 2007 naming nine females that were the first to do something in the United States. Although this sidebar is consistent with the content of the article (i.e., women's firsts), the information it presents is not necessary to understand the article about Sally Ride. The text features provide enrichment and elaboration, not scaffolding or guidelines to help readers glean the main ideas or themes.

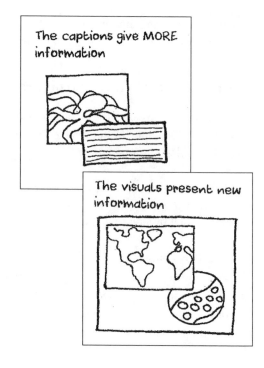

The captions give MORE information

The visuals present new information

A Strand of Difficulty: Knowledge Demands

There are several interrelated ways we've discovered that knowledge demands become more complex: the amount of prior knowledge a text expects a reader to bring, the degree of support a text provides to a reader to learn, and the sheer amount of information a reader is expected to absorb.

Prior Knowledge and Support

The amount of prior knowledge a reader is expected to bring to a text bears significantly on text difficulty. Easier texts will support a reader new to the topic, teaching vocabulary, concepts, and information as though they are all new and unfamiliar. For example, the level 3 article, "The Amazing Octopus," teaches the octopus's procedure for catching its prey step by step:

> An octopus catches its prey by grabbing it with its arms. To kill it, the octopus bites its food with its tough beak and injects it with a poison so the animal can't move.

Easier texts are written in ways that provide more support for readers to learn about an unfamiliar concept. Often, comparisons and examples are used to make an unfamiliar subject more accessible.

Harder texts, on the other hand, assume that the reader brings some background knowledge of the subject to the text. This might include basic technical vocabulary, essential concepts, and some scientific or historical background. The text introduces these terms and concepts without explanation or context, and the reader is expected to fill in what's missing. The level 5 text, "Lessons from the Deep," treats the octopus's hunting this way:

> An octopus catches its prey by grabbing it with its arms, sometimes using ink to disorient its victims first. To kill its prey, an octopus bites it with its tough beak-like jaws and injects it with venomous saliva, paralyzing it. Only one type of octopus, the Australian blue-ringed octopus, can kill a human with its poison.

The reader is expected to bring knowledge of the octopus's use of ink and of the concept of "venomous saliva" and is given little support around tricky vocabulary such as *disorient* and *paralyzing*. As texts become even more demanding, they might feel as though they are written to an audience that already has in-depth knowledge of much of the content, and there is very little support for the reader to learn the information.

Size of Text Chunks

The component parts of a text become larger as the text becomes more difficult. It's fair to say that as texts become more complex, the components that comprise those texts become longer. A description in an easier book is a sentence; in a harder book, it may span half a page. The same is true for an illustrative example, an explicit point, or even a question. Each may be longer and more layered in harder texts. In easier texts, the units of thought that comprise the text tend to be smaller and more self-contained. More complex

The text expects an expert reader / demands prior knowledge

As you already know...

No explanation is needed...

Experts agree...

texts tend to contain more elaboration, and within that elaboration, they may contain subordinate points, asides, or parenthetical comments that can sometimes take a reader off course.

In an easier expository text, content tends to be delivered in sentence-sized pieces. Let's look, for example, at a passage from the level 2 octopus text, "The Amazing Octopus":

> The octopus can squeeze into very small spaces because it has no bones in its body.
>   The octopus has eight rubbery arms that attach to its head near its mouth. The octopus's arms are covered in suckers.

This excerpt contains three ideas that relate to each other, but each sentence makes sense by itself, as an autonomous unit. Let's look, in contrast, at a snippet of Seymour Simon's *Earthquakes*:

> Why do most earthquakes in the United States occur in California? The answer lies deep within the earth. The earth's solid rocky crust floats on the mantle, an 1,800-mile-thick layer of very heavy, melted rock that moves up and down and around. Over the years, these movements have cracked the crust like an eggshell into a number of huge pieces called plates. The plates float slowly on the mantle.

In the first example, one self-contained bit of information is contained in the first sentence and a second bit in the second sentence. In contrast, the second passage contains five sentences, and the reader hasn't yet come close to achieving closure around the first bit of information.

Amount of Information

Another way that texts can get easier or harder relates to the sheer volume of information a reader is expected to absorb. Easier texts expect readers to hold on to a small amount of information. When more details are included, it is often evident that those details are there as examples only. The important information is clear, and the whole part is easy to sum up in a sentence. The following paragraph from the level 3 article, "The Amazing Octopus," provides an example:

> The octopus isn't just amazing physically. It's smart, too. Scientists have taught octopuses to learn shapes and patterns. Some octopuses in tanks have been seen "playing" games. They throw objects into currents in the water, then catch them again.

The main idea is explicit, and examples are given to support the reader's understanding. More demanding texts, on the other hand, ask readers to learn a lot of information. The texts often provide clues to help readers know what information matters the most and to help them hold onto the information. For example, the level 5 octopus article, "Lessons from the Deep," builds on the level 3 paragraph above:

> Considered the most intelligent of all invertebrates, octopus brains are still a mystery that offers scientists the opportunity to study a unique kind of complex intelligence. Scientists have taught octopuses to

learn to distinguish shapes and patterns. Some octopuses in tanks have been observed "playing" games. They throw objects into circular currents in the water and then catch them again. Another study found octopuses collecting coconut halves to use as tools, snapping the halves together when they were scared or wanted to hide.

The information for the reader to learn is more complex, and more examples are given to elaborate on the evidence for octopus intelligence. However, the most important information to hold on to is still clear to the reader. In the most demanding texts, on the other hand, the reader often gets the feeling that each detail is critical and can't be let go. Information and ideas are layered densely, making it challenging to discern what matters most. These texts often make allusions to or cite other texts, events, or ideas. In the level 6 article, "Lessons from the Deep," the complexity is evident:

> Considered the most intelligent of all invertebrates, octopus brains are still a mystery that offers scientists the opportunity to study a unique kind of complex intelligence. Running on a decentralized nervous system, two-thirds of which is distributed across its eight arms and away from the central brain, scientists are not sure exactly how octopuses experience the world. Though they are invertebrates, cephalopods exhibit affective, cognitive, and behavioral traits once considered exclusive to the higher vertebrates. The European Union recently made the octopus an "honorary vertebrate," to ensure they are legally protected against "pain, suffering, distress, or lasting harm."

Each sentence teaches new information, each piece of which feels important to hold on to. The text's reference to the European Union's legal document adds to the density of the ideas and information presented. The reader needs to determine what information should be taken in, and what, if anything, can be let go.

ASSESSING READERS AS THEY READ NONFICTION

How will this understanding of the progression of difficulty along these strands of nonfiction inform your assessments of your readers? Once you understand the ways the strands increase in complexity, you can assess where on the continuum of a particular strand your readers are, for the moment, and how you can help them to take their next steps.

Conferring with Readers Using Nonfiction Strands

You may find that as you confer with readers, you are able to determine where along each of these strands they are successful with nonfiction texts and where they could be served by some explicit teaching or some guided practice and coaching. You might choose to carry a copy of the strands of nonfiction as you crouch down next to a reader to confer. Balance listening and looking as you

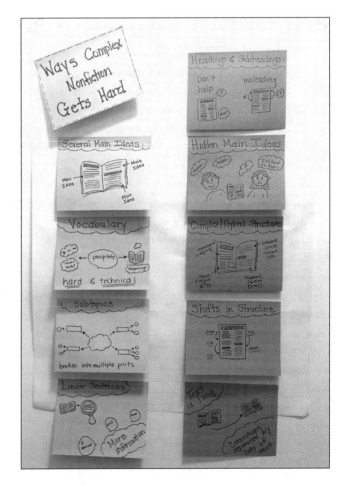

confer. You will want to listen for the extent to which the child is able to make sense of main ideas, tricky vocabulary, and complex structures and navigate the increasing knowledge demands of the text.

Scan the text the reader is holding to determine the ways that text is complex. Talk with the reader to learn more about the strategies she is relying on. "In what ways has this text been tricky?" you might ask. Then, after the reader has listed a few ways, you might say, "Will you tell me a bit about one of those ways the text has been tricky, maybe the one you're feeling proudest of tackling or the one you think you could use the most support with?" If necessary, you might prompt the reader to describe the strategies she's tried. "Whew, that's certainly challenging," you might say, wiping your brow in solidarity. "What strategies did you try? Which helped you the most?" Scan the strands of nonfiction as you confer, noting where along each of the strands the reader is able to be successful with nonfiction texts and considering next steps. Your research is likely to reveal more needs than you can tackle in a given conference, so you'll want to choose one to teach into, and record the rest as potential next steps.

Try Inventing an Assessment Tool

It may be that you, alongside some colleagues, will try your hand at inventing an assessment tool to help uncover the details of children's thinking along these strands of nonfiction difficulty. If you choose to go this route—and we never fail to be amazed by the insights, clarifications, and surprises that a well-designed assessment tool can bring—you may want to create a tool similar to the "Start with Assessment" performance assessment given to students at the start of each major reading unit in this series. You might, in that case, choose two short nonfiction texts at different levels and design a few prompts and questions to elucidate children's responses to each strand of difficulty.

When we've designed similar assessments, it has helped first to select articles that challenge students in similar ways, with one text providing more support than the second text. Then, we found it invaluable to read the text ourselves, spying on ourselves as proficient readers. At places where we noticed ourselves pausing and doing the work captured on the strands of nonfiction, we designed questions and prompts to elicit similar responses from students. We tried answering the questions ourselves to make sure they would yield useful data.

You may not be able to find a perfect prompt or question for each strand. There is no question, for instance, that will give you a quick answer to your questions about how a student is processing the increasing amount of content being delivered inside longer, more layered chunks of text. In those cases, you may find you simply need to pay attention to your students' reactions through the lens of that particular strand.

You may find that assessing students' understanding of a less explicit main idea is a bit simpler. Choose a nonfiction text that highlights this challenge, likely one where the main idea needs to be inferred based on the details provided in the text and where headings are either nonexistent or misleading. You'll find that asking a student what the article is mostly about can be very useful! As you read over students' responses, it will be clear if your students are able to synthesize information to arrive at an implied main idea, or if they become entangled in details and lose track of the main idea, or if they fall somewhere else along the continuum of understanding.

In the texts you select for the assessment, higher-level texts' features may not directly lead students to the main idea. In some cases, students may be lured to focus on less relevant details instead of building a general sense of what the text is about. This is hard work we're asking of them. Children who are just becoming comfortable using the text features to guide their understanding of a text's main idea may become flummoxed when they encounter potentially misleading headings or titles such as "Unfriendly Neighbors." When you are assessing this, you may choose a feature that is particularly apt to mislead students—this title, for example—and simply ask students to discuss how the title relates to the text's main idea. Children who are confused about the main idea will have difficulty moving beyond a literal interpretation of the title's meaning.

If you take this route, know that we have found it beneficial to sit with colleagues to analyze the results of these assessments. More information about norming meetings and analyzing assessments can be found in Chapter 2.

Whether you design an assessment tool to monitor your students' reactions to more complex nonfiction texts or you choose to assess these strands of complexity in individual conferences, it is invaluable to use the lenses of the strands to view what your students are doing. In either case, study what your children do with nonfiction now that you have a new, heightened awareness of some of the particular challenges they face. We hope this will increase, mightily, the precision and helpfulness of your assessments.

USING THE STRANDS OF NONFICTION TEXT DIFFICULTY TO CONFER AND PLAN SMALL GROUPS

Once you have data on your students, you will want to begin immediately putting it to use. We will detail a few particularly powerful ways reading workshop teachers have used these strands to power their instruction. This list of ideas is in no way exhaustive, and we look forward to hearing from you about additional ways you use these strands to target your teaching.

Using Annotated Texts across Levels

Many teachers find it useful to carry across several levels a collection of annotated texts that capture ways texts become increasingly complex. You could create this resource using the octopus texts, available in the online resources, which we designed to highlight ways the strands of nonfiction become complex. Or you could decide to take a text you love and rewrite it across different levels, referencing the strands of nonfiction as you revise it. Then, with your texts in hand, begin reading across them and annotating places of increased difficulty that you might want to highlight for children as you teach them a new strategy. When doing this work, we find it helps to read for one strand at a time, noticing first the ways a strand shows up in one text, and then reading the next level of text, noting ways the demands of the strand remain the same and ways the demands increase.

For example, when reading across several levels of the octopus text with the lens of language and vocabulary, you might first annotate several times in the level 2 passage where new words are used and the author gives a definition of the word in the same sentence. For example, you might annotate the line "Then, the octopus bites its food with its tough beak and **injects**, or shoots, poison so the animal can't move." Then, as you read the level 3 text, annotate the differences in language demands between the two texts. Where the level 3 text reads, "To kill it, the octopus bites its food with its tough beak and **injects** it with a poison so the animal can't move," you might add the note: "new word introduced without a definition; read the entire sentence to determine the word's meaning." Add your annotated texts to your reading toolkit.

As you prepare for small-group instruction to move readers whose assessment has revealed they need support with the same strand of nonfiction, consider ways to use your annotated texts to anchor your teaching. If you choose to teach using demonstration, you might scan your annotated texts quickly, looking for a place you marked that will allow you to teach the strategy you've identified readers need. After sharing the teaching point with students, you'll likely continue, saying, "Watch me as I . . ." and then pull out your annotated copy of the text and demonstrate how you try the strategy on that chunk of text. This

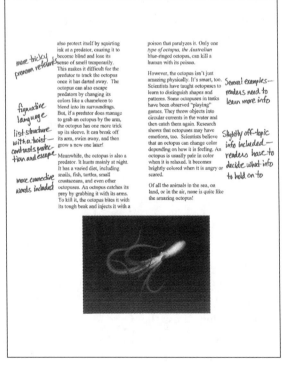

FIG. 5–4   Annotated versions of "The Amazing Octopus"

demonstration will be more supportive for your students if they are familiar with the text, so you might set aside a few minutes of read-aloud time to share with students the different levels of text in your toolkit.

Or you might decide to teach using inquiry, in which case you could pull out several levels of the octopus text and lead students in an inquiry, saying, "Let's investigate the ways the structure of the text is becoming more complicated." If you decide to go this route, you may choose to have students investigate copies of the text that have not been annotated, keeping the annotated texts as your guide throughout the inquiry.

Of course, there are other ways you can use the strands of nonfiction to guide your small groups. For example, your assessment might have revealed that a group of students can identify the main idea of a text when it is explicitly stated but are unable to determine the main idea of a text when it's more implicit. You might plan to gather these students together a few times. Choose a teaching point that matches what your readers need. Scan the conferring and small-group work sections of the nonfiction reading units for ideas, and consider borrowing units from other grade levels if you have readers who need wider-ranging support. You could even spy on the reading work you did while reading up the levels of nonfiction texts, noting the strategies you used and turning those strategies into teaching points to support your readers.

For the purpose of this small group, it will be important that all students are holding a text with an implicit main idea, so you might decide to provide all students with a common article that contains this complexity or decide to spend a minute scanning students' texts to be sure they contain parts that will allow them to practice the strategy you are teaching.

Teaching through guided practice will be particularly supportive in these situations. You will want to alternate between providing small bits of teaching and helpful tips and coaching readers one-on-one and in partnerships as they apply your teaching. After explaining to students what your assessments have revealed—so they understand why you've gathered them together—and naming your teaching point, you might say, "Let me give you a tip for finding an implicit main idea. It helps to notice words the author repeats exactly and similar words, synonyms. Often, the repeated words connect to what's most important in the article." Take a minute or two to coach students as they work independently to find the main idea, and then channel students to share with a partner how their work is going. If students continue to need support finding the main idea, layer in another tip. You might say, "The main idea won't be right there for you to find. Instead, you have to pay attention to important details, asking, 'What is the big idea these details are trying to show or support?'" You might draw from the list of prompts on pages 88–89 for coaching students in this work. Consider ways you can use guided practice to support students with other strands of nonfiction.

Prompts for Main Idea

Easier Texts

- This text is mostly about _____ . I know because it says _____ .

- A title for this might be _____ .

- I know this text is mostly about _____ because _____ .

- Which word tells you the main idea?

- The word or phrase that is repeated often in this text is _____ . That makes me think the main idea of this article is _____ .

- The most important point in this paragraph/passage/page/piece is _____ . I knew that because of _____ .

More Complex

- I learned _____ after reading this _____ (sentence/paragraph/ passage/page).

- The author discusses the topic by _____ . This represents the focus by _____ .

- The main ideas developed in this text are _____ .

- This section of the text could be called _____ because _____ .

- The main purpose of the sentence/paragraph in relation to the whole passage is to _____ .

- The details that best support the main idea of this text are _____ , _____ , and _____ .

- The main purpose of the sentence/paragraph in relation to the whole passage is to _____ .

- We can determine from what we read that _____ is important.

- The information from the text that determines the relationship between these two facts/events is _____.

- The result of _____'s idea is _____ .

- The interaction between these two people, ideas, concepts affected us today by _____ .

- The author indicates the result of these events by _____ .

You can use similar methods to support students within your one-on-one conferences. During any given workshop, you might confer with one reader using guided practice, basing your coaching on the strands of nonfiction. Then, you might confer with a second reader and offer a brief demonstration as support, showing the reader how you try the work using your annotated texts. During a third conference, you might use explanation and example to walk readers through how you ascertained the structure of another annotated text in your toolkit. Then, you could lead a fourth reader into an inquiry of how the main idea is getting more complex, contrasting the level 2 octopus text with the text she's holding to pop out the increasing demands of her text.

You might also teach small groups of students several prompts to support their work within a challenging strand of nonfiction. You might, for example, identify several of your students who are noticing structures throughout a text and using that information to guide their reading and learning from the text. In your small group, you might draw from the "Prompts for Structure" list on page 90, demonstrating how you use several of the prompts in a familiar text. In level 2, "The Amazing Octopus," for example, you might say, "Hmm, . . . I notice that there are some text features in this article. In this text, there are . . . photographs. They are there because . . ." You'll want to pause, letting the thinking work feel authentic to your students as you push yourself to say more, "They help me know what the parts of the octopus's body look like. The author writes about them, and then I can look at the pictures to help me understand." You can model one prompt or several, depending on your students and the level of complexity.

Once you have introduced several prompts and modeled how you might apply them in your own text, you might put them in the hands of your students. Prompts could be collected on a ring or kept as a stack of index cards. As partners read, they might keep the questions in front of them as they read, looking for relevant prompts and pausing to discuss them. Or they might read the text, then flip over one prompt at a time and answer the questions using text-based evidence.

Prompts for Structure ☀

Easier Texts

- The sequence of the text is _____ .
- The author presents the text in the beginning by _____ .
- The author compares _____ to _____ .
- It happened because of _____ .
- The author closes the text by _____ .
- The reason this occurred is _____ .
- The picture makes me think _____ . The caption helps me understand _____ .
- The text says the cause is _____ . The feature shows the effect by _____ .

More Complex

- _____ could be compared to _____ because of _____ .
- Writers used a certain type of text structure because _____ .
- _____ happened because _____ .
- An author used a timeline to represent _____ .
- The framework this author used to organize the information is _____ Chronological? Cause/effect? Problem/solution? Compare/contrast? Description? Directions? I know this because he/she does _____ .
- The author used a combination of structures such as _____ .
- The author organized (the paragraph/paragraphs 2 and 6/the whole text) _____ .

- The text features that help me collect information from the article are _____ . They are organized by _____ . This allowed me to see _____ .
- This text feature adds by _____ .
- The author used _____ structure because _____ .
- Part of the text used a _____ structure, but another part of the text used a _____ structure.
- The author signaled that the structure was changing by _____ .
- These parts fit together because _____ .

Most Complex

- The structure I used to help me hold on to the information in the article was _____ . I chose this because _____ .
- The author created a structure between the text feature and paragraphs _____ and _____ to help the reader understand _____ .
- The details reveal the structure is _____ .
- The author justifies his or her position by using the following structures _____ .
- The author uses structures to _____ . The purpose for this is _____ .
- The author chose to not use a clear structure because _____ .
- The relationship between the paragraphs could be defined as _____ .
- The impact of this organization was _____ .
- There were several structures in this text. They included _____ , _____ , and _____ .
- The author switched to a _____ structure in paragraph _____ . I think the author chose this structure here because _____ .
- The author signals the relationship of ideas by _____ .

USING THE STRANDS OF TEXT COMPLEXITY IN GUIDED READING

Your assessment data might reveal that students are poised to tackle new nonfiction complexities (or *to move to new levels of nonfiction*). If this is the case, you might decide to design a series of guided reading groups to equip these readers to handle increasing text demands. For additional information on guided reading, see *A Guide to the Reading Workshop, Intermediate Grades*, Chapter 8, "Small-Group Work: Developing a Richer Repertoire of Methods." If you decide to pull guided reading groups, it will be important not only to understand the strands of nonfiction, but also to understand the various ways they present themselves in nonfiction articles and texts. Analyzing a text helps you to anticipate the challenges a student might face while reading that text. It also gives you an opportunity to identify the ways the text is supportive, which you can then point out to students as added scaffolds.

Information from your analysis can be used to design your guided-reading text introduction. A text introduction to the level 4 octopus text might go as follows: "Readers, today you'll be reading an article about the octopus called 'An Animal Like No Other.' Right from the start, this is a little tricky. What does that mean, 'An Animal Like No Other'? As you read, the author will keep talking about the idea that the octopus is special and different, unlike any other animal on earth. The article will tell about how different parts of the octopus are special and amazing. What's challenging is that in easier texts, each new section of an article used to have its own heading. One would say 'Amazing Bodies,' and the next would say, 'Amazing Legs,' and you'd know just what the section would teach. Now you have to create your own headings in your mind as you read. When you see a place for a heading, draw a text box, and we'll talk later about what you could write in it."

You might decide to continue your text introduction and highlight an additional way the level 4 text gets challenging. "There's one other way the texts you're reading now are getting hard. Authors are using more sophisticated vocabulary. This author uses a lot of fancy vocabulary words, especially words to describe the octopus's body. Some will be names of body parts we don't even have! I've highlighted some of those words in your copy of the text. When you get to them, see if you can work to figure out what they mean. The text will give you the answers." With your text introduction complete, you can launch students into their reading, moving from student to student to coach in. You might pull from the "Prompts for Language and Vocabulary" on page 93. Then, you'll want to draw on your knowledge of the nonfiction strands to anticipate strategies to help students get through the text and plan possible discussion questions to pose when students are done reading.

Text Analysis of: "An Animal Like No Other" Level: 4

STRANDS OF TEXT COMPLEXITY	SUPPORTIVE	CHALLENGING
The Explicitness and Complexity of Meaning/Central Ideas/ and/or Author's Purpose	- Strong topic sentence that sets the stage for what the text will be about. - Paragraphs separate main subpoints, BUT → - each subsection has a clear topic sentence, BUT →	- The title is not explicit ⟩ requires inference ← to determine what text will mostly be about. - Greater density of information to navigate. Some tangential. → no headings - reader has to note the topic shifts
Language/ Vocabulary	- though it is generally clear what is being spoken ← about. - connective words highlight list structure on page 2.	- trickier pronoun referents ⟩ - some figurative language
Structure (including Text Features)	- Picture shows various aspects of the octopus being discussed, though not in great detail. Somewhat supportive.	- No caption to connect picture + text (labeled) - No pictures of more obscure body parts (siphon, gills, beak)
Knowledge Demands	- Most children have a basic knowledge of topic and some domain specific language (organs, hearts, suckers) - SOME WORDS easily determined or even defined	- Other, more difficult words (siphon, mantle) → OTHER WORDS left to the reader to figure out

FIG. 5–5

Prompts for Language and Vocabulary ✺

Easier Texts

- When I looked around the word _____ , I found the synonym _____ .

- As used in line _____ , the word helps me to understand _____ .

- When I look at the word in context, it clearly means _____ .

- This word, _____ , is used throughout the passage. It is used to help me understand _____ .

- The technical meaning of the word could be _____ .

More Complex

- I found the tricky word _____ . The clues the author gave to help me understand it were _____ and _____ .

- The word that can be used to clarify or contrast what the author was saying is _____ . One reason the author chose to do this is _____ .

- Is there another meaning for the word _____ that might fit here?

- This word might mean _____ , but it also might mean _____ . The meaning that fits best is _____ .

- The words that are repeatedly used are _____ . They impact the tone or the structure of the text by _____ .

Most Complex

- Some of the vocabulary I already know about this topic is: _____ , _____ , and _____ .

- A word part or root I recognize within this word is _____ . That part means _____ . So, I think this word might mean _____ .

- The words in sentence _____ create the impression that _____ .

- The words _____ capture the theme of the text by _____ .

- The author used the word _____ to impact tone, point of view, or mood by _____ .

Targeted book introductions are a key component of guided reading lessons, but you could also choose to give stand-alone book introductions to prepare a child for the challenges he will face in a more complex nonfiction book. To provide even more support, some teachers choose to provide students with a marked copy of the text, in which challenges are flagged so students know to pay extra attention to them. For example, if you plan to support a reader with the text *A Place for Fish*, by Melissa Stewart, you might highlight two complexities in your text introduction, based on the strands of nonfiction. Notably, you might draw a child's attention to the fact that the text boxes and illustrations across the book include vital information, as well as the fact that Stewart uses complex vocabulary, and the reader has to use the context as a clue to determine each word's meaning. You might also let students know a way the text is supportive. With *A Place for Fish*, you might highlight that most sections use a problem-solution text structure.

Prior to giving the book to the child, you might flag with a blue Post-it note all the places in the first third of the text where the reader needs to synthesize information between text boxes and illustrations, and leave the question, "How do these parts fit together?" on each Post-it note. Across the second third of the book, you might flag similar spots with blue Post-it notes, but leave the Post-its blank, so the reader is required to prompt himself when he gets to that section. Leave the final third of the book unflagged, and give the reader a few extra blue Post-it notes to flag places in the book where he notices text boxes and illustrations that include vital information that has to be synthesized with the main text. You could repeat this process using yellow Post-it notes to mark key words in the first two-thirds of the book. Then, as the reader makes his way through the text, he repeatedly stops and works through the ways the text is complex, moving himself along the continuum of each strand. This certainly takes time to prepare, but you'll find it provides an incredible level of support for your readers and quickly moves them from scaffolded practice toward independence. Students could mark one or two future texts this way until they are able to do the work with automaticity.

Chapter 6

An Introduction to the Learning Progressions

Y OU DRAW A CHAIR alongside a young reader and you say, "Tell me about your reading." The child starts to talk, perhaps telling you about a cool text box he has just read that shows the inside view of, say, a submarine. You listen, nodding and laughing enthusiastically, hoping your energy and interest will somehow be helpful. You ask about a few things you see in the illustration. The child seems on top of the various parts of the picture. You ask, "Is there anything you need help with?" and that question results in a quick discussion about a tricky word. Then the conversation is over and you move on, wondering whether you did anything to help and wondering what you could have done. This chapter—and indeed, the rest of this book—gives you your answer.

What you should have done was to listen to that youngster's remarks, thinking, "What is the work that this reader is attempting to do? What's a hugely important way I can help the reader progress along the skill trajectory of that work?

Let's rewind the conversation. The child has a book opened which chronicles life inside a submarine. The child is noticing a text box alongside the main text of his nonfiction information book. You need to think, "What is the work that he is doing, or almost doing?" You can't be totally sure yet, but if you are like me, your hunch is that for starters, the boy is synthesizing the content of the text box with the content of the larger piece. Your hope is that he isn't reading the text box as an unrelated text, but instead, that he is thinking about whether the information he has learned from the text box *adds onto* or *changes* what he read on the rest of the page.

Let's say that you know that the youngster is attempting to relate part of the text (the text box) to the main article. To help this child, it is important to know what this part-to-whole analytic reading looks like when it is done at a fairly low level and what it looks like when it is done at a more advanced level. That's where the learning progression comes in.

In third grade, as it turns out, a reader is expected to notice whether *the topic* the reader learns about in the two text parts is the same or is different. By fourth grade, when readers are asked to talk about the relationship between the parts and the whole, they can hopefully draw on a repertoire of ways in which two texts, or two parts of a text, go together.

When you press, asking "How does that text box go with the rest of the text?" you hope these readers have an internalized list of options to draw upon. Is this text box *an example* of a main idea, *a solution* to a problem, *an effect* of a cause, *an answer* to an earlier question? And by fifth grade, readers can ideally also note when there are parts of the text that feel somewhat extraneous to the main ideas/claims. Then, too, by fifth grade, youngsters are expected to use academic language to talk about the importance of one part to the larger text. Knowing this should give you plenty to draw upon in your conference. You can say to the youngster who is reading that text box about the submarine, "What I see you doing here is actually called analytic reading. You are thinking about how this one part goes with (or doesn't go with) the rest of the text. That's challenging work that skilled readers do all the time—not just with text boxes but with any part of a longer text. Can I give you some tips about how to do that work even better—tips you can use not just today but anytime you try to think part-to-whole?" Then you could teach in ways that made a difference.

Beyond this particular example, my larger point is that to help readers become more proficient with specific reading skills, it is important for you and your colleagues to draw on your own internalized understanding of the pathways along which readers develop. That knowledge will allow you to see what a youngster can do, can almost do, and will be able to do soon, and to move the reader along in forceful ways.

OUTLINING A TRAJECTORY OF LEARNING THAT IS VISIBLE TO EDUCATORS AND STUDENTS

The impetus behind the development of learning pathways came almost a decade ago when a TCRWP staff developer accompanied a group of teachers and a few administrators on a walkthrough of their K–8 school. This was in early October when most of the school was engaged in a fiction unit of study. Not surprisingly, children across the school were all developing theories about characters—work essential to any effort to read fiction—so the group honed in on this to understand how that work looked at different grade levels. What struck them was that although the texts the students were reading were different, the work that students did to grow theories about characters was remarkably similar. First-graders' books brimmed with Post-its like this: "Poppleton is a good friend because . . ." Eighth-graders' Post-its weren't very different: "Hester Prynne is a strong woman because . . ." That realization prompted our organization to begin clarifying the changing expectations for character work across the grades. Later on, the Common Core informed this discussion, leading us to include new strands in our progressions and to adjust the grade levels at which a specific skill is expected.

And as new and more rigorous standards call for new goals, it is important for you to understand the pathways to those new goals. For example, the hypothetical child who had been reading a text box about submarines was actually gesturing toward work that plays a big role in many of the new CCSS-aligned standards. On the new breed of high-stakes assessments, readers are time and again asked to identify the relationship between a part of the text—say, lines 67–69—and the whole text.

It will take some time and some practice before you and your colleagues are able to listen to a child talk about a text, read Post-its a child has left on an article, and be able to place the work that youngster is attempting to do on a larger map that charts the pathways to proficiency in reading.

Let's face it. As increasingly rigorous standards make new demands, kids today are being asked to do work that is staggering in its complexity. For the most part, the expectations make sense. How true it is that research today can't just involve plucking information out of a huge pile of sources, then sorting that information into categories. That definition of research sort of worked when our research sources were largely encyclopedias and textbooks, but in today's world, students are gleaning information from reading websites and watching YouTube videos. The authors of today's sources have not been screened for knowledge base or objectivity. It is critical that students grow up knowing that they need to evaluate the trustworthiness of a text and to consider the knowledge base, vested interests, or bias of a source. Research in today's world needs to include thinking about the different perspectives that the various sources take toward a subject so the reader can adjudicate between those positions, deciding to either choose a position or to overview the different positions.

It makes sense that fifth-graders are being asked to begin to do this sort of work—but the reading skills we're looking to cultivate won't emerge full bloom out of nowhere. Those skills will need to be developed, and for that to happen, you need to value the messy and incomplete early gestures children make toward skills that may only now be moving front and center in our thinking. Learning progressions allow you—and your children—to see the potential in a child's relatively simple conversation about a cool text box.

Then too, these progressions will help you unpack the standards and expectations placed upon you and your students. The progressions are aligned to globally benchmarked standards, but they are not limited to those standards. That is, some of the most essential reading skills are nowhere to be seen in the Common Core. Reading researchers agree, for example, that prediction is an essential reading skill, but it has no place in the Common Core. The same is true for envisioning and for monitoring for sense. These progressions retrieve those and other essential skills.

But the truly important thing about learning progressions in reading is that they are written for children. Many students today (and indeed, many teachers) are struggling to understand exactly what the new expectations look like. These progressions make every effort to translate the standards (and the essential skills that are missing from the standards) into kid-friendly, doable language. Their power comes because you can hand them over to kids, saying to youngsters, "This is a way for you to look at the work you are doing in your mind as you read and to think about ways to ratchet up the level of that thinking work."

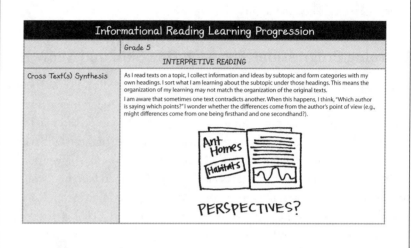

FIG. 6–1

You'll notice the progressions are written in the first person—in the "I" voice—as well as in student-friendly language. In the many versions of these progressions we piloted, and in our work with Ray Pecheone and Linda Darling-Hammond of the Stanford Center for Assessment, Learning, and Equity (SCALE), we learned that using "I" increases student accountability. It's not "someone," or "a reader," who needs to have done this work. The question is, did *I* do it?

Learning Progressions Focus on One Skill and Show How It Grows across Time

Progressions, like the one in Figure 6–1, focus on one skill and show the way it grows, or progresses, across time. In Part II of *Reading Pathways*, we provide a progression for each key skill, showing how each of those skills unfolds when reading narratives and when reading informational texts. We refer to the progression for each skill as a strand and imagine the progressions being put into kids' hands as strands so that students can work on a particular skill, pushing skill levels from a lower to a higher point. For example, perhaps students' fluency as readers of narrative texts can best be described like this: "I aim to make my reading voice sound like I'm talking or storytelling. I can do that out loud or in my head. I scoop up a bunch of words at a time. I do this in ways that make the story easy to understand." That is, for now, those students have achieved a second-grade level of proficiency in the fluency strand of the progression. With a little work, however, they can master the third-grade expectations: "I can read in my head and aloud in ways that help my listeners and me understand the story (e.g., changing my voice to show dialogue or a character's feelings). The new work I'm doing now is that I can do this even when I'm reading longer sentences."

Each column is meant to represent a years' worth of growth, with level 3 aligning to third-grade standards, level 4 aligning to fourth-grade standards, and so on. Within each category (say, "Monitoring for Sense" from the Informational Reading Learning Progression), several indicators are given to explain the skill work that is expected of a student at that level. Progressions are perfect for monitoring progress toward a bigger goal. By using progressions, students in a reading workshop can check to see how far they have come along the pathways toward meeting certain goals. And if they fall short, the progression can guide them in the right direction toward meeting that goal.

Learning Progressions Help You Connect Your Teaching across Disciplines

Learning progressions also allow you to connect the teaching you do in one part of your curriculum with the teaching you do in another part of the curriculum. For starters, once that child begins to talk about how the text box on submarines fits with the rest of the chapter, realizing that actually it is almost like a miniature synopsis of the entire chapter because everything a person does in a day on a submarine can be traced through that drawing, suddenly you have ground from which to teach kids to do similar work across other disciplines. "Now that you are so skilled at looking at how parts of a nonfiction text fit with the whole text, can you think about how this paragraph fits with the rest of the text? It feels sort of different than the rest of the text, so I'm wondering why it's here. What job do you think it is doing? Why do you think the author included it? And by the way, are you thinking in similar ways about parts of the historical fiction book you have been reading? Are there parts of that book that feel sort of extraneous to you at first? Have you been thinking about why the author included those parts?" Questions like this nudge a reader to read much more closely, more attentively.

Your Secret Toolkit: Learning Progressions Help You Be More Knowledgeable about Readers' Work

Progressions are helpful because they can act almost as cue cards, reminding youngsters and those of us who teach them, too, about the paths along which readers develop and about ways to make one's thinking work better. When listening to a youngster talk about a text, it would be a lot to both listen to that child's ideas and to also, at the same time, be able to keep in one's head the whole trajectory of, say, how readers develop skills in synthesis—and what work is a notch more challenging than whatever the reader seems to be doing just now. To teach well, it helps to have a sense of the pathways along which readers seem to develop toward skills that are important in this new twenty-first-century information age.

When I describe reading progressions to teachers, I say, "These progressions will be your best friend. They are your secret toolkit. They will help you feel vastly more knowledgeable about the work readers do in fiction and nonfiction across grade levels than you are now. They will let you assess your students' higher-order thinking, and they will allow you to give your students pointed, specific tips about next steps they can take. Once students do take those next steps, you can help them to transfer and apply that work between both fiction and nonfiction texts, realizing the work is similar even when the texts are different."

What we've found is that it is very helpful for teachers to know "This is the new work for third grade," or for fourth grade and so on. It's helpful to have a tool that encapsulates the most high-leverage new work that children need to tackle at each grade level. When your youngsters work with resolve to lift the level of the thinking they do as they read, they end up becoming a very different sort of reader. These ways of reading give children new power.

FREQUENTLY ASKED QUESTIONS ABOUT LEARNING PROGRESSIONS
How do we recommend using the learning progressions?

When your progressions are put into the hands of kids and used in formative ways, they are powerful teaching tools. Using these progressions will fuel enormous progress in your students' comprehension skills—and especially in skills that are important on high-stakes assessments.

As discussed elsewhere, it is wise to be cautious about treating them as truly objective measures of each student's relative strengths as a reader until students understand the expectations embedded in the progressions. A very skilled reader could think and write about a text in ways that *don't* align with the learning progression. You could rightfully ask, then, why we have a learning progression that suggests that fifth-graders, for example, need to be able to see several themes in a story and to quote from as well as paraphrase a text, and so forth. Part of the answer is simply that many of these are skills that the Common Core standards detail and what PARCC, SBAC, and state assessments appear to value. We want you and your students to be able to rely on these learning progressions, confident that the skills for which they will be assessed are baked into them.

But the logic for these expectations is more than that. For example, in general, as students move into fifth grade and toward middle school, they are being asked to be more aware of how texts are written from various perspectives and points of view. It is important for youngsters to grow up realizing that even the *language* that a person uses reflects that person's bias, tone, mood, and perspective. So the expectation that a fifth-grader, when providing evidence for a theme, will include specific quotes from the text is part and parcel of a belief that by fifth grade, children should be attentive to the fact that the actual choice of one word over another is significant and reveals a speaker/character/author's spin on a topic. This expectation also parallels the fact that by fifth grade, children should know that when synthesizing information from a variety of sources, it is helpful to keep track of the source of this or that piece of information. It's also worth noting that the expectation that children in fifth grade should quote from, as well as paraphrase a source, is aligned to the expectation that fifth-graders need to understand shades of meaning in language. The exact words a source uses matter.

See Chapter 7, "Performance Assessments," for more on the use of learning progressions in the classroom across the year, in both instruction and assessment.

What decisions informed what to put into the progressions and what to leave out?

The reading progressions focus on the skills that are most high-leverage for young readers. That is, if readers develop these thinking skills, *and* they are moving up reading levels at the same time, they'll do well. They'll do well on all these endeavors: state tests, book clubs and authentic reading experiences, and reading within social studies, science, and ELA. There is a lot of reading work which is interesting but that only pays off in certain texts—studying archetypes in fairy tales and fantasy, for instance, or using search engines in research. These progressions don't wander into those realms, but instead focus on the big work that will pay off in most texts.

The biggest decision we made was to include skills that are *not* included in the Common Core or assessed explicitly on state tests—skills such as orienting to texts, predicting, envisioning, monitoring for sense, and fluency. There is no question but that these skills are essential to readers' overall success. They are prerequisites to the skills laid out in the standards. They undergird all reading success, and mastering these skills is essential for both higher- and lower-level readers. When students tackle harder historical fiction, for instance, envisioning becomes important again, as does monitoring for sense.

A second group of skills that we included but that are not honored in the Common Core or on state tests are those that support critical thinking. State tests, including the new Common Core–based assessments, assess children's ability to determine, rank, and evaluate author's ideas and themes, craft, and structure and the details that support these. That is, they honor what the author did and what the author has to say, and they do not reward children talking back to texts or bringing in reading that may contradict an author's point of view. We believe it is important for children to learn to step back from texts and assess them critically—asking questions and determining their own stances in relation to the author's. So, you'll see a strand in the progression for questioning the text, developing one's own ideas, and reading critically.

How are these progressions aligned to the expectations of the CCSS, Partnership for Assessment of Readiness for College and Careers (PARCC), Smarter Balanced Assessment Consortium (SBAC), and to other state tests?

To make the decisions about what to leave out and what to include, we have developed a deep knowledge of PARCC, SBAC, and other organizations that are creating the state assessments our children will be taking in the years to come. TCRWP staff have participated in groups charged with writing both PARCC and SBAC assessments. *Pathways to the Common Core*, our book on the Common Core, was the best-selling book on that topic, and was #7 on *The New York Times* list of best-selling books in education for 2014. Our organization has closely studied the challenges posed to readers on those tests, as well as the limitations of these tests. It is important to us to be able to say with confidence that when you use these learning progressions to assess progress and guide instruction, the level of skill demanded on these learning progressions will match or exceed that demanded by high-stakes assessments.

You can be sure, then, that we know that by fifth grade, readers need to discern more than one main idea in nonfiction texts, to weigh and evaluate those ideas, and to correlate details that support each. That's solid reading work that you'll see on the PARCC and SBAC assessments—and you'll see it in the Informational Reading Learning Progression. You can be sure that we know how third-graders must be able to identify character change and also to name what caused that change. You see those expectations on the state assessments, and you'll find them embedded into the Narrative Reading Learning Progression. If PARCC and SBAC ask third-graders to identify *themes*, as well as *morals* and *lessons*, we used all those terms as well.

There's a *however*, and it's a big *however*. Doug Reeves warns that when you begin to align all of your reading work to specific state exams, you get in the rut of constantly revising that work as the exam changes in tiny ways. A year ago, a high-stakes test asked third-graders to identify a *moral*, and now they use the term *lesson*. We could spend our every minute trying to keep up with, not the Joneses, but the most recent iterations of high-stakes tests—and who wants that? Our hope, then, is that this series can help us all to aim not toward the standards or the high-stakes tests that are aligned to them, but beyond both, toward goals that are more enduring and authentic.

How are the assessments similar to those we have developed for assessing writing? How are they different?

We are very pleased with the contributions that the writing progressions, checklists, and rubrics are making to students' progress as writers. Everywhere, teachers, kids, and parents tell us that the writing checklists and progressions have provided new clarity for kids, allowing them to make tangible progress that in the end fuels yet more progress. Our goal is to do the same for reading, and the chapters ahead will give you and your colleagues a wealth of information about how to make this happen.

You'll note, however, that our reading progressions don't resemble the writing checklists all that much. Think about it this way (and there is no question that the logistics of checklists are easier than progressions). The fourth-grader who wants to be skilled at information *writing* need only look at a single checklist for her "to-do" list. (Of course, that may not be true because she may not be close to the fourth-grade expectations in writing, but at least in theory, she need only look at this one checklist). In *reading*, however, this same learner has ten skills to think about, and for each, she essentially needs a different progression! You are no doubt wondering why we don't use a checklist for reading, as we do for writing.

Think about this: when a child is writing an information text, she'd be remiss to leave out any of the major elements. That is, her writing will almost inevitably contain a beginning and an end. It will contain elaboration, transitions, organization, attention to conventions, and so on. So every time the child produces a piece of writing, she displays her aptitude at all the component skills. A checklist can help the writer to remember all the things she wants to do in concert with each other. So, a fourth-grade information writer could draw her pencil down a grade level–specific checklist, asking questions like "Did I remember to group information into sections and paragraphs to separate related information? Did I use a variety of facts and details such as numbers, names, and examples to support my subtopics? Did I get my information from talking to people, reading books, and from my own knowledge and observations?" Checklists are incredibly helpful when the job is to get something done or to not forget to do something.

One could never use all the reading skills at one time. If a reader is comparing and contrasting, that reader can't easily also interpret and envision and read critically. To some extent, the reader's work on one skill chases away the reader's work on other skills. The best way for a reader to use the progression, then,

FIG. 6–2A   A slice of the "Fluency" strand from the Informational Reading Learning Progression.

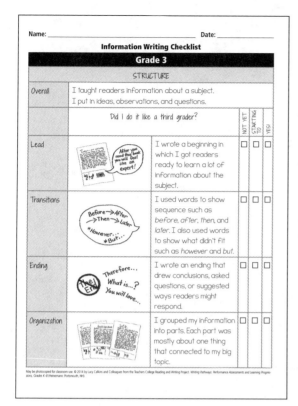

Information Writing Checklist

Grade 3

Name: _____ Date: _____

STRUCTURE

		NOT YET	STARTING TO	YES!
Overall	I taught readers information about a subject. I put in ideas, observations, and questions.			
	Did I do it like a third grader?			
Lead	I wrote a beginning in which I got readers ready to learn a lot of information about the subject.	☐	☐	☐
Transitions	I used words to show sequence such as *before, after, then,* and *later.* I also used words to show what didn't fit such as *however* and *but.*	☐	☐	☐
Ending	I wrote an ending that drew conclusions, asked questions, or suggested ways readers might respond.	☐	☐	☐
Organization	I grouped my information into parts. Each part was mostly about one thing that connected to my big topic.	☐	☐	☐

Information Writing Checklist (continued)

Grade 3

DEVELOPMENT

	Did I do it like a third grader?	NOT YET	STARTING TO	YES!
Elaboration	I wrote facts, definitions, details, and observations about my topic and explained some of them.	☐	☐	☐
Craft	I chose expert words to teach readers a lot about the subject.	☐	☐	☐
	I taught information in a way to interest readers. I may have used drawings, captions, or diagrams.	☐	☐	☐

Information Writing Checklist (continued)

Grade 3

LANGUAGE CONVENTIONS

	Did I do it like a third grader?	NOT YET	STARTING TO	YES!
Spelling	I used what I knew about spelling patterns to help me spell and edit before I wrote my final draft.	☐	☐	☐
	I got help from others to check my spelling and punctuation before I wrote my final draft.	☐	☐	☐
Punctuation	I punctuated dialogue correctly, with commas and quotation marks.	☐	☐	☐
	While writing, I put punctuation at the end of every sentence.	☐	☐	☐
	I wrote in ways that helped readers read with expression, reading some parts quickly, some slowly, some parts in one sort of voice, and others in another voice.	☐	☐	☐

FIG. 6–2B   Information Writing Checklist, Grade 3

is to take a strand of it on as a goal and to work with dispatch to progress along the progression in that skill. Meanwhile, when a writer writes an essay, for example, it is almost impossible for the writer *not* to do some version of each of the items on the writing checklist. It would be hard for that essayist *not* to include a lead, transitions, a conclusion, evidence, and so forth.

Progressions (see Figure 6–1) focus on one skill and show the way that one skill progresses across time. So, for instance, suppose you listen to a student read an expository text aloud. As she reads, her voice seems to follow the logic of the text, highlighting big points and quietly tucking in less important points. Then too, she shifts between an explaining voice and a storytelling voice as the text requires. This student is meeting all that is required of a fourth-grader when it comes to fluency, and you will want to look one square to the right on the progression to see what is required of fifth-graders. By doing so, you'll see what the next instructional steps might be for this reader, should you decide to teach into fluency. So, for instance, you'll see that fifth-grade informational readers use their voices "to add meaning to the text." They keep in mind what great science or history sounds like and "try to read like that, emphasizing the big points."

All of this, or just a small part, could become what you teach this student. For this reason, many teachers quite literally carry the progressions on their clipboards as they confer, comforted that they'll be able to account accurately for what students are doing and then teach them to do something more sophisticated.

Throughout the Units of Study series, you will find that the Informational Reading Learning Progression and the Narrative Reading Learning Progression play a large part in every book—from conducting initial performance assessments, to helping students set and meet goals, to informing the work you do each day. In the next chapter, I'll discuss the many ways these learning progressions can be used in the classroom—by you and by students, as an active tool—to fuel conferring, small-group work, and other kinds of teaching across the units.

Why are there no progressions for grades K–2?

The decision not to publish learning progressions for K–2 was a judgment we made just before the closing gate. The Teachers College Reading and Writing Project *does* have reading learning progressions that have been made for grades 1 and 2, but in the final analysis, we think primary teachers will be better off focusing on running records, high-frequency word assessments, sound-letter assessments, and so forth. (The exception is teachers whose students are very proficient.) The work of actually getting every reader making meaning as he reads is so gigantic and so critical that we don't want to distract teachers or students from those goals. Nor do we want teachers to have yet more assessments to conduct.

Then, too, learning progressions require that the skills for prior grades be detailed, and although we find it relatively easy to bring the level 3 to 6 learning progressions into grades 1 and 2, it is often far harder to detail what these skills might look like during pre-K and K years, especially considering the kinds of books they are holding during independent reading time.

Finally, we have found from the learning progressions in writing that this tool is most potent and helpful when it is ambitious, calling the students to dramatically higher expectations. The progressions are more challenging for the higher-level grades. Developing learning progressions that are appropriately challenging for every grade across a K–8 grade span is difficult, and the hardest part revolves around making the expectations for the younger grades be ambitious enough that they call on those children to do ambitious work. That is, when reading Frog and Toad, a reader can do work that is close to as sophisticated as the work that a reader, two years older, can do with *Sarah, Plain and Tall*. The smaller, easier book provides such scaffolding that, actually, a six-year-old can think in many of the same ways as we detail for older grades. If we were to bring those skills down to the K–2 grade levels, however, expectations for grades 3–8 would then be over the roof. As it stands, we are not convinced that our grade 2 learning progression is ambitious enough that it will be super-challenging for kids who are reading books like Pinky and Rex, and if a progression is *not* a stretch, it doesn't have enough teaching power.

We do think that learning progressions can be a potent tool for primary teachers whose students are well beyond benchmark levels, because those students need to be encouraged to think with depth and sophistication. But we encourage those teachers to develop their own learning progressions and not bring the upper-grade ones (word for word) into the K–2 grades, because that will make the tool far less potent in grade 3. If readers have already studied the third-grade progressions while in second grade, the tool will be old hat for them—yet actually, doing that level of work with third-grade level texts is a challenge.

Will it be important for me to use these progressions in the units?

You will want to use the progressions within each unit of study as teaching tools. In the chapters to follow, we write about ways you can do this. You'll want to do everything possible to recruit your students to embrace the purpose of the progressions; that is, these tools can have extraordinary power if students take them seriously and work zealously to live up to the descriptors. Your goal is to help students use them as ladders to sky-high levels of thinking, writing, and reading.

Ultimately, for the progressions to work their magic, *you* need to work magic and create a learning culture in your classroom. You'll need to recruit your learners to be invested in self-improvement. Any effort toward self-improvement will be more engaging if there is a respected scale for measuring progress and if learners are able to see and to learn from granular evidence of progress (or lack thereof). This is why athletes use stopwatches, yardsticks, and pedometers to measure their progress and set goals. And in the same way, your learners can use the progressions.

Before you can recruit your students' commitment to working with one of the reading progressions, you probably want to recruit their willingness to work on their reading in the first place. As I mentioned earlier, many of your kids probably come to you thinking that some people are born able to read really well, and others—well, that's just not in the stars for them. Your first job will be to turn that perception around. You might say, "Readers, you come to me able to read. You can say the words on the page, and you can construct meaning in your mind. But what I want to tell you is this: Reading well involves not just reading the words. Reading well involves being analytic and insightful in thinking about the text. Reading well is intellectual work that requires mental strength. And whether you read quickly or slowly, whether you read thick books or thin ones—you can do that high level of intellectual work. You can do it, if you work at it."

You'll find that most of our launch units talk up this growth mindset. "One thing about getting better as a reader is this: This is something you need to do *for yourself*. *You* are in charge of setting goals for yourself as a reader. Not your friends, your parents, or your teacher. That means *you* have to be the one who says, 'I want to become a better reader,' and then take the steps to achieve your goals."

Some teachers find that one way to create a sense of self-efficacy is to compare reading to a video game (or something else that students can relate to in their everyday lives). "When you play a video game for the first time, you acclimate yourself to the controls. Which button will make you jump? Which sequence of button strokes will make a lethal attack combination?" You might continue, "At first you're just trying to complete a level without running out of lives, but as you become more skilled you shift your focus to earning more and more points. You look at manuals, guides, and websites to get advice about how to succeed—until finally, you've earned the highest score. Imagine if you quit playing a video game the first time you died?! You would miss out on so much adventure! This is true of reading, too." Other analogies, like learning to play a musical instrument or learning to skateboard can work just as well.

Carol Dweck, in talking about what she refers to as the growth mindset toward learning, asks, "What do academically tenacious students look like?" She goes on to answer her own question. "They believe that they belong in school academically and socially. . . . They are engaged in learning, view effort positively, and can forego immediate pleasures for the sake of schoolwork. . . . They are not derailed by difficulty, be it intellectual or social. They see a setback as an opportunity for learning or a problem to be solved rather than as a humiliation, a condemnation of their ability or worth, a symbol of future failures, or a confirmation that they do not belong. This is true at the level of a given task and at the level of their studies in general . . . . They know how to remain engaged over the long haul and to deploy new strategies for moving forward effectively" (*Academic Tenacity: Mindsets and Skills that Promote Long-Term Learning*, 2014, 4).

Work Towards Your Goals

- Set your OWN goals

- Keep practicing- Don't give up!

- Give yourself time to improve.

- Keep track of your progress

Paul Tough, author of *How Children Succeed* (Mariner Books, 2013), concurs, adding, "When kids believe that they can change their intelligence, they actually do better. They work harder." (The full interview can be heard at http://www.econtalk.org/archives/2012/09/paul_tough_on_h.html; Google search term "Paul Tough how children succeed econ talk.") It is critical, then, to keep in mind that for performance assessments to be potent, they need to be accompanied by a belief that hard work yields achievement.

You'll see that these units of study support a growth mindset toward reading development. Time and again, instruction supports students who roll up their sleeves and tackle trouble, who work with resolve on the hard parts, who figure challenging things out, who aim to go the extra mile, who work with grit, perseverance, and resolve. This mind set is nowhere more clear than when it comes to the use of progressions.

How do I get to know the progressions before introducing them to students?

Before thinking about ways to bring the learning progressions to your students, take a bit of time to orient yourself to them. Say you will be using the Informational Reading Learning Progression. Lay it before you and choose a category on which to focus. Let's imagine you are a fourth-grade teacher and choose "Main Idea(s) and Supporting Details/Summary." Begin looking at the grade 3 main idea category in the progression, and then look at the same category for grade 4 and finally grade 5, each time asking, "What is new at this level?"

You'll immediately see a trajectory of learning you'll want to set students along. For instance, in third grade, students might simply locate a sentence that explicitly states the main idea in the text. By fourth grade, however, it is expected that students don't just identify a main idea—they summarize the text at intervals while reading to hold on to important information. This requires not only determining the main idea, but supporting it with relevant details. And they are expected to use the structure of the text to effectively determine the most important information. By fifth grade, students carry over the skills of the previous levels but are additionally responsible for doing all of that work for multiple main ideas. In other words, readers at this level are expected to sift the information in a text, ranking the importance of each piece and categorizing the most important information to support several important ideas taught by the text. Looking across levels can help you assess where students are, and this can inform the teaching you'll do next.

Informational Reading Learning Progression			
	Grade 4	Grade 5	Grade 6
	LITERAL COMPREHENSION		
Main Idea(s) and Supporting Details/Summary	As I read, I often pause to summarize as a way to hold onto what I'm learning, saying the main idea(s) of that part and linking it/them to related points. As I do this, I select points that are especially important to the idea.	I can figure out several important main ideas in a text, and I'm aware that sometimes those ideas thread through the whole text instead of being located in chunks of it. I can sort all the details in the text and weigh their importance so that I can also discuss important details that best support each of the main ideas.	I can figure out several important main ideas in a text and weigh and evaluate which of those ideas seems most significant in the text.
	I can use the primary structure(s) in the text to help me grasp what it mostly teaches (e.g., if it is organized as a main idea or supporting points or a claim and reasons, I can use either structure to help me determine importance and select supporting details).	I am careful to keep my own opinion separate from the ideas presented in the text. I also avoid mentioning minor details.	I am careful to include in my summary only what the text says, and none of my own opinions, ideas or judgments.
	I am careful to keep my own opinion separate from the ideas presented in the text.		

FIG. 6–3 "Main Idea(s) and Supporting Details/Summary" from the Informational Reading Learning Progression, Grades 4–6

In the end, taking time to orient yourself to the progressions will provide a big payoff. You will have a clearer sense of the trajectories of reading development that undergird the particular skills you are teaching. In addition, you will be equipped with teaching points and examples to use during conferences and small-group teaching. Once you've done this work, you will be ready to bring these progressions to bear on your teaching.

Chapter 7

Performance Assessments

BRINGING PERFORMANCE ASSESSMENTS AND LEARNING PROGRESSIONS INTO YOUR CLASSROOM

Picture this. Your students did the required performance assessment. They read the two assigned texts and answered the four questions, each on a half-sheet of paper. Whew! That's done. You stick the folder full of the kids' work somewhere and turn your attention toward tomorrow's teaching.

I want to say, "*Stop!*" I want to run out in front of your teaching, waving my arms like a crazy person, desperate to stop traffic. When I get your attention, I say it straight: "You need to use the assessments to lift the level of kids' learning."

Let me be clear. You do not need to take those assessments home and spend your weekend scoring them—although you might. You do not need to meet with teachers across your school and find some objective way for students to be scored across classrooms—although you might. Here's the one truly essential thing—the assessments need to propel students' learning going forward and to do so in dramatic ways.

In a world where people rarely agree on anything, there is unanimous agreement that the biggest problem with most classroom-based assessments is that too often, teachers conduct assessments and gather data, and then nothing is made of the data. This isn't to say it's the teachers' fault. When the process of conducting assessments is done for compliance reasons (as it so often is), and there is no perceived payoff, the waste of time and effort is staggering. Think of the days, hours, minutes spent preparing for and conducting performance assessments—for naught. Think of the waste of *children's* time—that most precious of all resources—and of their angst as well. For nothing?

The waste is especially dire because if the process of participating in performance assessments leads to nothing, then that effort will harden you and your children against ever wanting to participate in performance assessments again. So it is also imperative that you and your colleagues have a plan for using the results of the performance assessments in manageable, efficient ways that lift the level of student work and don't add too much work to your already overloaded plate. The good news is that this is actually possible to do. And better yet, performance assessments can not only guide instruction, but they can energize it as well.

Here's how to navigate this chapter. First, we'll give you a bit of history of the origin of our performance assessments and the way they are set up across the units. Then we'll discuss how to deliver the assessment in a no-nonsense, no-frills way. Finally, we'll end the chapter by explaining what many of us consider to be the most important part of this system—handing the performance assessments over to your students, along with a rubric, and teaching them to either assess the work they did or to study your assessments of it and then to *make it better* (this time guided by clear expectations as laid out in skill-based rubrics).

A Bit about Our Assessment System: Administering the Performance Assessment

For more than a decade, the Teachers College Reading and Writing Project has provided New York City schools with a system of performance assessments approved by New York State as measures of student learning. These performance assessments have included the running record system described earlier in this book. TCRWP also worked collaboratively with a team of other organizations to develop a set of performance assessments and rubrics that involve students doing argument and information writing about reading as a means of assessing both their writing and their reading. This work was done in coordination with Stanford's Center on Assessments for Learning and Equity (SCALE), Educational Testing Service (ETS), the National Center for Restructuring Schools and Teaching (NCREST), the NYC Department of Education (NYCDOE), and the United Federation of Teachers (UFT).

The assessments we developed, working in that fashion, are available on the TCRWP website. Many states use these as their approved measures of student learning. That process taught us a lot, and we're pleased that the performance assessments that are included in Units of Study in Teaching Reading benefit from the earlier iteration.

The process of developing the performance assessments associated with this series began not with the work on the assessments, but with work on the units. To decide on the units we would write, we identified high-leverage skills and then planned the teaching to support those skills. Then we devised a no-frills assessment to function as a pretest and as a posttest for some of those skills in the units (some skills— for example, fluency and vocabulary—are not easily assessed using this tool). We piloted the performance assessments in a dozen schools across the country and revised them a score of times, based on student responses, which we pored over. We also received feedback from Ray Pechone, from SCALE.

Of course, the performance assessments are nothing until you give them to your students. We suggest you conduct a preassessment very close to the first day of your school year. You will hesitate over the idea that on the first day of school, you'll say, "Welcome to my class. I want to start our year together by weighing and measuring you as a reader." Remember that you control the tone of this work. Shift the way you introduce these assessments so that you describe this as giving students a chance to "show off" all they know about reading.

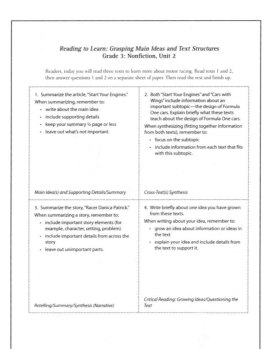

Reading to Learn: Grasping Main Ideas and Text Structures
Grade 3: Nonfiction, Unit 2

Readers, today you will read three texts to learn more about motor racing. Read texts 1 and 2, then answer questions 1 and 2 on a separate sheet of paper. Then read the rest and finish up.

1. Summarize the article, "Start Your Engines." When summarizing, remember to:
- write about the main idea
- include supporting details
- keep your summary ½ page or less
- leave out what's not important.

Main Idea(s) and Supporting Details/Summary

2. Both "Start Your Engines" and "Cars with Wings" include information about an important subtopic—the design of Formula One cars. Explain briefly what these texts teach about the design of Formula One cars.
When synthesizing (fitting together information from both texts), remember to:
- focus on the subtopic
- include information from each text that fits with this subtopic.

Cross-Text(s) Synthesis

3. Summarize the story, "Racer Danica Patrick." When summarizing a story, remember to:
- include important story elements (for example, character, setting, problem)
- include important details from across the story
- leave out unimportant parts.

Retelling/Summary/Synthesis (Narrative)

4. Write briefly about one idea you have grown from these texts.
When writing about your idea, remember to:
- grow an idea about information or ideas in the text
- explain your idea and include details from the text to support it.

Critical Reading: Growing Ideas/Questioning the Text

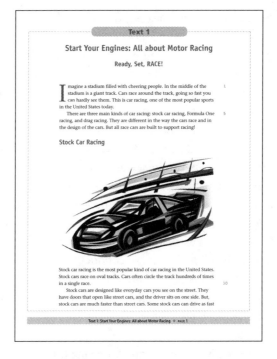

Text 1

Start Your Engines: All about Motor Racing

Ready, Set, RACE!

Imagine a stadium filled with cheering people. In the middle of the stadium is a giant track. Cars race around the track, going so fast you can hardly see them. This is car racing, one of the most popular sports in the United States today.

There are three main kinds of car racing: stock car racing, Formula One racing, and drag racing. They are different in the way the cars race and in the design of the cars. But all race cars are built to support racing!

Stock Car Racing

Stock car racing is the most popular kind of car racing in the United States. Stock cars race on oval tracks. Cars often circle the track hundreds of times in a single race.

Stock cars are designed like everyday cars you see on the street. They have doors that open like street cars, and the driver sits on one side. But, stock cars are much faster than street cars. Some stock cars can drive as fast

Text 1: Start Your Engines: All about Motor Racing ❖ PAGE 1

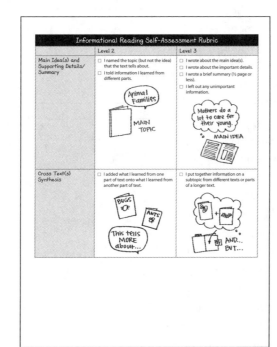

Informational Reading Self-Assessment Rubric

	Level 2	Level 3
Main Idea(s) and Supporting Details/Summary	☐ I named the topic (but not the idea) that the text tells about. ☐ I told information I learned from different parts.	☐ I wrote about the main idea(s). ☐ I wrote about the important details. ☐ I wrote a brief summary (½ page or less). ☐ I left out any unimportant information.
Cross Text(s) Synthesis	☐ I added what I learned from one part of text onto what I learned from another part of text.	☐ I put together information on a subtopic from different texts or parts of a longer text.

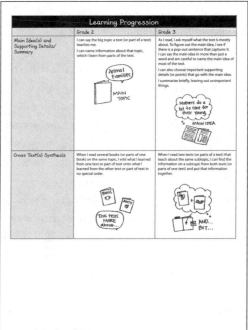

Learning Progression

	Grade 2	Grade 3
Main Idea(s) and Supporting Details/Summary	I can say the big topic a text (or part of a text) teaches me. I can name information about that topic, which I learn from parts of the text.	As I read, I ask myself what the text is mostly about. To figure out the main idea, I see if there is a pop-out sentence that captures it. I can say the main idea in more than just a word and am careful to name the main idea of most of the text. I can also choose important supporting details (or points) that go with the main idea. I summarize briefly, leaving out unimportant things.
Cross Text(s) Synthesis	When I read several books (or parts of one book) on the same topic, I add what I learned from one text or part of text onto what I learned from the other text or part of text in no special order.	When I read two texts (or parts of a text) that teach about the same subtopic, I can find the information on a subtopic from both texts (or parts of one text) and put that information together.

FIG. 7–1   Part of the Grade 3 Unit 2 Performance Assessment and Rubric

The truth is that the earlier in the year you assess, the lower the starting level, and therefore, the more progress the assessments will document. There is no more potent way to encourage future growth than to show past growth. "Look at how dramatically you are improving. I can just *imagine* what your reading work will be like by the end of the year. Amazing." Author and educator Peter Johnston reminds us in his book *Choice Words* (Stenhouse, 2004), "Once students have a sense that they are constantly learning, and are presented with evidence of that learning, teachers can ask not only about the details of their learning histories, but about the details of their futures, and the plans they have for managing those futures." By conducting a performance assessment as close to the start of the year as possible and then gathering data at other intervals, you and your students will be able to see evidence of growth—and evidence of the effectiveness of your teaching.

Each performance assessment begins by asking students to read one or two texts (depending on the unit and the skills being assessed). These are generally short, accessible texts, and at times include short video clips. If you are conducting an assessment before an informational unit, you will give students nonfiction texts and ask questions aligned to the Informational Reading Learning Progression. Similarly, if you are assessing prior to a narrative unit, students will read narrative texts and answer questions aligned to the Narrative Reading Learning Progression.

You'll want to set aside one reading workshop period for giving this assessment. While students could probably write essays about some of the questions asked, we recommend you limit the amount of writing they do by giving each student four half-sheets of paper on which to write their answers.

We expect you will read aloud the texts to any students who can't read them themselves, making sure those students also have copies to refer to when answering the questions.

You might question reading aloud to kids—Is that fair?—and frankly, we wish we'd rewritten the assessment texts at an easier level so that you had the option of using that. We didn't, however, and in the end, the goal is not to assess reading level (the running records accomplish that goal), but instead to get at children's comprehension, and you can't glimpse that without the reader being able to access the text.

Argument and Advocacy: Researching Debatable Issues
Grade 5: Nonfiction, Unit 3

Readers, today you will read three texts about cellphones in schools. Read text 1, then answer questions 1 and 2 on a separate sheet of paper. Then read the rest and finish up.

1. Summarize text 1, "Cell Phones Raise Security Concerns at Schools." When summarizing, remember to: • write about more than one main idea • include carefully selected details to support each main idea • keep your summary brief • write about the ideas in the text, not your own opinions. *Main Idea(s) and Supporting Details/Summary*	2. Read lines 6–8 from text 1, "Cell Phones Raise Security Concerns at Schools." An undercover investigation by police found that at least 24 devices had been stolen over two months at the school, according to nbcphiladelphia.com. Why is this line important to the text? When writing about how one part of the text fits with another, remember to: • explain how the part in question fits into the whole structure of the text and with the main ideas • use academic language: This part explains/describes/supports/introduces . . . • include evidence or details from the text to support your explanation • write just a few sentences. *Analyzing Parts of a Text in Relation to the Whole*
3. What is the author's point of view in text 3, "Cell Phones Should Be in Schools"? How does your knowledge of the point of view help you think about the text's content? When analyzing point of view, remember to: • name who the author is, as well as his role/age or the group he belongs to • discuss how the author's points are influenced by the above • write about why the narrator probably thinks or feels the way he does. *Analyzing Perspective*	4. Based on this packet of texts, decide whether cellphones should be banned or allowed in schools. Imagine you are going to write a letter to your mayor and convince him or her that your position makes the most sense. Map out a plan for your persuasive letter to the mayor, making sure you reference the texts. (You do not need to write the actual letter, just your plan.) When synthesizing among texts, remember to: • pull together relevant and important information from different texts (or different parts of a longer text) • organize that information. *Cross-Text(s) Synthesis*

FIG. 7–2 Grade 5 Unit 3 Performance Assessment

Each unit's assessment will contain four questions—skills that are central to the upcoming unit and are high leverage. In grade 3, for instance, you'll see that you assess *prediction*, because that skill is foundational to later reading success. In grade 5, however, you won't assess prediction, moving instead to skills such as considering the author's point of view. In grade 5, Unit 1, *Interpretation Book Clubs: Analyzing Themes*, you assess a student's ability to analyze the parts of a story in relation to the whole, analyze author's craft, determine themes, and compare and contrast themes across texts. This is not to say that these are the only skills taught in this unit—not by a long shot—but they are the most integral to narrative reading for fifth-graders reading at benchmark. Similarly, before beginning the second nonfiction reading unit in the fifth-grade series *Argument and Advocacy: Researching Debatable Issues*, students are asked questions after reading three articles entitled "Cell Phones Raise Security Concerns in Schools," "New York City Mayor Changes Cell Phone Policies in Schools," and "Cell Phones Should Be in Schools" (see Fig. 7–2).

The questions on each performance assessment serve to identify the work that a student is doing with a particular skill. They act as prealerts to your students, highlighting some of the skills in the upcoming unit that are especially important. As you progress through a unit, a minilesson on perspective, for example, will carry extra importance because it aligns with a question that's already come up on the performance assessment. The results of the assessment, then, will also serve as an important alert for you—letting you know skills that you'll probably want to support with vigilance within the unit. Setting out a clear goal rallies students to work toward that goal, so we suggest you administer the first assessment at the start of the year and then again at the beginning and end of each new unit of study. You'll find everything you need to do this in the online resources that accompany this series.

Don't delay conducting your initial assessments. Start tomorrow, before you read beyond this chapter; there's not a lot you need to know to pull this off! It is important to students and their parents (and to you as well) to be able to look back on the journey traveled, saying, "Look at where you started and contrast that to where you are now!" Imagine the parent-teacher conference with, say, Michael's parents. You bring out Michael's first attempts at writing about his reading and say to his parents, "This is what your son's writing and thinking about characters in fiction looked like at the start of the year." Then you lay his most recent writing alongside the performance assessment, saying, "Look! *This* is the kind of thinking he was doing just the other day!" With an internalized sense of the learning progression guiding your discussion, you'll be able to explain to Michael's parents the new work that he is already doing and the plans you have for Michael's next steps.

Decisions You Need to Make So the Performance Assessments Work for You and Your Students

As students become experienced with these performance assessments, we expect you may want to teach them to score each other's, working in partnerships. There are reasons for doing this—and reasons against. It will save you time (no small advantage) and make it more likely that students regard the performance assessments as existing for growth purposes. On the other hand, if your school or district treats these assessments as high-stakes and it is important to document growth over time, you will probably need to assess children yourself. Kids will not fully understand what all the questions are asking them to do, especially on the pretest, and their misunderstandings will not only lead them to answer in less than an ideal way, but also it will lead them to have trouble seeing any problems in the way they have answered. Your assessment will be necessary to signal, "No, you aren't getting this." It could even be that by the time the posttest comes, students know enough to be more critical of their answers and they do worse, not better, because now they know what the question is asking. As the student becomes more aware, then the level of his work may not appear to go up at all, and if teaching so that students have an impressive curve is important to you, those results may not be obvious. For these reasons, then, if students' scores are high-stakes for you, you probably should *not* recruit kids to do their own self-assessing.

Either way, you will want to teach into the idea that assessments can give valuable feedback. Ask students whether any of them have ever tried to get better at something and done so by keeping score, working at the thing, keeping score again. Have they tried bouncing a ping-pong ball (or a tennis ball) up in the air off a racket, counting the number of bounces they can pull off? How about jumps on a pogo stick? It's hard, right, but did they get better?

You can change the references to anything you see your students doing in the schoolyard—kicking balls, shooting hoops. The point is to acclimate kids to the fact that they'll be assessing their own reading work using a learning progression, and they are apt to find that the first time they try a skill—say, summarizing or comparing and contrasting or thinking about author's craft—it will be like the time their tennis ball bounced off the racket into a tree. I can almost promise that the first time most of your students try their hand at some of this work, their efforts won't qualify as meeting grade level standards.

If one question you need to answer revolves around whether children should score their own work or not, the next question revolves around whether you want the questions themselves to include bullet points that spell out for students how they are expected to answer a question. That is, if the question reads, "Compare and contrast the way the two texts develop the theme of overcoming loneliness," you have a decision to make about whether you want to add bullets that spell out for kids what they are expected to do to provide a reasonable response. Do you want to include bullets such as these, or do you want to see if the child knows to do these things without you spelling them out?

- Be sure you write about similarities and differences.
- Discuss the content of the two pieces.
- Discuss also the craft decisions used to develop the theme in the two pieces.
- Be sure to support your answers with examples (and citations) from both texts.

There are again reasons to provide the bullets—and reasons not to do so—and our general advice is to remove this scaffolding when you think it is reasonable to do so and to make these decisions in concert with other teachers from your school so that everyone handles this the same way.

When you remove the bullets, there will be a time when a child's score is knocked way down because she doesn't write about, say, the differences as well as similarities, contrasting as well as comparing. Your readers will probably be dismayed by this. They'll protest, "But, but, but I *could* have done that!" That may be true, but you'll be asking kids to score the work they *actually* did on the performance assessment, not the work they could have done. In life, you and I will not always be there to remind each learner that "compare and contrast" means discuss similarities *and* differences. That's why we suggest you eventually refrain from providing the support of the bullets during these performance assessments. The kids will mess up—and, ideally, they will learn.

This won't just be about comparing and contrasting, of course. When the performance assessment asks for students to provide evidence to support a theme, for example, chances are, if you don't caution them otherwise, their evidence will all come from the ending of the text. But on these performance assessments, if a reader supplies details only from the ending of the text, this will knock that reader down on the progression. Our point is that eventually, you will want to let kids make these mistakes and receive this feedback.

On the other hand, it doesn't seem reasonable for kids to all flounder because they have no idea what you are asking for in a question, so for the first year or two with these assessments, we imagine you will provide the bullet points. When you withhold them, we only caution you not to draw definitive conclusions from the students' mess-ups, because a very strong reader could temporarily get a very low score on these progressions, before that student wakes up to the expectations that are embedded in the questions.

If You Decide Children Should Assess Their Work— Or If You Do that Assessment for Them

If children self-score, you will want them to work in partnerships to study their efforts. Working with a partner, a child will hold her writing about reading—say, her summary of an article on tornadoes and hurricanes—against the progression (or a shortened progression we are calling a *rubric*, on this day), asking, "Does my work most closely resemble level 1, level 2, level 3, or level 4?"

Because students will be working in partnerships, they can tell their partner which level they believe their response is, and their partner can agree or disagree. I cannot emphasize enough just how important it will be for you to encourage—require in fact—that students *prove* their thinking with evidence. That is, it simply can't be enough to say, "Yup, I got a level 4!" and move on. Instead, you will want students to get into the habit of looking between the progression and their own work, pointing to an indicator on the progression, and then showing their partner where they have done that exact thing in their own writing.

They won't be perfect at self-assessing, especially at the beginning. They'll think they are discerning nuanced themes when you do not think they are! They'll think they've moved up a whole level in considering author's craft when they really aren't even at the level they thought they were to begin with. As you teach your units of study, though, and children become more sophisticated and knowledgeable in their skill work, they'll also become more discerning about their own work. As they begin to carry this knowledge up the grade levels, they'll begin each year with more assessment literacy.

If you score for your children, you will want them to study their work with a partner to determine the source of your score—and to revise their work to alter that score right away!

Questions to Ask When Self-Assessing

* Do I have evidence?

* Which level does my work match?

* Am I missing any parts of that level?

* What could I have done that I didn't?

Either way—for children to score or for them to study your scores—they will need an accessible, simple rubric. For example, for this first question in the fifth-grade *Tackling Complexity: Moving Up Levels of Nonfiction* unit, note the learning progression and the rubric (see Figure 7–3).

It is important for you to know that the rubric is not any different than the full learning progression. It is just shorter and only measures the objective observable results that will show up in the product. Children can use this rubric, and perhaps some exemplar responses, to self-assess. If you are using *Writing Pathways*, your children have probably been self-assessing their writing already.

Along the way, or at the end of a unit of study, you have the option of giving a postassessment. You and the children should see growth, and if there is trouble, at least you'll know it well before children will face higher-stakes assessments, when there is still plenty of time for you to plan reinforced instruction. If the trouble seems surprising, double-check that the assigned level of text wasn't too hard.

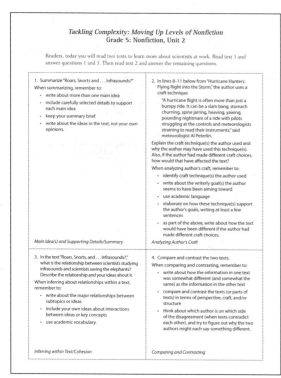

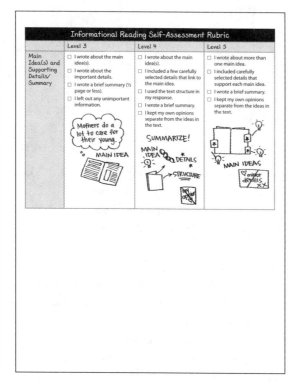

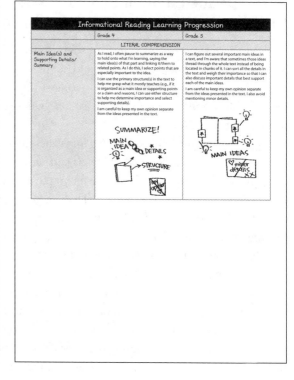

FIG. 7–3

Use Learning Progressions to Help Give Your Students a Vision for Growth as Readers

After children's responses are scored, you and the children are apt to think, "Yikes. Gulp." You will probably know in your heart of hearts that some of your students *can do better*. For example, your strongest fifth-grade reader may have answered a main idea question by jotting what the text was mostly about and then supporting that inference with a detail that seems to have been somewhat randomly chosen. Meanwhile at the fifth-grade level, students are expected to identify multiple main ideas, when they are present in a text, and to choose supporting details that best make that point. "Is this really an accurate measuring stick?" you'll wonder. "Why are *two* main ideas so all-important?" The good news is that the learning progressions spell out the descriptors in such a way that students will be able to revise their first efforts in fairly quick order.

Once students are not assessing but revising their work, informed by the progressions, you should be able to glimpse their power. But even then, the goals that are captured through these are not the only goals. Our suggestion is to remember that the goal of the learning progressions is to support development. They also weren't written by God. Fallible human beings put these together, and they are open to critique and revision. Add your own deeply held values.

When you put the relevant strands of the learning progressions into your children's hands and invite kids to immediately try to revise their initial responses, chances are that many of them will be able to do more than they did without feedback. This will be especially true if you and your colleagues decide to omit the bullet points that spell out exactly what is called for in a strong response. So although their first accounting may feel like a kick in the gut, their energy will quickly rise as they see that, in fact, doing standards-based work is entirely doable and within their grasp.

This work with performance assessments is not meant to encompass all that your students need to learn to do as readers. That is, four questions, asked about an article or two, a story or two, won't encompass all of the grade level expectations that will be important for your students, but this work will serve as a wake-up call, alerting them to a few of the skills that they will learn over the course of the upcoming unit and pointing out some of the important work that will soon become second nature for them.

At the end of the unit, you will probably decide once again to give students a performance assessment that assesses the same skills you measured at the start of the unit, and your students and you will be able to look to see if there has been notable improvement. In Chapter 8, I'll discuss what happens in the interim. That is to say, between the initial and the final performance assessment for the unit, the really important thing will be for students to become accustomed to using the strands of the learning progressions to ratchet up the level of their reading work.

Lucille Clifton, one of America's greatest poet laureates, once said to us, "Nurture your image of what's possible. You cannot create what you cannot imagine." The learning progressions contained in this book will give you what you need to provide students with a vision for the work they'll aim to create, and we'll provide you with the tips and methods, both in the next chapter and throughout the units of study, to make those learning progressions effective, inspiring, and dynamic learning tools in your classroom.

Chapter 8

Students and Teachers as Agents of Change

Teaching and Learning Informed by Learning Progressions

Y OU HAVE ADMINISTERED the performance assessment and have either asked students to assess their initial thinking using rubrics or done this yourself. Then, presumably, you have shown (or plan to show) students the larger learning progressions that apply to the skills they are working to master, asking them to raise the level of their initial assessments. What now? While many students were immediately able to raise the level of their work using a slice of the learning progression, not all could. This is important data that suggests these students will need more focused, intensive instruction. In all cases, you'll want to help students self-initiate using these progressions in more independent ways in their independent books, in book clubs, and in partnerships.

This chapter will help you learn about ways you can embed the learning progressions into your everyday teaching. I hope this chapter helps you imagine how you and your students can be *on fire* over the learning progressions. You are probably raising your eyebrows and asking, "Seriously?" Frankly, the secret to success lies in the manner in which you introduce them to your class. See if you can catch some of our excitement as you read this chapter.

GETTING STARTED: PROGRESSIONS AS A TOOL FOR SELF-ASSESSMENT AND GOAL-SETTING ACROSS A UNIT

As we've piloted and published books and assessment systems in both reading and writing, one thing about assessment has become crystal clear: student performance says as much about our teaching as it does about our students' skills. Perhaps more. We *cannot* simply look at low scores, at student performance assessments, or Post-its that are far below grade level, and say, "Well, these students don't have the background." "These students don't have the work ethic for success." "These progressions are totally unrealistic." What we *must* say is "What can we do to teach these students more effectively?" We *must* ask, "Have we granted each student in our care every possible opportunity and support to grow?"

One of the most important things you can do to help students grow is to have a crystal clear vision of the goals toward which they are working. The progressions can help to name these goals, putting into straight talk a lot of qualities of thinking and reading that might otherwise be hard to grasp. Now the challenge is for students to connect with and "own" the progressions, or for them to adapt them, so that students form a *vision* of what thoughtful reading looks like. As John Hattie, the author of a meta-analysis of over 800 studies of the factors that most influence student achievement, says, "Goals have a self-energizing effect if they are appropriately challenging for the student, as they can motivate students to exert effort in line with the difficulty or demands of the goal."

Once you have let your students know that the learning progressions exist, you and your students will want to use them regularly. The progressions can function as coteachers, helping with almost anything you are hoping to teach or your children are hoping to learn. Recently, I visited Kara's fourth-grade classroom. The year had just launched and students were beginning with a quick study of reading habits, including writing about reading, as well as character work. Kara called for the class's attention, with copies of the "Inferring about Characters and Other Story Elements" strand of the learning progression in her hand. "Readers," she said, "I'm impressed with the voice you are bringing to your writing about reading. It is clear that you have made your writing your own. I want to talk to you about *what* you are thinking and writing about as you read, though." Kara handed out a copy of one thread from the "Inferring about Characters and Other Story Elements" strand of the narrative reading progression for grades 3, 4, and 5. This thread shows increasing expectations for students' work with character traits. Kara asked each student to read along as she read about the work that they were expected to do.

Referencing the fourth-grade expectations, Kara said to her class, "As you've been thinking and writing about your reading this year, will you put your thumb up if you've been keeping in mind your character's main traits?" Lots of children signaled that they had been doing this. Kara pressed on. "Now let me ask you something different. Be totally honest! Put your thumb up if you have been thinking about ways that your character is complicated, like ways he (or she) is different on the outside than the inside or different in one setting, or in one relationship, than in another." Not a single thumb went up.

FIG. 8–1 "Inferring about Characters and Other Story Elements" strand of the Narrative Reading Learning Progression, Grades 3, 4, 5

"Thumbs up if you've been thinking about your character's deeper motivation—about what drives the character. Have you been mulling over why characters make the decisions or take the actions they do, thinking what really drives them?" Scanning the room, Kara put the continuum down, having made her point.

After reminding the class that they need to draw on all they have learned so that their entries and thinking about books are as smart as possible, Kara suggested the class study together an entry that represents fourth-grade level work. She channeled the class to work in pairs to study what the author (a child from a previous year) had done in relation to the characters' personalities, motivations, and relationships.

The class talked about what they saw not only in the fourth-grade expectations but in fifth-grade expectations as well. "Do you think you could revise your work so that it is a level 4, like the Post-it we just studied?" Kara challenged them, and of course the students were game. As they worked, Kara looked over their shoulders, taking note of the work they were (and weren't) producing. Some attempted a level 4 Post-it but fell short, while others seemed ready for more challenging terrain.

After students worked for a bit to raise the level of their writing about reading, Kara called for their attention again. "Many of you, in the blink of an eye, have been able to raise the level of your writing about reading to level 4, which is end-of-the-year fourth-grade work! My hunch is that this level of work is not yet second nature to you, so I'm going to suggest that each of you reread level 4 on the learning progression and do some underlining or annotating of parts you will need to remember. Then talk with your partner about what you are going to do over the next few days to make sure you do your absolute best thinking about characters."

Over the next day or so, Kara returned to the students' work, asking them to think together about ways they could actively work toward the new goals they'd just set. Perhaps some would decide to put yellow Post-its at intervals in their books as nudges to do some of that work. Perhaps the entire class would resolve that at the end of each day's workshop, students would leave their most thoughtful Post-it or entry on their desk so the teacher (and actually, any peer as well) could read and respond to it.

When you try this work with your students, it is enormously helpful if you recruit them to give advice. "What could you do to make sure that these goals become second nature to you? How could you get the practice and support you need? Will each person bring in a frame to put on their desk and spotlight their best work from the week? Will kids all post their best work on a square of the bulletin board?"

You and your students can plan occasions for reassessment. Of course, during conferences, you and the student will look at ways her work around the highlighted skill has changed, but you will want to consider making more formal appointments to reassess. Some teachers schedule days when different tables from the class leave their work for the teacher to study in the evening. Perhaps one table leaves its work on the teacher's desk every Monday, with flags highlighting what they consider to be their best work.

Then too, don't underestimate the importance of partners in this process. Partners can share ideas and check up on each other. "Let's take a look at the goals you've set for yourself," you might teach partners to ask each other. "How are they going? Can you show me where you are trying new work?" With a little training and support (like that provided by the chart below), you've turned each partner in the room into another teacher.

HELP STUDENTS CRYSTALLIZE VISIONS OF GOOD WRITING ABOUT READING: USE BENCHMARK EXAMPLES, DEMONSTRATION WRITING, AND PROGRESSIONS IN TANDEM

It might be helpful to take a step back and consider the steps that you can take to get to the point where the learning progressions are ingrained as a part of the daily life of your classroom, as they are for Kara's classroom.

Demonstrate by Using the Progression to Create Your Own Writing about Reading

Self-assessment, like any other skill, must be taught. One very effective way to do this is through the use of demonstration. If you have access to a document camera, overhead projector, or Smart Board, use that tool to enlarge your copy of the progression.

Consider taking a Post-it you've written about the class read-aloud and writing it a few notches below the grade you are teaching. Then, show students how you use the learning progression to name what makes for a level higher. Model thinking back to your read-aloud, with progression indicators in mind, trying to write the best Post-it you can. Then, invite children to help you write the next level up. Again, allow students to review what makes for, say, a fifth-grade inference, interpretation, summary, or the like. Then, with their own best Post-its, challenge them to do the same work. You might also show them a prewritten bit of writing "up-the-ladder," with descriptors naming what makes each level higher than the next.

Level	Grade 3	Grade 4	Grade 5	Grade 6
Inferring about Characters and Other Story Elements *Character Traits*	I can develop ideas (theories) about the kind of person a character is. I know this means talking about a character's traits (personality), and I'm careful not to confuse the way a character feels for a trait. When a character makes a decision and does something, I can usually figure out why, based on what I know of the character and what happened earlier.	I keep in mind that characters are complicated. For example, I might think about how the character is different on the outside than the inside or in one part of the story or one relationship than another. I'm interested in what *really* drives a character to make the decisions or take the actions he or she takes. What does the character *really* want? I know that a character's action will sometimes seem small (closing a door) but will actually signal a deeper meaning.	I can see places in a story where the characters are not what they seem at first. For example, the character might say or act as if he or she doesn't care, but readers see signs that he or she really does. That is, I see hidden sides to characters. I know that what drives the character (his or her motivation) can be complicated. There may be several things that drive or pressure a character, and often he or she is pulled in conflicting ways.	I continue to develop theories about main and minor characters, thinking how they are affected by other story elements such as the plot, setting, issues, and conflicts.
Sample Response	Kek is hopeful. He thinks his mom will come find him. And he gets excited about living in America. Like he gets excited about the TV and when he first sees his new bed he jumps up and down on it.	Kek tries to make the best of things. He ignores Dave when Dave tries to tell him "we aren't sure where your mother is." He believes his mom will come, even though he's not sure that's true. Readers can learn from him because no matter what happens, Kek has hope and believes things will work out. It seems like remembering his mom and her love gives him hope.	Kek is a little like an ostrich with his head in the sand. He doesn't want to face what might be the negative truth so he refuses to believe it. Like when Dave tried to tell Kek that they weren't sure where his mother was, Kek says right away, "She's fine . . . she will come" without even thinking twice. It's like everything is so new and scary in this new place, he is too afraid to even think of what the negative might be. He's kind of showing that a person can only handle so much change all at once, but his hope gets him through.	Kek responds to challenges by remaining hopeful, despite facing great odds. The author seems to use the torn blue and yellow scrap of cloth to represent Kek's hope— he is constantly gripping it at the start of the story. When Dave mentions his family, that is the first time Kek feels the cloth and the author describes it as "soft as new grass after good rain"—a hopeful image. Later, when Kek starts to lose hope and feel afraid, he uses the cloth to wipe away his tears. Yet, right after he feels afraid, in the next poem he thinks of his mother and feels "hope's embrace."

FIG. 8–2

Introduce the inquiry to students. Suppose you are working on raising the level of students' abilities to notice character response and change. "Today," you might say, "we'll each be asking ourselves, 'What level Post-its am I tending to write?' and then, 'How can I make them better?'" In partnerships, kids can once again study their Post-its against the mentors you created.

As the unit progresses, you'll want to keep the momentum around rubrics and goal-setting going, taking time now and again both to model and to ask students to self-assess and set goals. The learning progressions are incorporated at multiple points across each unit, giving students opportunities to develop their assessment literacy skills. Some days you will devote an entire minilesson to this work. Other times a mid-workshop teaching, a share, or even just homework will focus on this work. Use your own demonstration examples as much as students need, making sure the examples are created using a text that students know well (such as your class read-aloud). This will help students focus on the work you are demonstrating on each Post-it, rather than the book itself.

For example, for a third-grade class in the midst of a biography book club unit, I might say, "I've been reading the biography *Mrs. Harkness and the Panda*, by Alicia Potter. One thing I'm thinking about as I'm

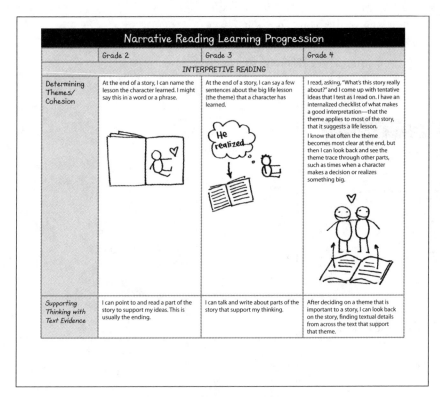

FIG. 8–3 "Determining Themes/Cohesion" strand of the Narrative Reading Learning Progression, Grades 2, 3, and 4

reading is the big life lesson the subject of my biography might have learned. So far I've jotted down 'Follow your dreams.' I'm going to compare my jot to the 'Determining Themes/Cohesion' row of the Narrative Reading Learning Progression." I might read the third-grade column of the "Determining Themes/Cohesion" strand to the class, demonstrating the way I use an item from the progression as a goal, holding it in my mind as I read.

"Hmm, . . ." I began. "It says I'm supposed to be writing a few sentences about the big life lesson, and I only wrote a few words. My goal should be to try to stretch my idea into a few sentences. Now that I know *what* I need to do, I should figure out a plan that tells me *how* to meet my goal. A few sentences, anyway. Well, I guess I could write a little about why I think Mrs. Harkness learned the lesson that she should 'follow her dreams.' That seems like a plan. I'm going to a write a few sentences about the big life lesson by explaining *why* I think my idea is the big life lesson."

Then I said to the class, "Do you see that I'm making plans not just for *what* I need to think and jot about, but also *how* I will accomplish my goal?"

As much as possible, encourage students to look between your demonstration texts and other examples of good work they can learn from. "Ah," you might say, "as I look between my jots and the rubric, I'm noticing that following the structure of the text is an important part of summarizing at the fifth-grade level. I've made copies of some of the work I did, structuring my ideas in a different way, so that you can use it as a mentor if you'd like." Put a stack of your examples (or the fifth-grade exemplars) in an area in the classroom, encouraging students to take one if they, too, are working to restructure their summaries. By doing so, you

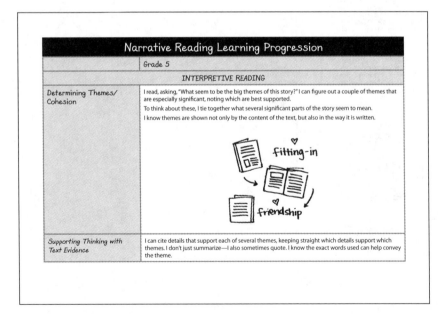

FIG. 8–4 "Determining Themes/Cohesion" strand of the Narrative Reading
Learning Progression, Grade 5

are establishing an environment in which benchmark exemplars become personal coaches of sorts. These exemplars may be used to illuminate the qualities of strong writing about reading in a particular strand and to help students envision the work they are setting out to do as readers.

Emphasize the Importance of Being Truly Honest with Yourself

Since your goal is to encourage students to raise the level of their work (rather than pretend they are doing work they are not), you will want to make a big deal out of the fact that you didn't just glibly say, "Yes, I did this. Yes, I did that." You might make an aside, saying, "What if I'd just checked 'Yes!' for the requirements of fifth-grade structure, saying, 'Oh, I did that'?" You can act as if it would have been a calamity had you merely dismissed the prospect of making a plan for your notes. "If you were my partner, and I said, 'Well, I sorta did that,' what would you say?"

One youngster recently piped in, "I'd say, 'Well, actually, you only did *part* of this.'" Continuing to play the part of the mistaken student who keeps trying to get off the hook, you can protest, "No, no, I *almost* always make a plan for my notes before I read. Just this one little time I didn't do that." Shaking your head in feigned protest, say, "I don't need to practice it more. I know how to do it, I just don't always. So I'm totally at the fifth-grade level!"

You can fire the students up in indignation so they agree that helping each other and themselves reach for high standards is the moral thing to do. Affirm any student who says he will remind his partner (and you) to aspire toward greater heights. "You are so right! I hope everyone is realizing that it is important for you, as the partner, to not just gloss over your partner's work, saying 'It's good.' You really want to study the nitty-gritty of it. Partners need to say to each other, 'Where's the evidence that you did that?' and then, 'What else could you try?'"

Stay Positive—Encourage Students to Be Thoughtful Self-Assessors

You may want to do yet more encouraging, in which case you could say, "And readers, if you find yourself at an earlier level of the progression, remember, that's *okay*. That's positive! That means that you are a really thoughtful self-assessor. You're being honest with yourself, and you are assessing your writing about reading and saying, 'I know I can get better. I have the support of my class, and I know so much about reading, and my teacher can help me with that.' And this whole year is about getting better at things. If you self-assess and find a bunch of 'not yets' for yourself, that just means you are on a course. We all have next steps to take."

After demonstrating how a reader can self-assess by doing this with a strand or two, you'll want to pass the baton to students, giving them a chance to self-assess using the progression and their own responses.

Partners Can Ask Each Other...

"Where's the evidence?"

"What else could you try?"

"Did you try it more than once?"

COACH STUDENTS IN USING THEIR GOALS WITH THE PURPOSE TO IMPROVE

As your students begin self-assessing with the progressions, you'll want to coach into their work. If you have given them the charge to underline the instances where they found evidence showing they accomplished something, and they mark evidence that doesn't actually fit the descriptor, you'll want to teach them to be more accurate. If kids try to excuse themselves by saying things like "I was just being sloppy in this response. I *usually* do this thing on the progression," assure them while holding them accountable to what they see: "By the next self-assessment, you'll be better already! But don't alter the facts of this assessment. Be strict with yourself."

You'll also want to coach into students' revision. Once students identify where their response falls on the progression, the next steps should be clear. The progression lays out the elements of each level explicitly, so that each student can take steps immediately to add on or rewrite their response to meet the next level's descriptors. Once the responses have been rewritten, they can also become mentor texts. Kids can tape them into their reader's notebook or place it in their folder for future reference.

If kids' responses fall at the lowest level of the rubric, or even below that, reassure them that they can take action to change that in just a few minutes of work. Often this reflects the prior teaching a student has received, which you can let the student know. Say, "You haven't been taught a lot of this, so you didn't know that was what you should be doing. Keep this rubric with you as you read, so you'll start doing the items on it really quickly! Pretty soon you will be moving up the levels. Let's mark on the calendar that on Friday, in two and a half weeks, we'll assess again and see how your work has improved. Until then, keep practicing!"

Help Improve Student Agency

Once students have deliberate goals in mind, it will be important to help them think about how their use of time changes. The goal is to improve student agency so students learn to work for long stretches of time toward goals they have decided matter. We've found it's possible to explicitly coach students toward agency. You might say, for instance, "It is time for you to get started on today's reading time, but before you go, will you think, 'What goals will I be working on?' Once you've decided on your goals, will you ask yourself, 'What do I need to have out in my work space to help me accomplish what I want to do?' Think about your reading space as a workbench in your garage. If you set out to accomplish a goal at that workbench—to build a birdhouse—you need your tools nearby. It's the same with reading, and with writing about reading." Students should eventually learn to gather tools that make sense for them. You might designate a place in the classroom where students can easily access charts, Post-its, or other tools and organizers. Students can also set up a section of their notebooks to collect material and tools related to their goals.

You will need to tell students that their workspace will look different because they are working toward goals—but also, the actual pages on which they are writing about reading

will look different as well. When readers hold themselves accountable to meeting certain goals, they are not apt to spend time just reading, reading, reading, and their pages will reflect their new work habits. For instance, if a reader is working on cross-text synthesis, she might tape a duplicated copy of an exemplar entry into this section of her reader's notebook and then annotate it to detail what exactly the mentor reader has done. Then, alongside that, she might "mirror-write" a matching entry about her own text. If she has a few pages of her notebook designated for work on cross-text synthesis, she could also list the specific strategies she aspires to use and add the page numbers from her notebook to show where she has used those.

After students have been working for ten or fifteen minutes, you could pause and remind them to work in goal-driven ways. You might say, "Readers, can I stop you? I just stopped by Rob's desk, and he said he was pausing his reading to ask himself, 'Am I accomplishing my goals?' Right now, would you each stop and ask yourselves that same great question? Look back at the goals you set, and if you're not achieving them yet, ask, 'What tools can I use to do so?' Remember, you can use the exemplars, your progressions, the charts around this classroom, or your partner or someone else nearby to help. Right now, make plans for what you will do."

Of course, this is just one example of this kind of instruction; your classroom will have its own culture and feel. No matter what, though, have in mind that your goal is for students to learn to work hard. In Malcolm Gladwell's *Outliers* (Little, Brown, 2011), when he looked at the conditions that led to extraordinary success, the unifying factor was that someone gave the student an opportunity to work hard. Peter Johnston, in *Choice Words* (Stenhouse, 2004), also reminds us to cultivate a language of independence over a language of obedience. All of this adds up to helping students see what it means to take charge of their own growth as readers.

When I work with teachers I often say to them, "If your students' reading skills are not visibly, dramatically improving after a few weeks of instruction, you are doing something wrong." When you provide students with constant opportunities to read, and when you actively and assertively teach into their best efforts, their development as readers will astonish you, their parents, the school administrators, and best of all, the students themselves.

Coaching students into holding high expectations for their own work and to working hard to meet these is no small goal, and teaching this way is very challenging. Yet is it not worth every ounce of energy we can muster?

Make Goals and Working toward Them a Big Deal

With students working hard to set and achieve meaningful, substantial goals, you'll want to find ways to celebrate their progress along the way. Celebrate the goals. Make a very big deal of them. Allow students to decorate their checklists or doodle along the sides. Just as you worked hard to help students take ownership over their reader's and writer's notebooks, you'll want to help them feel a sense of pride and ownership over their progressions and goals.

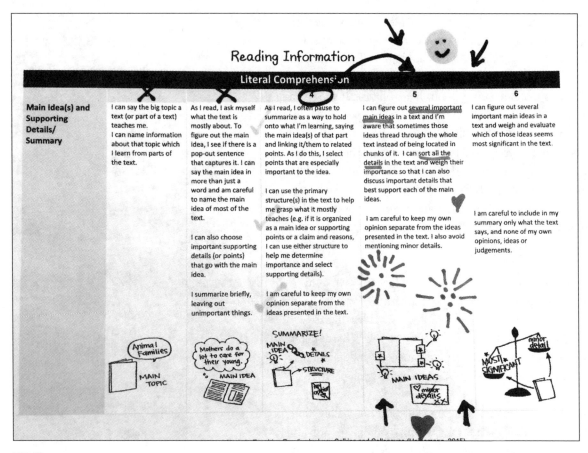

FIG. 8–5

One way to make a big deal out of goal-setting is to say, while students work on their self-assessments and their goal sheets, "Let's make these public, so that you can study what other readers have designated as work they can do well and work they need to work on. You might look over at a classmate's goals and say to yourself, 'Hey, he needs help on something that I can do well. I can help him with that.' Or 'She sits at my table. We can work on this together.' Say, 'If I have a skill, it's my responsibility to help my classmate who needs help with it. That's how I'll be a good member of this reading community.'"

Another way to make students' goals big and important work is to set up each student to create a wall-sized timeline of her goals. On a long scroll of paper, each student hangs her writing about reading in chronological order, alternating the entries with intermittent goal sheets. When visitors come to the classroom or on parent-teacher conference days or on "Meet Our Goal" celebration days that you set up, each student can help a visitor "walk along the pathway of the student's learning." If you do this with your class, one interesting thing you will find is that goals for one type of reading tend to apply also to other types of reading. For example, a student whose goal is to work on summary in a narrative unit will often find that he can also gain from working on summary when reading nonfiction. This allows for a continuity of goal-driven work across a sequence of reading units.

This may sound like all fluff and no substance, but it's more important than you may realize. It is a very big deal if self-assessment sheds light on achievements and yields goals, and if that process is celebrated and transparent. This makes it far more likely that students will actually note what they haven't yet done in their reading and that they'll think about what they need to work on, talk about it, and actually aspire toward meeting those goals. It is tremendously important that your class regards achievement as obtainable by all and as the result of hard work, perseverance, and help from others, not as something that comes from one's DNA.

USING THE LEARNING PROGRESSIONS TO INFORM YOUR TEACHING
Form Small Groups Based on the Performance Assessment Results

While your students are studying their work and setting their goals, you'll be studying right along with them and developing goals of your own. You might begin by gleaning data from the performance assessment results to help plan for responsive conferences and small groups. You might also examine students' responses, strand by strand, between the performance assessment and the day that students self-assess. Or you could collect students' responses one strand at a time, studying both their original responses and their revisions. Either way, the process of sorting and grouping their responses by similar needs should be quick and straightforward. Your efforts will fuel your teaching for the next few weeks.

You can lay each student's response next to a slice of the progression it aligns to, determining where it falls. Repeating this process with each student's response will leave you with groups of students who have similar next steps on a particular skill. You'll get a sense of the patterns across your class, seeing where most of your students fall. You'll also be able to spot outliers who need immediate support with this skill. After students' responses are sorted into levels, you might revisit each pile, looking for similarities in the responses students generated and identifying small groups with similar needs. Record these groups for yourself, and get the responses right back into the hands of your students for self-assessment or as mentor responses.

Noting where your students currently fall on the progressions gives you a sense of how they'll respond to the big work of the unit and allows you to teach in ways that are responsive to your students'

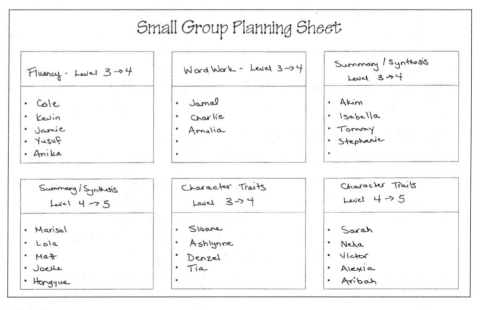

Small Group Planning Sheet

Fluency - Level 3→4	Word Work - Level 3→4	Summary / Synthesis Level 3→4
• Cole • Kevin • Jamie • Yusuf • Anika	• Jamal • Charlie • Amalia	• Akim • Isabella • Tommy • Stephanie
Summary / Synthesis Level 4→5	Character Traits Level 3→4	Character Traits Level 4→5
• Marisol • Lola • Matt • Joelle • Hongyue	• Sloane • Ashlynne • Denzel • Tia	• Sarah • Neha • Victor • Alexia • Aribah

FIG. 8–6

current levels. Using the progressions to guide this work, you can differentiate your instruction to meet students where they are and identify a clear trajectory of teachable, concrete steps to help them improve.

Use Learning Progressions to Help Judge Students' Reading Work and Determine Next Steps

All the talk about catching teachable moments and thinking on your feet works well for teachers who feel they are experts in the teaching of reading. Malcolm Gladwell's bestseller, *Blink* (Little, Brown, 2007), explains that it is a mark of expertise to be able to make judgments in the blink of an eye. However, the reverse is also true: for people whose expertise lies elsewhere or is not fully developed, making judgments quickly is harder. If you and your colleagues have not received support in the teaching of reading, it can be challenging to look at a student's entry and to recognize the traits of good work. And the catch is that you and your colleagues need to teach reading long before you become experts.

It helps to know that judgments and diagnoses do not come out of the clear blue sky. Instead, both come from knowing that there are progressions of learning that undergird a reader's development. Remember that when you give feedback, your goal is to teach the *reader*, not the book. Before you can give that feedback, you need to place the reader's current work and skill set (what the reader is doing) somewhere on a learning progression. When you give the reader feedback or suggest next steps, you are helping the reader go from where she is on a learning progression toward whatever you believe might be next steps for her.

The learning progressions provided in this book are critically important to your readers' development, and they can also help you and your colleagues grasp some fundamental truths about ways to give young readers feedback. There are, of course, many other learning progressions in the world, and it would be a mistake to think that *all* of a reader's development can be reduced to the learning progressions that are at the core of this resource. However, our progressions illustrate a trajectory of skills we believe to be essential. It is a big deal for you to grasp that to coach a reader toward next steps, moving the reader from where she is now to where you believe she can get to next, you need to think about that reader's place on a trajectory.

Conferring Using a Learning Progression

As I drew a chair alongside Maya, I looked at my conference records and noted that the last time we had talked, she'd resolved to note the techniques the author used to craft the informational text she was reading and to think about the author's possible goals. When we began talking, Maya eagerly explained her work, telling me how she had used the sentence frame "The author used _____ in order to accomplish _____" to structure her thinking. I complimented her on that work and also on how she'd tracked her goals and progress in a special section of her notebook.

As she showed me her entries cataloging the author's goals and techniques, I noticed that, though she could identify the technique and the goal, these entries were very brief, as if she was not at home writing her thoughts at any length. She stuck strictly to the script. Maya named the craft move she saw an author using, and that was it. This was something I'd seen in other children's entries as well.

I turned to my learning progression to help. I glanced at the relevant row for "Analyzing Author's Craft"—that's where Maya's work had centered—and saw that a next step might be to teach her to ask herself, "How would the text be different without this?"

This teaching point seemed entirely doable for Maya. I thought quickly about whether to illustrate that point by giving an explanation and example of the work but wasn't sure that I had an exemplar for that particular skill. So I opted to teach through demonstration, doing the work of "writing about reading" aloud for Maya, to show how she might elaborate on the craft move and its effect on the text and on her as a reader. Maya had many examples in her reader's notebook to choose from, so by using one of these examples, I would still leave her with plenty of work to do.

I asked Maya to find a spot in the text where she had noted that the author made a comparison. In Seymour Simon's *Our Solar System*, she pointed out the line, "If Earth were the size of a basketball, the sun would be as big as a basketball court." I asked her to figure out the author's possible goal in using this craft move. To help, I directed her to a chart the class had made earlier in which we listed possible goals authors might have—they might be aiming to hook the reader or to provide background knowledge. Maya quickly identified "Help readers grasp an abstract idea or describe/show the scale/parts of something" as a goal the author was trying to achieve.

I then reminded her that there are prompts readers use to help themselves elaborate on their ideas. I jotted the prompt, "How would the text be different without this?" on a Post-it. Then I thought aloud, asking myself the question and writing a response in the air. "Hmm, . . . Well, if the text didn't have this comparison, and Seymour Simon just told me how big the Earth and the sun are, it wouldn't mean anything to me. Like, I'd know that they were big, and that the sun was bigger than the Earth, but since the numbers are impossibly large, I don't really understand what they mean. But with this comparison, I know how big a basketball and a basketball court are, so I can picture the size difference and understand it." I looked at Maya, and asked, "Do you see what I did? I used the prompt to help me think about what it would be like if the text didn't have this part. Then, I thought about how having the craft move there helped me as a reader. Do you think you can try that?"

I coached Maya on another example she had noted from her text, using lean prompts to help her say more. I decided to channel her to try this work repeatedly, building her muscles for elaborating on the author's craft moves. I pointed out that what she was doing was making her writing about reading more sophisticated, using her writing to explore both the author's intentions and the effect the text has on her as a reader. And I suggested that once she had practiced that, she might be willing to think about what the author might have done differently and the effect those other choices might have had. I reminded her

FIG. 8–7

that if she was game for doing that work later on, her learning progression, with its descriptions of higher levels of this work, could probably help her get started.

Partnerships and Small Groups Can Help Build Incredible Incentive around Newly Developed Goals

There are many reasons to teach your students by leading small groups. First, this is the only way you will be able to reach many students often. Think about the amount of feedback students are accustomed to getting when they play video games. They tilt their handheld, they push some buttons—and then bing, bing, bing!—the feedback comes, right then and there. If your teaching and your feedback are only reaching kids

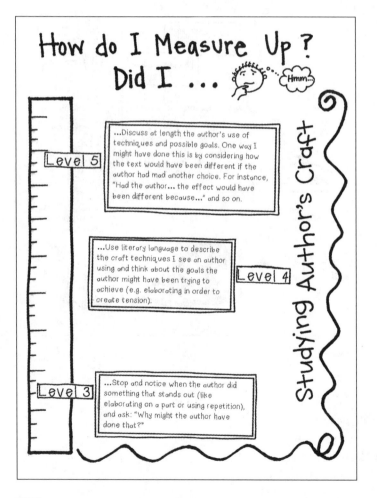

How do I Measure Up?
Did I ... Hmm...

Studying Author's Craft

Level 5
...Discuss at length the author's use of techniques and possible goals. One way I might have done this is by considering how the text would have been different if the author had mad another choice. For instance, "Had the author... the effect would have been different because..." and so on.

Level 4
...Use literary language to describe the craft techniques I see an author using and think about the goals the author might have been trying to achieve (e.g. elaborating in order to create tension).

Level 3
...Stop and notice when the author did something that stands out (like elaborating on a part or using repetition), and ask: "Why might the author have done that?"

Thinking and Wondering in Response to Reading

- "I wonder if . . ."

- "Could it be that . . ."

- "This makes me think . . ."

- "I'm realizing . . ."

- "This might be important because . . ."

- "Probably they . . ."

- "It much have been . . ."

- "For example . . ."

- "Probably after awhile . . ."

every two weeks or so, that's just not enough. You'll have the assessment data at your fingertips telling you that there are a few of your students who have begun comparing and contrasting several texts and could profit from thinking not only about the content, but also about their focus and perspective. Instead of working with each one of them individually, repeating yourself, you can opt to convene them in a small group.

Making Your Small-Group Work Effective

- Begin these small groups by talking for one or two minutes, channeling readers to try something. Then give students a few minutes to work (alone or in pairs) as you circle among them, coaching into one reader's (or one partnership's) work after another. Talk to the whole group for another minute before you leave to work with the next small group. Allot the majority of the time for students to work and you to coach into their work.

- During the initial talk to the small group, be direct. You have called them together because . . . why? You'll probably be saying, "Because I think your reading (or your writing about reading) will get a lot stronger if you . . ." You are teaching them about ways to improve, or playing out next steps, so don't mince words.

- When you coach into students' work, you will usually use lean prompts to provide running commentary or quick guidance, often said into an ear as the readers keep working. "Keep adding to your mental movie!" or "Remember to cite text evidence." Aim for your commentary to lift their level of work a notch but not for it to solve all problems.

- When you coach into group members' work, remember that you are teaching toward a goal or two—and pursue the goal(s). Don't be sidetracked by every other possible goal. You are trying to help the writers practice more skilled work on the *one trajectory* you've chosen to address.

- If you refer to a mentor text, try to be sure it is already familiar to the writers. Now is not the time to introduce a brand new text.

- Encourage readers to do whatever new thing they are doing not just once, but repeatedly. This may mean doing that work on a series of pages, a series of chapters, or across several texts. It may also mean that the readers do that work on Post-its across a text, then return to their notebooks to write long about their best thinking.

- Although some of your small-group instruction will resemble the teaching point and guided practice portion of a conference, it is important for you to think broadly about small-group work that can support students' progress toward goals they set—or you help them to set. Don't imagine that all groups are variations of one-to-one conferences done to scale.

Many teachers seem to worry about small-group instruction. "I haven't planned how it will go," they say. But the truth is that you can lead a small group in a fashion that is very similar to the way you lead a one-to-one conference.

You will recall that after looking for a moment at Maya's work, I supported the way she'd begun to do something—and encouraged her to do it in a more sophisticated way, in a way that was one step up on the learning progression. That's a fairly easy conference to lead—and an equally easy small group. You could tell a small group of students that you noticed they had places in their books where they noted an author's craft moves, and you could point out that it helps to say a lot about what you notice. To illustrate, you could show them an example of an entry where Maya had done so. You could say to the members of the small group, "Could you locate places from your own notebook where you've noted the technique an author was using, and maybe the goal the author was trying to accomplish?" After the members of the group have located those places and shared them with each other, you could tell them—as I told Maya—that simply noting those places isn't enough. Instead, readers need to elaborate, explaining how the technique the author used affects the reader. You could ask all the members of the group to start with one technique they've noticed from their texts—say, "Providing examples of the main idea"—and think about how the text would have been different had the author not decided to do what he did: "If he hadn't included these, then readers . . ."

For example, suppose a group of third-graders are reading across the same topic, say polar bears, and you pull up to their table and hear them discussing their reading. You listen for a few minutes and hear students basically showing and telling the facts they have read. That is, one student says, "I read that polar bears actually don't have white fur." Then the next student says, "I think it is very interesting that they can run as fast as a horse if they want to, but only for a little while, and usually they walk very slowly." You might pause the students and give them a bit of the synthesis strand to hold onto. You can tell them first to look between the second- and third-grade levels and to mark the differences between those levels. Help students to notice that while in second grade, synthesis can mean adding onto what you have learned from a text or different texts on a topic in no special order, in third grade, the expectation is that you will pull out and discuss subtopics.

Then you can ask the students to look at the progression while you repeat back a bit of their conversation to them and decide if it is second- or third-grade level. Students will likely notice that yes, they have just been adding on about what they learned from different texts in no special order, and you can then involve them in figuring out what subtopic the group wants to discuss. Does the group want to discuss body features, for example, or polar bears' behaviors or their eating? Then have them restart their conversation, and assign a student to be on the lookout for if students stick to a subtopic or if they begin just adding on in no special order again. If you have an iPad or other device, you could also have students record a bit of their conversation and then play it back while they study the progression, asking themselves if they made sure to work to meet third-grade expectations. You might also record another group discussing texts across a topic (or a fourth-grade group from a colleague's classroom) and let this group of students listen to it

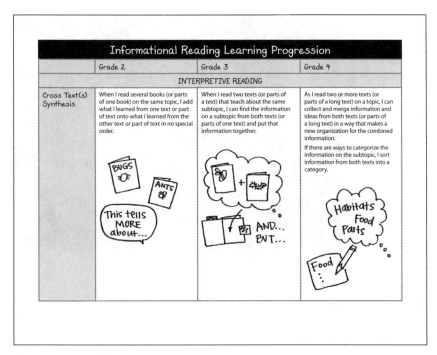

FIG. 8–8 "Cross-Text(s) Synthesis" strand of the Informational Reading Learning Progression, Grades 2, 3, and 4

as a mentor text of sorts, again with the progression in hand, considering how to ratchet up the level of their own conversation. Let students know that in a few days, you will want to record *them* and use *their* conversation as an example for others of what a conversation that meets third-grade synthesis expectations sounds like (and hopefully, very soon, fourth grade!). Tell them that before the end of the unit, you plan to bring a recording of the group to a *fourth*-grade classroom as a mentor text for that class. Imagine the excitement and the determination to meet that ambitious expectation! When you return in a day or so, expect to hear a conversation that sounds more like this:

Student 1: Let's discuss things that polar bears can do that really only they can do.

Student 2: Well, one thing they can do is lay down next to the ice for hours, just waiting for one seal to come. They don't get cold, and they don't give up.

Student 3: It makes me think they are very good hunters.

Student 2: Yeah, they are patient.

Student 1: Oh, I can add onto that! I have more about how they hunt. In this book it says that seals lay on floating ice, and polar bears can just swim up all quietly and then pop up and eat them!

Or say you have a group of students who are ready to do more advanced compare-and-contrast work. Before you gather students, you can first ask them to do a bit of writing to compare the texts they are reading and then gather them for a small group, with that writing. You might first show them a chart, which comes from the strand of the learning progression for compare and contrast for second and third grade. This chart would not only include description for the expectations of each level but also an example of good compare-and-contrast work for that level, ideally from your read-aloud. Students would likely be familiar with the expectations at these levels and mostly mastering them.

You could give students a minute to self-assess their work and be sure it is truly meeting all that they know to do. Then you might let them know that today you are going to show them a way to raise the level of their work even higher, and you can reveal the fourth-grade expectations for compare and contrast, saying, "Do you see that at this level, you don't just compare *information and ideas* you learn from the different texts? You also compare how those texts are written—the author's choices?" You can provide a quick model of what this sounds like for students and then involve them in looking back in their books and revising their compare-and-contrast work. You can leave students working as you go to confer with other students, then return to check on the first group.

If you notice that students have had trouble with this work, you can gather them again in the next day or so and do some shared compare-and-contrast writing. That shared writing can be left with students as mentor writing as they continue to push themselves to keep considering author's choices as they compare and contrast. Another day, you might borrow a fourth-grade colleague's craft cards and introduce a few of these to the group, showing them some common goals and techniques that authors of informational texts use and pushing them to use these to help with their compare-and-contrast work.

> Snakes by Melissa Stewart and Snakes! by Time for Kids are both showing that snakes are very cool animals. But they teach in different ways. For example, Melissa Stewart starts her book by asking questions. Like she asks, "What is long and round and slides on the ground?" She wants you to say "snake"! The Time for Kids book starts out by telling you about an animal slithering through the forest and how you can't see it. Then it says it is a snake! Both books get you hooked and try to surprise you.

Rufus Jones, the great American Quaker, once said, "I pin my hopes on the small circles and quiet processes in which genuine and reforming change takes place." I've often shared that quote with teachers, reminding them to band together with colleagues to outgrow their own best teaching. But the truth is that small circles and quiet processes are as necessary for students as they are for you and me.

How the Progressions Can Inform Your Day-to-Day Teaching in Other Ways

Use the Progressions to Inform Your Read-Aloud

As you plan your read-alouds, you make careful decisions about the prompts and questions on which to focus. By thinking about the demands of the text itself, your knowledge of your students' reading skills, and the major goals of your current reading unit, you craft a read-aloud that reteaches, reinforces, and propels the level of your students' reading work. The reading learning progressions can be another resource you keep beside you as you plan.

Recently, I was working in a fourth-grade classroom that was reading *The Egypt Game*, by Zilpha Keatley Snyder. Based on conversations with the teacher, I knew that her current unit of study relied heavily on students developing their inferencing work. As I prepared my read-aloud, I consulted the "Inferring about Characters and Other Story Elements" strand of the Narrative Reading Learning Progression. Several items popped out to me. Fourth-graders are expected to keep in mind that characters are complicated, pay attention to the "why" of characters' actions or decisions, focus on moments of difficulty, and know that sometimes a character's small action has a bigger, deeper meaning. These indicators became the tent poles of my read-aloud.

I began, "I wonder about the false eyelashes April bought for herself at the beginning of the book. The author seems to keep bringing them up a lot, so they must be important. Can you keep April's false eyelashes in mind as I read the next section? I'll want your help growing some ideas after I read." I continued to read aloud *The Egypt Game*, stopping after the part where April changes her overall appearance by getting a haircut and stops wearing the false eyelashes.

"April has made a big change in the way she looks! Turn and talk to your partner about what you think this change might mean." Partners discussed as I listened in. Simone began, "She seems to have stopped her 'grown-up act.' Maybe she's just trying to be a regular kid now."

Simone's partner, Saniyah added, "Yeah, her haircut looks more like a regular haircut now, instead of her hair all piled up on top of her head."

I chimed in, "What about the eyelashes?"

Narrative Reading Learning Progression

	Grade 3	Grade 4	Grade 5
	INTERPRETIVE READING		
Inferring about Characters and Other Story Elements *Character Traits*	I can develop ideas (theories) about the kind of person a character is. I know this means talking about a character's traits (personality), and I'm careful not to confuse the way a character feels for a trait. When a character makes a decision and does something, I can usually figure out why, based on what I know of the character and what happened earlier. 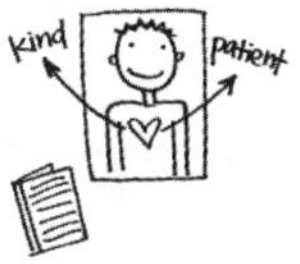	I keep in mind that characters are complicated. For example, I might think about how the character is different on the outside than the inside or in one part of the story or in one relationship than another. I'm interested in what *really* drives a character to make the decisions or take the actions he or she takes. What does the character *really* want? I know that a character's action will sometimes seem small (closing a door) but will actually signal a deeper meaning. 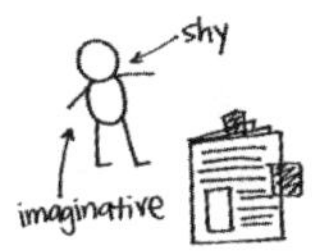	I can see places in a story where the characters are not what they seem at first. For example, the character might say or act as if he or she doesn't care, but readers see signs that he or she really does. That is, I see hidden sides to characters. I know that what drives the character (his or her motivation) can be complicated. There may be several things that drive or pressure a character, and often he or she is pulled in conflicting ways. 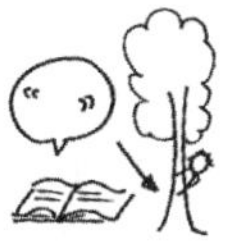
Character Response/ Change	I notice how a character changes across the story (for example, the character's feelings, traits, motivations, or behaviors might change). I think about what key moment(s) in the story caused the character to change. 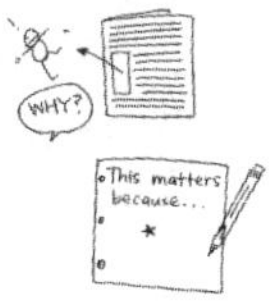	I notice how a character changes across the story. I think about many possible causes of these changes, including other story elements (the problem, the setting, other characters, and so on). I know that what a character learns about life can often be the theme of a story. 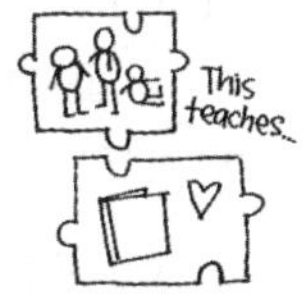	I can notice small, subtle changes in characters in addition to more obvious ones. I know that the causes of these changes may also be subtle or complicated. I think about how a character's change is important to the whole story. I am aware that characters can represent ways that people can be—the bully who is insecure, the boy with feelings locked inside—and that when a character changes or learns something, this can teach readers about ways that people like that character deal with challenges or issues. 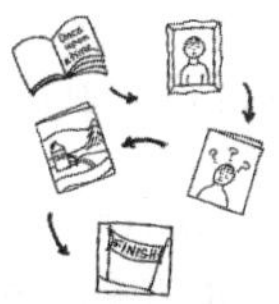
Supporting Thinking with Text Evidence	I support my ideas with details from the text.	I support my ideas with details from several parts of the text. I discuss how those details actually *do* support my ideas.	I support my ideas with specific details and quotes from several parts of the story. I select these because they are strong and they actually do match my points. I discuss how those details and citations support my ideas.

FIG. 8–9 "Inferring about Characters and Other Story Elements" strand of the Narrative Reading Learning Progression, Grades 3, 4, and 5

"Oh, yeah! The eyelashes are gone too!" Saniyah exclaimed.

I called the class back together, "Class, I want to share out something that Saniyah and Simone were discussing. They were saying that April might be trying to look like a regular kid now instead of trying to act like a grown-up all the time. They also noticed that April's false eyelashes are gone. Readers, I want to let you in on a secret: sometimes a character's action can be a clue to a bigger, deeper meaning. I'm wondering if this might be one of these times. Something so small as not wearing false eyelashes might actually tell us something big and important about April. Right, now I want everyone to stop and jot about this idea, and then we'll share out."

Student started jotting in their reading notebooks. I moved among them, peeking into their notebooks, I read jots such as:

> Maybe the eyelashes were April's way of staying connected to her mom. Since she took them off, maybe she's going to be more connected to her grandma now instead of her mom.

> The fake eyelashes made April stand out. Kids made fun of her. Maybe she's going to try harder to fit in now.

> April was kind of pretending before. I think she's not going to pretend to be someone she's not anymore.

Through this read-aloud, I set students up to practice the work required of fourth-graders. This scaffolding of skills will lead to students trying out the same work of paying attention to times when small actions might actually signal a deeper meaning in their own texts and to growing to be more sophisticated readers.

Develop Centers that Provide Opportunities for Students to Interact with the Progressions

The more students interact with the progressions, the more comfortable they become with the expectations. The more students are comfortable with the expectations, the stronger they will be to achieve both the goals you have set for them and the goals they have for themselves as readers. Centers are a high-interest, engaging way for students to read, process, and try out the skills described in the progressions.

One center might be "Jot Cards." In this center, students work with the "Analyzing Parts of the Text in Relation to the Whole" strand of the Informational Reading Learning Progression.

I was able to observe as two partners, Kai and Vikram, began their work at the "Jot Cards" center.

"It says here we're supposed to take turns reading parts of the rubric," Vikram said. "Can I go first?"

Kai replied, "You went first last time. It's my turn now. Level 2 says, 'I can talk about the order of the events or steps in a text. I can say how a part fits into an order, or how it says more about the main topic. I can answer the question of what came before or after.' Okay, your turn!"

Vikram replied, "No, it's not. The task card says you have to explain what that means to you. Then it's my turn."

Kai explained what level 2 meant, saying, "This means that you have to think about how parts of the text fit together. Like, is the part what happened first, next, or last? Now, go take your turn."

The boys continued in much the same way for each level of the rubric, second through fifth grade. They were reading a level and explaining what it meant, in their own words, to their partner. This was obviously not the first time the boys had encountered this strand of these progressions.

Next, the partners read the book at the center, *The Moon Book*, by Gail Gibbons. After reading, Kai and Vikram spread the jot cards face down on the table. They took turns picking a card and deciding which level of the strand the jot represented.

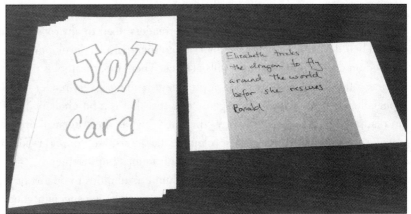

"My card says, 'The part about something hitting the earth is what happened first.' So, it talks about a part of the text. Umm, . . . it doesn't really say how it connects with the whole, and that's what level 3 says. So I think this is a level 2 jot," Kai explained.

"Yeah, I agree. It also doesn't say anything about why the author chose to put it in, so it can't be level 4 or 5."

The students continued to analyze each jot card, sometimes agreeing, sometimes disagreeing, but the conversation this center generated was priceless. What I found most effective about the work of these two boys was that they were talking not about the plot of the books, but about the skill and thinking work that was evident on the jot cards. After continued practice, these students will become much more metacognitive in thinking about the work they do as readers.

The center described above was focused on crystallizing these third-graders' knowledge of reading expectations across four grade levels, grades 2 through 5. Not all centers need to have this broad of a scope. Centers could instead focus on solidifying the grade level expectations for one grade level, pushing the students to pursue all of the thinking demanded of third-graders. Another option would be to develop a center that focuses on moving students up one level, possibly from third to fourth grade, within one strand.

ANTICIPATE THAT CHILDREN WILL PROGRESS ALONG A TRAJECTORY OF SKILLS AND COLLECT DATA ON THAT PROGRESS THROUGHOUT THE UNITS

As you mull over the performance assessments and the kids' revisions, I urge you to keep in mind that when you teach reading, as when you teach writing, you won't teach one particular skill until all readers have "mastered" it. Remember to think of skill development as having a trajectory, a learning pathway, and to teach so that all your readers progress along that trajectory. Expect that your teaching should be powerful enough that individual readers will be able to see themselves progress along the trajectory of a skill in noticeable ways. But you needn't expect that there will come a time when you say, "Okay, all my readers have mastered inference"(or determining importance or critical reading or any other aspect of reading).

So you also needn't persevere, teaching the same skill on and on and on until everyone "gets it." This curriculum is a spiral curriculum for a reason: readers need to always work on an orchestration of multiple skills. Their development of one skill relies on their parallel development of other skills, and we cannot be focused on developing all of our skills at once. Then, too, mastery is not the goal, because in fact, none of us have totally mastered the skills of proficient reading. Every reader continues to develop reading skills, especially when trying out a new genre or a text that is a bit challenging. I work hard to envision when I am reading the directions to fix my computer! Just as no writer will ever say, "I've mastered writing with voice," or "I'm done working on developing characters," so, too, no reader will fully master the skills you are teaching in reading. The goal, then, is continuous improvement.

If you collected baseline data on your children's abilities to do any of the skills that you are especially highlighting in a unit, then you and your students will be in especially good positions to watch for progress and to hold yourselves accountable. Teachers, the most important accountability will be your own. You will absolutely want to make sure that your children progress in dramatic ways. In early October, you can't watch, right then and there, to see if all your children can perform well on a standardized test. But if you have a sense of learning trajectories that kids follow to learn to summarize, compare and contrast, and synthesize with increasing sophistication, then you should certainly be able to hold yourself accountable for teaching so that every one of your kids progresses along those trajectories. And the important thing is that a reader can be reading a level J book or a level Z book and can still progress along those trajectories. It won't be the case that your teaching is applicable only to a few of your readers.

Chapter 9

Record Keeping

Developing Effective Systems for Teachers and Students

R EADING LOGS, goal sheets, reading notebooks, performance assessments, Post-its, observational data, and more. If you have a strong reading workshop up and running, then odds are that you have enough data to sink a ship. While your students are creating goals and devising systems for meeting them, you too are attempting to keep track of their progress and associated data, as well as your instruction and its correlation to that progress.

When my colleagues and I begin working with a school, one of the first questions teachers ask us is "How do people keep track of all the data? What do other people's conferring sheets or binders look like?" And if you are anything like the teachers I know best, you've probably tried five, ten, *dozens* of systems and found, much to your dismay, that each is as cumbersome and limited as the next. I look at their desks, piled high with logs and reading notebooks, Post-its hanging from every available surface with notes and reminders. I wish more than anything that I could say, "Ah, here, *this* is the solution you've been looking for." Unfortunately, it just isn't that easy. Who was it who likened teaching students to leading a school full of minnows? In today's world, you not only need to lead that school of minnows, but you also need to keep accurate records of each minnow's progress! As a reading teacher, one of the greatest areas of growth and transition will be to collect data in a way that allows you to make use of it in the most potent ways.

To help you get control of your data, this chapter will address aspects of data collection and record keeping, offering practical, time-honored ideas for ways to track student progress across the year. But, alas, it won't offer the one magic answer. As I wrote in *Writing Pathways*, "All record-keeping systems are like relationships: they take work" (Heinemann, 2013).

THE IMPORTANCE OF RECORD-KEEPING SYSTEMS: CLARIFYING WHAT THESE SYSTEMS NEED TO ACCOMPLISH

It is my hope that you'll come to see data, in all its forms and iterations, as a life force of sorts in your classroom—something that informs every instructional choice you make with your readers. As you assess each reader individually, constructing a sense for that particular reader's learning pathway, you'll also need to ensure that each reader has goals that are within his zone of proximal development, a clear sense of ways to work toward those goals, and a constant stream of feedback that enables that reader to refine, extend, adjust, or accelerate his efforts.

You'll want to develop a portable, efficient system for carrying your assessment information, on the run, as you move among your readers. To accomplish this, it helps to be as streamlined and as organized as possible, to have access to the information you need at your fingertips, and even to create "cheat sheets" of sorts that help you remember all that you want to teach and do.

If you think for a moment of the different roles that record keeping needs to play when you are teaching reading as opposed to teaching writing, it will quickly be apparent that the demands on your record keeping are far greater in the reading than in the writing workshop.

So the question you need to ask is this: how can you devise a form of reading records that functions, for young readers, similarly to how medical records function for patients in a hospital. This, of course, is not a new question, and there are many reading researchers who've developed systems (see Myra Barrs' *Assessing Literacy with the Learning Record* for one impressive example). My sense is that the record-keeping systems that have been the most common and well used are tailored especially to K–2 readers, where a good deal of the record keeping revolves around ascertaining the reader's stage of development (preemergent, emergent, beginning, early transitional, late transitional, and so on), and around helping readers draw on the cueing systems (including graphophonics, syntax, and meaning) to read fluently.

Once readers are in or beyond the intermediate stage of reading development, there are fewer agreed-upon developmental pathways along which teachers can track a reader's progress, and most instruction supports intellectual work that can be subsumed under the catch-all term *comprehension*. Think about it: if a teacher is really going to watch over a proficient fourth-grade reader's reading growth, is it enough for the teacher to look for broad, general indications that the reader is "comprehending"? Is it enough for our records to say, "Yep, she's comprehending this book. Yep, she's comprehending that book." We simply can't settle for this level of record keeping for our intermediate-and-beyond readers.

DEVISING AN EFFECTIVE RECORD-KEEPING SYSTEM FOR YOURSELF

There are some goals that I recommend you aim toward when devising a plan for yourself. An effective record-keeping system will allow you to:

- Hold yourself accountable to teaching in ways that have traction.

- Collect and consolidate large-scale data so you can see patterns and trends across a class (or all your classes) to teach whole-class and small-group instruction in response.

- Track an individual reader's progress, seeing evidence of growth (or lack thereof), so your upcoming work with that reader can be informed by what you see and so that reader knows you are attending to his progress.

- Help readers track their own progress toward goals by teaching them to record what they are learning, what they are working toward, and achievements they've made.

Hold Yourself Accountable to Teaching in Ways that Have Traction

There will be times when you teach, and the results come in just as you hoped. Bingo! The kids' work improves before your eyes. Sure, there will be some students who need reteaching, but still, there will be times when the results provide concrete evidence that your teaching worked. Continue on course. Then again, there will be times when your teaching doesn't yield the expected results. Your students' thinking and writing about their reading stay mired in the same problems. In that case, you'll need to respond appropriately.

First, check those expectations. Remember that no one week of teaching will allow all students to master a skill. If you teach a lesson on understanding the perspective from which an author writes and you see evidence of improvement, but many of your students are still not at grade level standards, you can still feel great about the results of your teaching. Your intention is not for students to improve miraculously so that overnight, they all perform at grade level. Your goal is *progress*, and that progress should be visible. That's all. And sometimes there won't be progress. The good news is that when you look at the results, when you study your students' work or listen to them read and discuss their reading, you will be given the feedback you need to improve that portion of your teaching. Perhaps the results aren't there. Then you know you messed up, or we, your curricular guides, messed up. So you will alter something: reteach with more power and fidelity, tweak your methods, choose different examples, speed up or slow down. You will, in any case, do something differently, and again, you'll keep your eye on the results.

For this cycle of continuous improvement to happen, first and foremost, you need to regard your students' progress (or lack thereof) as feedback *on your teaching*. If your students are having difficulty analyzing the perspective from which a nonfiction text has been written, instead of thinking, "My students are really dense about perspective," or "This curriculum doesn't teach perspective," say to yourself, "I haven't taught perspective well enough yet." Then think about how to alter your instruction. A word of caution: don't feel that you need to engage in perfect assessments to harvest this benefit. Remember, imperfect data on a just a random sampling of students is a lot better than none at all. If you wait until you have perfect data, analyzed perfectly, chances are you'll never get off the starting block. The more you study the data and get to know your readers, the more insight you'll have into your next steps and theirs.

Collect and Consolidate Data So You Can See Patterns and Trends and Teach in Response

Patterns that Inform Small-Group Work

Administering performance assessments and running records to all your students at regular intervals across the year will not be the hard part of these assessments. The challenge, instead, will revolve around studying the data of each one of your students and making meaning from it, letting it shape your instruction.

The important thing is that you will want to mine your collection of scores to find students who would benefit from similar sorts of support. For example, you might locate four students who especially need help with something—say, analytic reading—as shown by lower scores in many of the traits that reveal that skill. (In this instance, analyzing parts of a text in relation to the whole, analyzing author's craft, and perspective all contribute to the category of analytic reading.) Meanwhile, you might also decide that many of your students could use help with supporting their thinking with text evidence or word solving. In this fashion, you divide students into a few groups.

Depending on the number of students in your care, you might find it helpful to use a spreadsheet and a color scheme including red, yellow, green, and blue. In this color scheme, red is below expectations, yellow is approaching, green is meeting, and blue is exceeding. List student names down the left-hand column, allowing three to four rows for their data entry points for the year. Next to their names, create a date or month column to track when the assessments were completed. Then list the categories assessed (orienting, determining themes/cohesion, etc.) across the top of the spreadsheet. When your spreadsheet is complete, you can add a data filter, a feature that allows you to narrow down and sort your data, to the top row with the categories. This will enable you to group your kids for small-group instruction.

It will be important to devote some of the workshop time to need-based groups. You may decide to keep a few groups consistent over a stretch of time, teaching cycles of small-group work to provide students with repeated practice of a particular skill. Your data can set you up to do this. For example, if you decide to work with one group of readers who need help with word work and with another group who need support with analysis of point of view, you might set up a folder for each group, including copies of their responses to the performance assessment for a particular skill and the rubric for each student in each group. You can also put into each folder some mentor examples you've created or scaffolds to help with that group's particular aims. This will make it easy for you to show students examples of what they have done in their writing about reading, as well as how they can improve.

Another advantage to students working in groups is that on one occasion, you might rally members of a group to help one reader review his work and set goals, doing this work with one group member in such a way that all the members of that group get help doing similar work.

On another occasion, you might channel all the members of the group to look between their initial performance assessment response and the entry or jot they've just written to check that they are improving in whatever goals they've decided to tackle. Of course, many of these needs will not be genre-specific, so members of a group can also look at their goal—say, supporting their thinking with text evidence—across

Research	Teach/Next Steps
Sept 12 When asked to talk about the characters I notice the student has difficulty generating single word descriptions as an idea about the character's dominant trait. Student says: nice	Play close attention to where the character is talking and think what kind of a person would talk like that. You can carefully read a section of dialogue between two characters. Ask yourself, "What does the way they are speaking to each other say about the kind of people they are?" Go back in three days.
Sept 14 When asked to talk about the characters I notice the student still has difficulty generating single word descriptions as an idea about the character's dominant trait. So needs more help. Did try to follow up what was left. Student says: The character likes to do a, b, c which means he is	Notice the way the character interacts with other characters in the scene. Ask yourself, "What kind of person would act that way?" Go back in three days.
Sept 20 When asked to talk about the characters I notice the student could generate single-word descriptions as an idea about the character's dominant trait but could not follow the character throughout the text and think about what that trait says about what that person does and says. Also note that he is reading a book a week need to push volume which is what he had difficulty with last year as well look back at last year's notes.	Readers get to know their characters just as we get to know a new friend. We watch and think about the new person. We ask, " What kind of person is he/she?" We get to know our characters and really care about them like they are friends or family. If you had to call home and tell someone about this new person what would you say? Go back in five days.
Sept 28 When asked to talk about the characters I notice the student now can follow the character but misses things sometimes as he tries to follow the untagged dialogue. Also notice again too little reading.	Readers pay attention to what a character does, says, thinks, and feels. When we pay attention to all of these details we can grow an idea about what kind of person the character is. Find places to stop and think. You can write your thoughts on post its. Then you can read over your post its to grow an idea about your character. Also let me show you the chart you used last year to remind you to keep reading and to read read read your volume challenge chart. Let's remember what you did! Go back in four days but check in in two.
Oct 4 Still needs push but is now noticing traits but he has tried. When asked to talk about the characters I notice the student has difficulty generating single-word descriptions as an idea about the character's dominant feelings.	We can watch what a character does and says on the outside, imagine how her words would sound, think about the expression on her face and movements to guess how she feels on the inside. Go back three days.
Oct 12 When asked to talk about the characters I notice the student has difficulty generating single word descriptions as an idea about the character's dominant feelings. Students missed the message the last time that's okay do it again.	Readers pay attention to what characters say and how they say it to learn more about them. The words a character says can show us if he/she is angry, frightened, happy or sad. Did he or she cry, scream, whisper . . . Go back in four days.

FIG. 9–1   Conference notes of Jose, Level P

all of their reading life. These folders would, of course, also house notes you take or observations you make, records of the small-group instruction, and of the work readers do in class, so that you can easily recall what you taught and also hold students accountable to actually doing what they agree to try.

One challenge arising from combining your notes into small-group folders is that they won't then be filed in individual writers' folders. Presumably, after the small group has met for a cycle, or a short sequence of times, the group will be disbanded, at which point you'll get at least some record of that group work into each of the members' individual records. (No one said this is easy!)

Some teachers keep their notes about individual students on Post-its, stuck to one sheet of paper in the small-group folder. When the group is disbanded, those Post-its for the individual student can be moved to another sheet of paper for that student, housed in a binder or folder that contains student-by-student data. Other teachers have used apps for iPads or Android to address this. The Confer app lets you assign students to skills, and then it groups them into small groups and records your notes. Evernote is also a good system for this because you can create a note for each student, photograph his work with your iPad, and then the app automatically tucks this into that student's note.

Track an Individual Reader's Progress to See Needs and Evidence of Growth

In addition to creating systems that will allow you to see and record the needs of groups of readers, you'll want to have a place to record research and work with individual readers. Again, you will need to decide what is workable, given the size of your student load.

Imagine yourself carrying a simple pocket folder, with one pocket for each of your readers. What would that folder contain, and how would you use it to inform and fuel your teaching? As I've mentioned, there is no one *right* answer to that question. There are, however, useful suggestions that many teachers we've worked with have found beneficial. You might, for example, carry a sequence of sheets on one side to record data in short, at-a-glance references for where the student is and where he's going next. One of these sheets could contain some quick reference facts to feed your teaching of this child:

- Data from the reader's initial and formative assessments, such as running records and performance assessments—perhaps the documents themselves and perhaps just the analyses of strengths and needs

- Data for when the child needs to be reassessed with hopes of progressing to another level of text difficulty

- "Next steps" or goals you have for the child—most likely gleaned from an analysis of performance assessments and ongoing research in conferences, which might even be in the form of learning progressions, with specific goals circled across the various skills

- A copy of the student's goals for himself

- Spelling inventory data
- High-frequency word data, if relevant

The other side of the folder might be dedicated to ongoing data collection throughout the unit. We'd recommend keeping the dated record sheets from your conferences and small groups on this side, with compliments, teaching points, and next steps recorded for each conference (more on record-keeping systems for conferring and small groups below). Then too, some of these notes might be collected at home or during prep time, as you study students' reading notebooks, Post-its, and so on.

No matter what, you will want to be sure that students keep complete collections of their thinking and writing about reading, including capturing some jots, presumably in their reader's notebook. Some teachers who are carrying an especially large number of students require that students assume responsibility for a major portion of record keeping, with students recording pointers learned and the plans made after each conference or small group. Those teachers can then look back on the students' records when reminding themselves of prior teaching, studying the notes on a conference or a small group, alongside the evidence of the work the reader has been doing. Of course, if students lose their reader's notebook, complete with all those records, that becomes a big problem.

A potential solution, if your school has access to computers or tablets, is to create a shared document file, such as Google Docs, with each student that serves as a digital version of a reader's notebook. Both you and the student can add notes to record her goals, small-group and conference teaching points, and next steps. You can also add resources to help the students work toward their reading goals—a chart, a list of prompts, a mentor entry—and you can access these from multiple locations. This builds a bridge between the student's reading life at home and at school and allows you to review all of this information from the comfort of your couch or your kitchen table, without carrying a stack of notebooks home with you. Even better, the digital file can't get lost (as long as it's backed up).

Many teachers make binders or folders with a section for each student. These can house your notes from your work with each student, their running records, copies of their performance assessment responses, prompts related to their band of text complexity, and anything else that helps to shape your knowledge of the student's learning trajectory. And then there are those who keep all of their notes on their tablets or computers—Evernote and Notability are great for that. Snapping pictures or scanning in assessments and student work can help to build a digital portfolio for each student. Whichever way you choose, you will want to be sure that this system enables you to look back at a reader's progress often, so that you can help your readers do this as well. You want readers to get into the habit of expecting that you will follow up on their goals, holding them accountable for actually working toward those goals and improving their writing.

Conferring Table – Week of: 11/17, 11/24   NF Reading Goals

Ashley	Avery	Bea	Christiana	Dylan	Ege
ELL Guided Reading – vocabulary ⓒ ✓ SG	Determining main idea ⓒ (OK) SG	Bringing F strategies to NF ⓒ *transit. baggie SG	Taking notes in an organized way ⓒ SG	Determining main idea ⓒ X SG	see Ashley ⓒ ✓ SG
Eliana	**Felix**	**Finn**	**George**	**Giuliana**	**Hassan**
organization – note-taking ⓒ SG	separating notes into categories / sub-headings ⓒ SG	Technical vocabulary – personal word wall ⓒ SG	Main idea in a small section of text ⓒ SG	see Ashley ? interest level ⓒ	Determining main idea ✓ (structure X) ⓒ SG
Isabella	**Jack**	**Julia**	**Kurumi**	**Margaret**	**Monica**
Determining main idea → Boxes + Bullets ⓒ SG	organizing notes for sense ⓒ (OK) SG	Determining main idea ✓ ⓒ C	see Ashley ✓ Give new baggie ⓒ SG	Determining main idea ⓒ ✓ SG	Determining main idea ⓒ SG
Naomi	**Olivia**	**Sive**	**Soraya**	**Tavo**	**Tyler**
Finding key details vs. details ⓒ SG	✱ Not missing important information ⓒ SG	Technical/ unfamiliar vocabulary → personal word wall ⓒ	Determining main idea ⓒ X SG	Boxes + Bullets to organize notes ⓒ SG	ⓒ SG

SG = small group   C = 1 on 1 conference

Small Group Notes

Students Names: Soraya, Monica, Bea, Tyler (club)

Topic: Club expectations/working together

Session 1: Making a plan for how to read together

11/11
- Preview 1st (predict)
- stop to talk when you need to digest info.

  ✱ S not talking/reading?

Session 2: Debates during club talk

11/14
It's ok to disagree - this happens in real life
→ If you feel strongly about your point, support it w/ proof from your text

  ✱ T/M argument → OK

Session 3: Maintaining same subtopics

11/19
Keep the same subtopics book after book -
Keep adding to your notes in each area

  ✱ Hard organizationally for S, M

Session 4:

Small Group Notes

Students Names: Finn, Julia, Naomi, Hassan

Topic: Text structures

Session 1: Boxes + Bullets vs. sequential

12/1
✱ In sequential order, events are presented in the order in which they happen   (all OK)
✱ Boxes + Bullets has a main idea + lists details

Session 2: Compare/contrast

12/8
Determine the structure of a compare/contrast text → signal words
  ✱ F, H Had a hard time w/ signal words

Session 3: Cause + Effect

12/15
✱ Differentiating btw. what's the cause + what's the effect? □ → □
✱ Group had a hard time ↑

Session 4: Cause + Effect vs. problem/solution

12/22
✱ w/ problem/solution, the problem gets solved   (all OK)

FIG. 9–2

Conferring and Small-Group Record Sheets

Conferring and small-group record sheets can be useful in many ways. They can function as cue cards, reminding you of things you hope to teach your readers. If you sometimes aren't quite sure what to notice or teach toward in a student's reading, you can look at where the student is in the learning progression and record in the margins of your conferring record sheet the work that the student should be tackling. Then, if nothing emerges out of a conversation with the child, you can use the cue sheet as a reminder of possible topics to address.

When designing your conferring record sheets, include enough content from the appropriate progression to remind you of what to teach. Of course, your goals extend beyond the progression; you are also teaching into reading habits and behaviors, building a reading life and social structures that support reading. So allow room on the sheet to jot down your observations for several students. We've provided you with a few examples of ways you can organize your conferring record sheets, but you may wish to adapt and change them to suit your particular needs.

Because a record sheet like this allows for records of multiple conferences and small groups to be laid alongside each other, it is possible to look across notes, rereading and considering the progress of the reader. You can see the notes about several conferences or small-group meetings at a glance. Another benefit is being able to identify what areas you most frequently address with the reader and what areas tend to be overlooked. For example, you might notice that you've had three conferences about main ideas/summary with a reader, but only one about habits. The reader might need work with main ideas, but of course, you could support that work through a conference about the reader's behaviors. ("Do you tend to read a chunk of your nonfiction text, then pause to sum up for yourself what that chunk was mostly about? That would help you.")

HELPING STUDENTS DEVISE RECORD-KEEPING SYSTEMS FOR THEMSELVES

It is not only the teacher who needs to look back on a reader's work and see progress—or lack thereof. Students, themselves, need to be able to do this. Specifically, they will want to recall what you and others (including their reading partner) have taught them to do in conferences and small groups. They will also want to recall the goals they set for themselves or that you set for them. If readers are going to be accountable for actually living up to those goals, it is important that they are recorded, the aspirations set onto the page. Students need a record-keeping system of their own to keep track of all of this valuable information.

You will want to help guide students to keep track of what they're working fervently to improve, making it easy for kids to pull out this reminder of their goals. Some students set up a system by designating the final portion of their reader's notebook as a "Goals, Plans, and Reflections" section. Allow your students the freedom to invent wonderful ways to create such a section. Some will simply fold down a page about three-quarters of the way through their notebook, and others will find their own ways to create a boundary.

Some students staple two notebook pages together to create a pocket for their learning progression as the first page for this section, adding pictures or illustrations to make it celebratory.

Many teachers have become exceptionally good at helping students feel ownership of their writer's notebooks. Students decorate those notebooks, carry them to home and back, pull them out while on a bus or in the doctor's waiting room to jot a quick entry. Similarly, you'll want to help students feel this kind of ownership of their reader's notebooks as well. Let the sky be the limit when it comes to designing their own system for goal-setting.

Usually the first portion of this "Goals, Plans, and Reflections" section is a reflective entry in which the reader thinks about the collection of goals that he has adopted and his plans for meeting those goals. Talk to the child about how you organize your life in ways that support your efforts to live up to a goal. You might say, "I have this goal to eat healthy. If I keep ice cream or cookies at home, they are the first thing I'll go for when I'm hungry! So, I make a plan to buy only the healthiest foods when I'm at the grocery

FIG. 9–3

store—veggies, fruits, and other good stuff. So now, when I reach for a snack, because I planned ahead, I only have healthy options to choose from. Readers also need to make plans for how to keep their goals in mind as they read."

Each student will take to this work differently. Perhaps one reader decides to place Post-its at predetermined intervals in his book as a reminder ("Remember to think back over and summarize the parts of the story that relate to what I'm reading now!") and institutes a habit of doing a quick mental summary whenever he reaches the end of a chapter. You might suggest he add another step, such as doing a quick recheck at the end of each reading period to make sure he's lived up to his goal.

You might also set goals as a class. If you have been focusing, for example, on the "Inferring about Characters and Other Story Elements" strand with your fifth-graders, you might say, "If you have been paying attention to when characters make decisions, but you have not been thinking about their motivations, you must decide whether this should be a major goal or if you could just jot a note that says 'motivations' to remind you to do this work. However, if something on the progressions is an area you need more support with or maybe something you could learn more about in a small group—for example, thinking about the interaction between a character and other story elements—then you could create a major goal sheet and put those items on it." Students cannot focus on all of their reading skills at once. Instead, guide students to the goals that will make the most difference in growing their thinking as they read.

If your students have a "Goals, Plans, and Reflections" section of their notebook, you can use this section as a place to record your conferences and small groups. In a conference, of course, it will be critical for you to skim through this goals and plans section of a student's reader's notebook, using it (and the reader) as a tour guide through the reader's work. As students tell you how their work is going, you will also want to hold in mind the work you asked the reader to do: the reader's own goals, the previous efforts to meet those goals, and so forth.

This also might be a good place for you to add in your own conference/small-group notes for students so they have a placeholder not only for their own goals, but for what you are doing with them as well. Depending on your students' ages, you might ask them to write their own records of conferences and small groups, or you might do this yourself. The important thing, either way, is that students then jot down the page numbers of their notebooks or number their Post-its, showing they have worked toward this goal. For instance, if a student's goal is to become more skilled at thinking about the relationships within a nonfiction text (Is there a cause-and-effect relationship, a claim-and-reasons relationship?), he might number this as goal 3 in his notebook. Then, on each Post-it where he jots a bit about the relationships with nonfiction texts, he could jot a quick 3 to identify the goal. This way, when you check back in with him, it will be easy to see where he has worked on various goals.

Which brings me to an important point: it will be critical that your conferring with a student shine a light on the importance of goals. You might even decide to have one of your first questions relate to the child's goal work. "Let's take a look at the goals you've set for yourself," you might say. "Can you show me where you've been working on them?" Or "As I look at my conferring notes, I see that last time we worked on noticing more about ways different parts of nonfiction texts relate to each other. Can you show me where you've practiced getting stronger at this work?" In this way you send a crystal clear message to the readers in your classroom—goals are not merely things they set on a passing whim. Instead, goals are something they commit to, as readers and students, to working on getting better at. If you make a point of checking in, I promise students will take their goals all the more seriously!

Of course, this system has a few limitations. The first is that you will only be able to look at this section when you have a student's notebook in hand. Often teachers decide to collect all reader's notebooks every Monday night (or one table full of reader's notebooks every Monday night) so then, as they look through this record of a reader's deliberate practice, they can think about the week ahead. The digital reader's notebook housed in a shared document system, such as Google Docs, discussed earlier in this chapter, is another option.

Whatever system you and your students invent, you can be sure of one thing: you will need to revise it! Your needs and purposes will change, and your systems for collecting data will need to change as well. If your record-keeping system hasn't changed for a while, focus on what information you are getting from it—and ask whether that is still the most pressing information. If not, what information do you need, and in what form can you collect it? Has a colleague already figured this out? If so, what has she tried? With this information, you will be off and running, reinventing and re-collecting, ready to interpret what you've collected to tailor your teaching more exactly to what your students need.

HELP STUDENTS USE READING LOG DATA TO DEVELOP GOALS

Students' reading logs contain a treasure trove of information that you can use in conferences and small groups. You'll want to look at logs within your day-to-day conferring and research, and to look between logs and running records. Then you can put together all that you know about that student to form a theory about her as a reader. In a conference, you can look at a book log together with students, noting times when reading was high-volume, more pages than usual, and times when reading was low-volume for the student. You might notice patterns in the child's reading. Maybe he reads quickly through realistic fiction, while expository reading seems to be taking forever.

Of course, there will be students who pad their volume of reading, hoping to please you. It is important that reading logs are used only for information to fuel conversations and instruction, not to accumulate points or rewards. Donalyn Miller, in *Reading in the Wild* (Jossey-Bass, 2013), suggests that one option is to institute reading logs at the start of the year as a way to establish baseline goals and expectations for reading volume and stamina, but then to scale back the emphasis on logs as the year goes on, to avoid fueling an obsession with reading too quickly. Logs can be brought back from time to time for the purpose of reflecting on how long and how much each student is now reading, and tracking growth.

Another way to help students maintain these records with vigilance is to show them how to become researchers of their own reading habits, poring over their own and each other's reading logs to deduce patterns. Encourage readers to count up the pages read or the minutes spent reading in one week, and then

Date	Title and Author of Book	Time Reading in Class	Pages Read in Class	Time Reading Out of Class	Pages Read Out of Class	Finished or Abandoned	Level
1/5/06	The Spiderwick Chronicles, Vol 1, Diterlizzi	9:30-10:00 Or ½ hour	1-18	4:00-4:30 ½ hour	19-43		
9/8	Felita	9:50-10:10 (20)	13-27 (14)	3:40-4:15 (35)	27-60 (33)		P
9/9	"	test		9:00-9:05 (20) 10:10-10:30	60-83 (23)		
9/10	"	test		10:10-10:30 am 10:30-10:50 pm	84-105	Finished!	
mon 9/11	That's So Raven	10-10:15 (15) (3-3:20)(20)	4-14 15-35	3:40-4:10 (30)	35-65		? P/Q ?
9/12	"	20 mm	66-81	10-10:15 7-7:15am 30	82-105		
9/13	"	30min 9:30-10:00!	106-140 !	3-3:20 10:30-11:00 50	141-end!!	Finished!!!	Q ?
9/14	Raven II	35mm! 9:25-10:00!	4-44!	½ hr on train 20min before bed	44-88		
9/15	"	32mm	89-124				

Name: Sarah   Class: _____

Goal: I need to bring home 2 Ravens this weekend

FIG. 9-4

contrast that with data from the next week. Eventually, they can do the same for one month, contrasting it with the next month.

Of course, the reason to notice patterns in one's own data is to learn from those patterns. If a child notices that she reads almost twice as much one week as in another week, some important questions are "Why? What explains the sudden rise in her reading volume? How can she continue to create those conditions for herself?" These questions are especially important because the data collected in a reading log may be used as an impetus to changing behavior. The child can at any point resolve to read longer and more. This matters. Just as it is important for you and me to feel as if we can draw a line in the sand right now, starting today, and resolve to change our ways, so too it is important for kids to realize this.

Let Students in on the Research that Can Help Them Analyze Their Data

I think it is wise to share research findings with youngsters, asking them to join you in figuring out whether those findings have relevance for their lives.

Reading Rate

You may decide to recruit kids to join you in researching their reading rates. Then once each child has established his words per minute, you can share guidelines from the research for evaluating that rate. That is, without telling children your purpose, you could set them up to mark the starting place in their book and then to read, stopping after two minutes, and you could use this measurement to help them to calculate their words per minute. Then you could show children Harris and Sipay's (1990) guidelines for thinking about reading rate based on levels of text difficulty. These researchers suggest:

J–L: 85–120 words per minute

M–O: 115–140 words per minute

P–R: 140–170 words per minute

S–U: 170–195 words per minute

T–V: 195–220 words per minute

V–W: 215–245 words per minute

If some of your youngsters are reading much more slowly than the research suggests is advisable, you may want to assess their fluency, which includes not just the speed with which a child can read, but also expression, prosody, and parsing. For example, you might make a list of students whose reading rates are slow and check to see if they are reading in very brief phrases. Listen to them read and check off whether they are reading in two-word phrases or in three-word phrases. You could also note which of these readers attend to punctuation and which do not. As you do this, you'll probably reconsider whether you have established just-right reading levels for these readers, because one of the preconditions for a level being just right is that this is a level at which the child can read with fluency (which includes an attention to punctuation and phrasing).

If you've decided that fluency is holding back a reader, you will want to show the reader the data that you've collected, contrasting it with what research indicates would be data the readers could aim to achieve. You could let them know tips that researchers say can help. For example, sometimes when children are reading slowly, they are running a finger or a bookmark under the words or mouthing the words as they read—all habits that slow down a reader's rate and that can be set aside. Many children who read slowly are in fact doing constant little check-backs as they proceed down the page, rereading often a score of times while reading even just a single page of print, as if worried that some name, some detail, might get past them. These children need to be encouraged to read on unless something is really confusing and to trust that the important things that the reader needs to hold onto will usually recur anyhow. Many children who read too slowly need help phrasing and can be encouraged to reach for larger chunks of words, taking in longer and more meaningful phrases at a time. It can help to reread a familiar text aloud multiple times, paying tremendous attention to the meaning of the text, trying to read it in ways that allow the meaning to really shine through.

My point, right now, is not to summarize methods for supporting a child's fluency so much as to suggest that we benefit from letting children join us in collecting data on their reading and join us also in working with resolve to strengthen their muscles as readers. And the good news is that after working for a few weeks, children can collect more data and look for indications of growth. If a child's data suggests he is growing, then it is critically important to use that data to help him develop a self-concept of "I'm on my way as a reader. I keep growing and growing. This year looks like it'll be one of those growth spurt years."

Reading Volume

You may also decide to share data (Gentry) that suggests that children who are reading books at particular levels will generally complete those books within predictable lengths of time. Allington points out that many level M books—and remember, the Magic Tree House series is level M—contain approximately 6,000 words. Readers who can handle level M books will tend to be reading at least 100 words per minute, suggesting that one of these books should require no more than an hour of reading. If children are reading an hour or two a day, that suggests that a child reading level M books will read at least seven books a week. Meanwhile, many level R books are closer to 50,000 words, the word count for Gary Paulsen's *Hatchet*. Readers who can read this level of text difficulty will tend to be reading at least 150 words per minute, suggesting that they'll tend to be able to read one of their level R books in six hours—and that certainly, readers will complete these books within a week. The important thing to realize is that children reading at lower levels of text difficulty need to read closer to a book a day than a chapter a day!

It is likely that some readers are creeping through books, reading exponentially more slowly than these figures suggest. I strongly suggest you talk to these kids about what you notice. Say, "I want to talk to the two of you because I'm noticing that you both have been reading something like sixteen pages a day in school, and a bit less at home. You should know that some scientists have studied what kids need to flourish as readers, and they're suggesting that kids need to read at least twice as many pages a day as you are reading. They're suggesting that a reader like you should be aiming to read close to thirty pages a day in school and the same amount at home. I know that must sound crazy to you. It is so much more reading than you are doing, but I am wondering if you'd be game to try for this. I mean, these researchers—these scientists—have studied thousands of kids, and they are really sure that the amount of reading you're doing isn't enough. Would you be willing to really push yourself and see what's possible? We could talk tomorrow about what you discover." When I've talked like that to kids, it has often happened that the next day, the kids gallop into the classroom, calling, "We did it! We did it!"

Of course, it is not a small thing to help kids ramp up the amount of reading they're doing, and you and the youngsters may need to talk about how to make this possible. One way is to interview youngsters

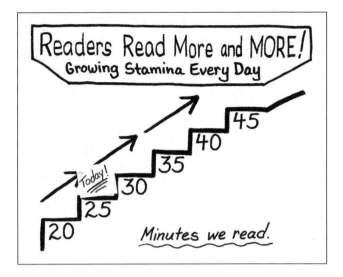

who are getting a lot of reading done. (Ideally, there will be some readers who do not read especially challenging text levels but who do make time for lots of reading, so these children can become famous for their time on task.) You can help youngsters learn that the way to get a lot of reading done is to carry books everywhere, using stolen moments to read. It means making time during the prime time of the day for reading and not just relegating reading to those weary moments before bed. It means disciplining oneself not to watch TV or play video games or talk on the phone constantly, and perhaps even asking parents or caregivers for help establishing boundaries. You'll also want to be sure that you don't teach as if the goal is a measured increment of time each day for reading. Be stunned when a child never reads for three times the required length of time. "I'm so surprised. Don't you ever get so drawn into your book that you can't put it down and you read way on and on?"

These are just general guidelines, but the powerful thing about them is that they high-light some of the most important aspects of teaching reading well. Again, the data can reveal patterns that are easily shared with kids and easily addressed. So often, the term "data-based instruction" has been used to pull young people away from reading toward text-prep exercises, but in fact, data-based instruction can rally kids to exponentially increase the time they spend reading.

ASSESSING WIDER READING LIVES

We encourage you to assess your entire class using the Building a Reading Life Progression (see Figure 9–5). You'll notice that the document is a series of flags. These flags represent situations that you might see in your classroom—not individual children. They are a way to triage the class, thinking through the work that the majority of the class needs, and needs *now*. This document seeks to go beyond reading level into reading behaviors, helping you to notice patterns and address them so that children are engaged readers who move up levels of text complexity. The *if . . . then . . .* statements under each flag are intended to help you to do this work and do it quickly.

We made this chart in part because we often noticed teachers, inspired by attending a workshop or staff development, focus on a very specific aspect of their workshops. For example, one group of teachers was intent on inserting interludes for "stop-and-jots" into book clubs so that students would pause when the conversation lulled to jot their thinking in ways that reinvigorated their conversations. While that was a beautiful thing to do, in that particular school, students were reading just a book or two a month! The much more important focus for that school was on volume of reading. So you might think of the Building a Reading Life Progression as a "first things first" document. It's a way to peek into your classroom and to prioritize the most important things, giving you a lens to focus on the things that need your urgent attention.

Of course, there is no magical formula to the particular combination of behaviors included on the progression. While we believe that these areas are important, they are not necessarily the most important

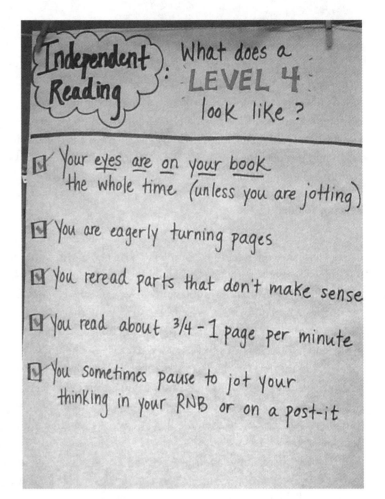

Building a Reading Life Progression		
Red Flag Situation	**If you see . . .**	**Here is a sequence of things to address . . .**
Engagement and independence	• Kids going to the bathroom/sharpening pencils during reading workshop • Kids reading for a short time, then putting books down • Kids abandoning books • When asked to read aloud, kids' reading does not sound like talking—they are not reading to punctuation, and the reading is choppy	• QUICKLY assess and **match readers to books—you must get books that are within reach into their hands.** • Develop a plan for inspiring the community (e.g., do community circles around books, have frequent reading celebrations, show video clips about people helping each other to inspire). • Get high-interest, popular, easy books into readers' hands (series/books by author). • Do book introductions and have kids do book buzzes to build up level of excitement; have kids make recommendation charts and basket labels ("Books that Will Make You Cry and Cry," "Anna's Faves!," "Stories to Make You Shiver!"). • Show clips from *Vimeo.com/TCRWP* and say, "This is where we will be in Jan!" • Do lessons on finding tons of within reach books. • Do lessons on fluency and helping readers to outgrow choppy, robotic sounding reading. • Set class goals to read ____books by ___ (and have celebrations when it happens!!).
Volume/stamina (looking at logs)	• Kids only reading at school/only reading at home • Kids jumping from book to book • Kids reading one book for longer than it should take (e.g., J book—more than 10 minutes, see chart earlier in chapter) • Kids reading less than 10–12 pages in 15 mins. (need to read ¾ of a page a min.)	• Be sure readers are **matched to books**. • Be sure you are giving readers protected reading time EVERY day. • Do a minilesson about how reading is like running. We need to set goals so we can read strong, fast, and long. We can use Post-it notes as goal posts and mark our books. • Coach individual readers to outgrow early reading habits. • Give readers time in share to discuss, analyze their logs, and problem solve. • Talk directly to kids and have them set ambitious goals.
Partner Work	• Partners looking away from each other • Partners' conversations running out of steam quickly—one partner speaks, then the other, then they are "done"	• Have partners read aloud parts to each other that they love. • Teach partners ways to encourage and support each other ("Wow, you read so much more than yesterday!" "Oh, you are trying another book by James Howe—awesome!" "It's so cool that you have a plan for what to read next!" "That part was tricky for me too—let's look at it together!" "Let's recommend this book to ____!") • Do lessons on ways you can share your reading with a partner. • Model partner talk.
Ways Post-it notes are used to support/extend reading	• Kids have few or no Post-it notes in their books	• Teach readers to use Post-it notes as goal posts so they can read more. • Teach readers to mark cool parts they are dying to talk about. • Teach readers to mark parts that are confusing for them. • Be sure materials are easily accessible to students.

FIG. 9–5   A portion of the Building A Reading Life Progression. See the full progression in the online resources.

areas of focus for your specific classroom. We invite you and your colleagues, then, to collaborate and to revise, reflecting on your own teaching and creating a document that reflects your own priorities and meets the needs of your classroom and your community. The most important thing is not the specific indicators and suggestions on the progression; it is the power of a community of colleagues thinking and reflecting on their teaching and generating ways to make it even better—together.

Chapter 10

Tap the Power (and Avoid the Harm) of Large-Scale Data

S CHOOLS ACROSS THE COUNTRY are being told that "data-driven instruction" is a good thing, that this will improve teaching and learning across the school. People who actually work in schools, however, know that it is more accurate to say this: adopting a stance of data-informed instruction makes a difference, and that difference can be for the good or it can be for the bad. That is, there is no question that data can be a powerful tool—and this makes it very important that people take great care to use data in ways that work for the good.

In this chapter, I want to suggest ways to use reading data to support positive change in schools. I'll take up questions about how to use data to predict and track progress, to see otherwise hidden troubles, and to make instructional decisions that are informed by how children seem to be responding so far to current instruction. The schools we work with most closely take assessment seriously, collect many different kinds of reading data, and share data openly and generously. This means that we have been able to compare thousands of children as readers over the last decade. You'll collect and study some of your reading data within the context of your particular school environment. Other data, though, you'll want to be able to compare with data of children outside of your school, studying your peer schools to get a sense of how reading is going overall in your building relative to others. While we can't give you, here, the intense detail and analysis that we would if you were participating in AssessmentPro, the online database most of our schools use to track and share their data, we can highlight some of what we've learned from analyzing that data and encourage you to work in similar ways within your own district and region.

There is a great deal one could talk about in relation to data—how to collect data, what to collect, what's most worth analyzing, what trends we have seen. In this chapter, we'll tackle only the major questions that come up first when we engage with a school around the use of their data.

WHAT COUNTS AS READING DATA—AND WHAT KIND OF DATA SHOULD YOU COLLECT?

Standardized Tests

No matter what your standardized test is (AIR, ACT, PARCC, or SBAC; a Pearson-authored exam, a state-authored exam, or if you're an independent school, the ERB), it will provide you with some significant data.

If it's a state exam, that data may arrive late, months after children took the assessment. It may be that the results are accompanied by rhetoric suggesting incorrectly that this year's teacher is somehow responsible for the results. (David Berliner, who has researched that question extensively, suggests it is more accurate to suggest that this year's teacher is responsible for 10% of this year's results.) The data may be "supported" by misleading spreadsheets that suggest students struggled with a particular standard, when in fact what happened may have been that kids couldn't read (or didn't have time to read) that passage. Still, your standardized test can tell you something about how children do in relation to each other. It will give you the most useful data for children who read at or near grade level, because the texts will be normed to that level, and it will be progressively less useful and nuanced for children who read well below or well above grade level. So there is a lot to be cautious about with this kind of reading data.

There are two questions to ask before proceeding: How good is the new breed of tests? Do they assess what most people value in readers? Certainly, the goal of these new tests is to assess interpretive and analytic reading and not just literal comprehension. It is open to debate, however, whether higher-level skills can be tested through multiple-choice formats. Yet until tests are given to a sampling of students (as the NAEP is) or are given only during select years (as in most other high-performing countries), the price tag for tests that do not rely mostly on multiple-choice questions will be prohibitive. This means that it is likely that the United States will continue to rely on assessments that are, by design, somewhat constrained in what they can measure.

The Teachers College Reading and Writing Project has twice created online sites to collect and organize feedback on the new breed of assessment. Also, we often meet with test-makers and regularly advocate for better tests. We encourage you also to take the initiative and speak out on the question of whether your high-stakes assessment actually assesses what you and your colleagues value in reading, because this is an issue that affects the entire education landscape.

While encouraging the development of better tests, it is also helpful to learn ways to help students succeed on your current texts. Until the new breed of assessments came out, one could surmise that children who didn't pass the standardized tests were likely to struggle with the reading work of middle and high school. The results of those assessments could then be used as a red flag to alert parents and educators that a particular child needs extra support. This, of course, should be news to no one, however. The second reason that standardized test results merit attention is that if you were somehow *surprised* by which children did or didn't demonstrate proficiency, this suggests you need better methods for observing your children. That is, you can use the data as a catalyst to revisit how your school is implementing its formative and performance assessments. If you're doing thoughtful, calibrated assessments, you shouldn't be surprised by your standardized testing data. Scores of schools tell us that their results on high-stakes tests are 95% congruent with their expectations. If the results are wildly different for you, take a close look at your delivery of running records, your observations of students, and your other means for other performance assessing.

If a teacher says to me, for instance, that based on a running record, a child in third grade reads at level U, and then I note that the child didn't pass the state reading test, my thought would be, "I'm a little doubtful about that U! Let's do a running record together and talk with the child about the book she's reading, and see if she's really reading U with deep comprehension. Because something seems off here." That is, you can use your testing data to help you triangulate with other data and raise red flags when your data doesn't coincide.

If the test your students are taking distinguishes tasks so that some are based on reading fiction, poetry, or nonfiction, you may be able to see which child or which class of children was more successful with a particular genre. By the time you get the data, for instance, the child may have been in a rich poetry unit that came after the test, or perhaps the child moved up reading levels and now would be able to tackle those fiction questions more easily. Still, you can look for patterns. You can study question strands, and if there is a cluster of questions that your students seem to get wrong, it might be a red flag for you. When we studied high school data from the PSATs in one school system we know well, for instance, we noticed that students were missing virtually all the questions on the science and historical texts. That was a red flag that kids weren't reading enough authentic texts in the content areas. You may see similar trends, which you can investigate. Do *investigate*, however, because there can be mitigating reasons. For example, on one test that we know well, the last question on the test is usually poetry, so when the results which come back always say that kids do less well on poetry, teachers know that the problem could lie less in their children's abilities to read poetry and more in the length of the test.

There's one more way that testing data can be useful, and again, you have to be cautious about it. The data can let you track long-term trends and progress across your school, across grades, across classrooms, and so on. For example, perhaps there is a teacher whose students seem to make exceptional progress. Might it be worthwhile to observe what's going on in that classroom? Perhaps there are a few classrooms where the standardized test scores and students' running record levels are especially out of sync. Might it not be a good idea for someone who knows a lot about reading assessment to help those teachers inquire into the situation?

If your school recently adopted a reading workshop, you will want to watch the consequent changes in data. Schools connected with the Teachers College Reading and Writing Project show statistically significant evidence of our impact on student achievement. In many states, they are winning recognition as the best in the state, even, and certainly the high-implementation reading workshop schools in a district tend to outperform other schools. In a recent study conducted by an outside statistician, the statistical analysis of city-wide data over the past three years revealed that the Teachers College Reading and Writing Project implementation brings clear and consistent improvements in the performance of all students at all grade levels and within all populations. A broad range of statistical controls and robustness checks verified that these findings were not the result of bias in the types of schools enrolled or the students who attend the schools that adopt RWP work. Instead, results demonstrate with a high degree of confidence—99.9% in fact—that RWP programs bring measurable and independent improvements to student performance. In the next few pages, we'll explore some of this data. If you'd like more information on this study, you can refer to the full report on the TCRWP website.

In New York City, students in high-implementation Reading and Writing Project schools outperform other students by a wide margin, and this is true even on the recent CCSS-aligned tests which rocked New York State because of the exceedingly high percentage of students who failed the test. For instance, while only 27.2% of NYC students scored within the upper two proficiency levels in 2013–2014 (meeting or exceeding proficiency standards), 38.1% of RWP students achieved these levels. Of course, one would wish for results that are far better than those, but even before this particular CCSS assessment was given, parents and children across New York State were warned that pass rates would be exceedingly low. The fact that RWP pass rates were 38.1% when the city average was 27.2% is significant.

This trend is consistent for all available data and by all available subgroups (ELLs, IEP students, boys, girls, and so on): fewer RWP students fall below or lie at the basic standard than other students, while more RWP students achieve or exceed proficiency standards.

The chart at the right represents the comparison of scores on the brand new English language arts (ELA) exam (see Fig. 10–1). As you may know, New York State was one of several states to first to take the plunge into the newer versions of the Common Core standards exams. What you will notice first is that both years, significantly more students in Teachers College Reading and Writing Project schools scored at grade level standards. You should also view the growth from one year to the next as our students became adjusted to the new demands of the standards. In short, students in RWP schools outperformed their peers across the city and across the state, year after year—and this is true after controlling for all other factors.

The chart at the right shows the predicted ELA scores for median students at each grade level (see Fig. 10–2). This is based on the data of over 700,000 students across New York City, and it highlights the fact that students in Teachers College Reading and Writing Project schools continue to score higher on the new New York State exams at all grade levels.

The charts on page 163 represent the expected proficiency levels of students across multiple subgroups for the two most recent academic years, controlling for key factors (see Fig. 10–3). You might notice that student performance is likely to increase for students who belong to RWP schools. For example, students' chance of scoring in the upper two levels of proficiency (3 and 4) increases from 18.7% to 34.1%. These

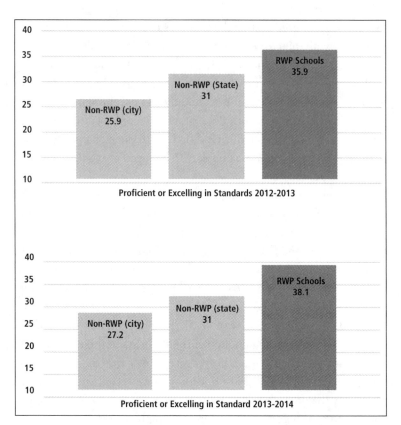

FIG. 10–1   Percent distribution of ELA proficiency by year for RWP, city, and state schools

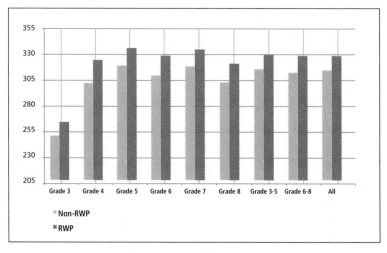

FIG. 10–2   Median scores at each grade level

charts also demonstrate that RWP work is successful with all subgroups of learners. With RWP involvement, ELL students and students with IEPs outperform their peers in other schools. In fact, RWP schools with Special Education Nest Programs scored double what other schools with the same programs scored.

Having said this, I need to caution you that there have certainly been a number of schools that implement a reading workshop and the scores don't shoot up for the first two or even three years. But after that initial time period, scores do usually increase substantially and they stay up. Research suggests that the adoption of new initiatives can result in an implementation dip, so you need to understand that that may happen.

So, yes, you will see patterns in your data, and you'll think about what the data shows. Here's why you have to be cautious with the data from standardized tests. First, the tests themselves are rarely exactly the same from year to year. In New York State, for instance, in certain years, our test changed dramatically, becoming much harder. The same has been true in many other states recently as higher, CCSS-aligned standards have been adopted. In those instances, you couldn't possibly compare the results from the year before that change to the year after it, because the results, while both purportedly showing proficiency on the state test, really measured proficiency on profoundly different exams. Then too, in the 2015 testing cycle in New York State, extremely high percentages of children opted out of the test, and this skewed data. Then, too, the data will be most useful for children who read near grade level. It's hard, for instance, for an English language learner who is in the early stages of English acquisition to show progress when all the texts are at and above grade level. There will be other data you collect that will show the progress along the way for those children, and once children are closer to reading at grade level, the tests will be more nuanced. Look at your patterns, ask yourself if the testing data makes sense to you, and above all, collect other data so that you can build a more complete picture about the reading growth of children, classrooms, grade levels, and your school.

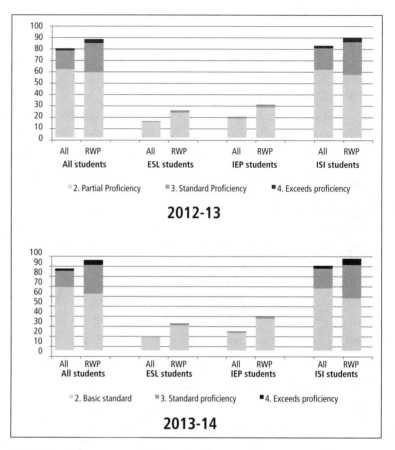

FIG. 10–3   Subgroups across two school years

Running Record Reading Levels

You'll certainly want to know how children in your class and school are moving up reading levels. By collecting and studying running record data, you can see when children are moving rapidly and when they are stagnating. You'll see pockets of trouble—a child who has stayed at level M for months and months or a whole class that is working at the same level. You'll see signs of progress—children who are moving steadily forward. You'll see responses to intervention, including how children are responding to an increase in small-group work during class or to outside-the-classroom supports.

My colleagues and I think that until students reach fairly high levels of proficiency, running records are a way to track a good proportion of what matters most in reading. The ability to read increasingly complex books seems to us to be a very big deal. This is especially important because our data suggests that if a teacher focuses on increasing the levels of text complexity in which kids can read with comprehension, fluency and accuracy, that work will have a spillover effect in ways that raise students' abilities to comprehend deeply (something that running records do not show) and on students' scores on high-stakes tests as well, which in this all-too-real-world of ours has real consequences. We have tracked the correspondence between students' running record scores and students' scores. It is very strong.

We suggest, therefore, that you not only collect and record reading levels systematically across the school, but also that this data (without student names on it) is transparent and available to parents and teachers across the grade levels. That way, a fourth-grade teacher can compare her students' fall reading levels with their earlier spring reading levels. This allows this teacher and everyone else to track summer reading growth and loss, measure growth or loss, and so on.

You'll get more information than simply a level when you conduct running records, of course, and I discuss that in Chapter 3. The data changes so rapidly that we suggest recording running record levels at the classroom level, so the teacher has a record of how children are evolving and she can build small-group instruction. There will probably be times during the year when that data is harvested at the school level. But in the interim, keeping track of the changing levels for each student will probably be too much, too finely grained, and too quickly changing for this to be recorded at the school level save for when the school decides to harvest the data.

Performance Assessment Data

It is important to realize that running records alone don't show the whole picture of what matters in reading instruction, and this is especially true once kids can read at levels K/L/M and above. A child might be able to say the words in a complex text with intonation and to answer a few low-level questions, but in today's world, kids are expected to be able to write on the test about the craft techniques an author used and the effect of those techniques on the story. A reader is expected to be able to synthesize several texts, to analyze the structure of texts, to note the way several texts advance a similar theme, how each text develops that theme differently, and so forth. The reason my colleagues and I place so much weight on performance assessments is that they, in fact, allow us to measure higher-level comprehension. Once readers can read with some degree of proficiency, this is what matters most.

Your performance assessment data should show how your readers are growing with high-level thinking skills. For us, that means the ones we trace on our Narrative Reading and Informational Reading Learning Progressions. The levels your students achieve will vary based on other decisions you make. For example, are students self-scoring (which will inflate scores)? Also, do you provide the students with bullet points that detail exactly what each question requires, or do you expect students to know that if they are asked to compare and contrast, they need to write about similarities and differences? Again, the presence of bullet points will lift scores. Maximum growth will be evident if you provide fewer scaffolds. One way or the other, however, you will want to be sure you see growth over time.

Our belief is that these performance assessments are most useful for readers themselves and that they'll trace their growth by literally moving their reading responses across a rubric that is a kind of yardstick for growth in a skill. Although you may decide to record students' levels for each skill assessed, using the reading progression as your tool, we can't say whether that is the best use of your time. It's clearly useful for readers to study their own reading responses and strive to improve them and for you to study student work to tailor instruction. Whether it's worth documenting each of these levels is not clear, because hopefully they are changing rapidly in response to instruction and student agency.

Informal Reading Data

You will gather this data as you confer and observe students and as you study work done by students, such as Post-its, logs, reading notebooks, and projects. Don't underestimate the value of the ordinary artifacts of reading that students produce daily in your classroom. Students' reading logs will not only give you insight into their volume, but they will also show you what kinds of books children are choosing and whether they are following up on series, authors, and genres. Their daily Post-its and notebook entries will give you insight into their thinking and their habits. Their projects will tell you a lot about their engagement and growth. Education innovator Tony Wagner once advised me to encourage schools to assess what matters most. Doug Reeves gives similar advice, telling schools that if they don't want to be measured solely by their standardized test, then they should be sure to measure what they *do* value. In some schools, that might be evidence that children are becoming avid readers. In others, it might be that they are applying lessons learned in their books. In still others, it might be that they can recommend books well. In any case, use the artifacts that are the daily fare of reading workshop to see how reading is going for your students.

HOW DO YOU LEARN THE MOST FROM YOUR READING DATA AND APPLY THAT KNOWLEDGE WISELY?

The first way to make data-informed instruction a force for good is to make sure the data that is at the center of that equation is data you value. The next way to make data-informed instruction a force for good is to make sure that people are willing to learn from the data. No one is going to learn from data if it is perceived as being used to fire teachers or to humiliate them. David Rock, an expert on cognitive coaching, points out that human beings are still animals, and as such, we have animal instincts. If we are afraid for our lives, we close down. We become guarded, shortsighted, less flexible, and less insightful. We have less peripheral vision, and we become less intelligent. It is crucial, then, that any school that hopes to use data-informed instruction as a force for good become accustomed to a stance that welcomes people saying "I don't know how to . . ." "I worry that I'm not . . ." "I need help on . . ." "I notice I'm not doing a good job at teaching my kids to . . ." "I'm thinking I might try . . . I don't know if it will work."

Some school leaders reward not the teachers who claim to know a lot but rather those who are willing to be risk takers and public learners. One school I know makes a huge fuss not over the teachers who are willing to mentor other teachers (valuable as that is), but instead, it makes a fuss over the teachers who ask to be mentored on one dimension or another of their teaching. Roland Barth, who started The Principals' Center at Harvard, once came to Teachers College and said to the 200 TCRWP principals who had gathered to learn from him, "Here is my question to you. What are you learning about this year? More specifically, *when you are in school* this year, what are you learning about? And most of all, *who knows about that learning?*" He went on to stress that schools need to be places where everyone's learning curve is off the charts. The principal needs to be learner-in-chief. Dignifying the stance of "I have so much to learn. I'd really like to think with others so I can get better at this," is one of the best things a literacy leader (whether that person is officially or unofficially a leader) can do.

So your first work is to actively foster a culture of continuous improvement. Your approach to data, then, will be one that supports transparency and reflection and response. Everyone is on a journey. The data can help raise questions and can inform discussions and further investigations and observations that end up affecting routes, detours, and return trips.

I've already written about one of the important lenses you'll want to apply, which is to look for inconsistencies in your data so that you don't rely too heavily on certain assessment data that may be skewed. If there are large discrepancies between your running record data, for instance, and how it correlates with testing data, you'll probably want to look at your implementation of running records. If your performance assessment data seems to you to suggest that your children are summarizing well, discerning main ideas, and supporting those with details, but they didn't do well on short responses or on those tasks in your standardized test, you might want to rethink your expectations (How good is good enough?) and to compare expectations across those tasks.

Look as well for subgroups of children who may not be flourishing, and be open to the messages you can glean from your data. Let the data shock or surprise or nudge you. Otherwise it isn't doing any good at all. When looking at movement in reading levels, for instance, how are your English language learners progressing? Are children with IEPs meeting the goals laid out in their IEPs? Do you have gender trends? In your school, is there more movement in some classrooms or grades than others? Are reading logs and notebooks showing that one particular teacher is getting kids to read a lot more than in other classrooms?

Hopefully, in your school, you have strong, courageous teachers who are willing to speak up and admit that the data results are not what they wish they were. If one teacher comes to a study group and says, "My kids' results on that performance assessment were horrible! I wanted to throw half of them out and pretend those kids had been absent today, but figured instead I'd bring the whole sad story to you," that makes it okay for everyone to say, "I feel the same," and "Let's think what we can do differently."

There is a lot of research that suggests that when teachers across a grade level are willing to observe the teachers whose children are making a lot of movement on one kind of data or another—when teachers use the data as a reason to go study the work that teacher is doing—those schools become places of continuous learning. Of course, when you do go to observe in classrooms where the data shows movement, be careful to be alert to different kinds of data. Sometimes, for instance, a teacher may do a lot of specific test prep that helps children move forward on the tasks of the state test (that year), but meanwhile, the children haven't read a book all year, their reading logs and notebooks are bereft, and they can't hold a passionate, literary conversation. So either target specific data and ask "How did you specifically achieve that?" or look across data for overall healthy profiles of readers, and ask "How did you achieve all of that?"

WHAT SYSTEMS MIGHT YOU USE TO REPRESENT YOUR DATA: WHAT CHARTS AND GRAPHS ARE MOST USEFUL?

Some data is best viewed as artifacts. Reading responses, for instance, can't really be captured well just by a number. You and your students will want access to the actual responses to see how to best improve them or to use some as exemplars. Some teachers, especially primary teachers, like to keep on file the actual running record, so they can see children's patterns with MSV. Studying the cueing systems a student relied on for individual miscues and self-corrections will yield much more information about the way that student is processing text than simply knowing the number of errors or self-corrections overall.

Other data is best viewed as visual representations. If you enter your reading levels and testing data into a spreadsheet, for instance, you'll be able to generate a variety of helpful graphs and charts. Schools we work with closely tend to enter their data on AssessmentPro, the aforementioned online database that the Project has developed. The advantage of that system is that it not only lets teachers enter data on their own readers, but it lets them know how that data compares with thousands of other readers. We'll look at some of the charts and diagrams that teachers and schools have found particularly helpful.

Independent Reading Levels (Compared to Benchmarks)

Figure 10–4 will assist you in determining overall reading levels and reading health. You might choose to show a class or a grade level or the overall school. Figure 10–5 is a graph that represents the overall reading levels broken up not by grade, but by subgroups of male, female, children with IEPs, and English language learners from a sample school. In comparing the two charts, you might notice, for example, that the ELL students have made significant progress or that the girls have made greater gains than the boys. This kind of graph will help you get a big picture of needs and progress and plan your supports, study groups, and staff development. Sometimes you may need this data for district or state accountability as well.

Instead of school-level charts, you may also wish to look at reading levels by grade level. Figures 10–6 and 10–7 show the results of a fourth-grade and a fifth-grade classroom, indicating the distribution of students at, below, and above benchmark.

September 2014 Benchmark Levels

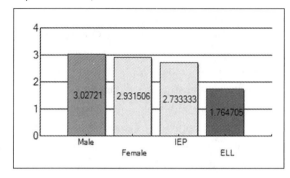

FIG. 10–4 September 2014 benchmark levels

March 2015 Benchmark Levels

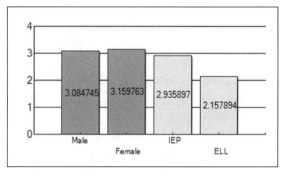

FIG. 10–5 March 2015 benchmark levels

Fourth Grade—March 2014

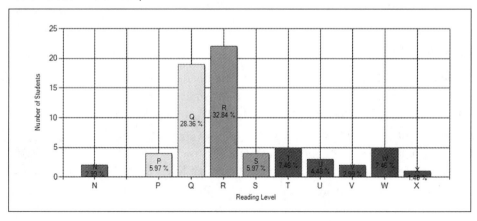

FIG. 10–6 Fourth grade 2014

Figure 10–8 narrows the lens of data even further, revealing the reading levels in one specific classroom. This gives a teacher an instant bird's-eye view of how the children in his care are progressing. In AssessmentPro, when you click on these kinds of charts, it will pull up individual students. The information in this chart, along with an individual student's data, allows teachers to easily consider seating, partners and book clubs, and small-group work.

Figure 10–9 provides a classroom-level overview of all of the assessments students have taken. This overall class data reveals important patterns and next steps. For example, in studying this chart, it is clear that the class has mastered letter sounds and identification. However, the class is below benchmark in reading level. This data indicates that the students have strengths in phonics but not comprehension. They've become word-callers, and the instruction in this classroom needs to address the significant, classwide need for instruction focused on comprehension and moving up the levels of text complexity.

Figure 10–10 provides a different way of looking at classroom-level data. It shows two assessment windows and students' independent reading levels plotted against the benchmark levels in each assessment window. If you examine the chart, you'll notice that the level 1 students made significant progress. The level 2 students stayed fairly consistent, but one student moved up to a level 3. The chart allows you to track the students in your classroom from one benchmark period to another. This allows you to see in a concrete way the progress (or lack thereof) made by your students.

Testing Data

It can also be helpful to compare the correlation between reading levels and proficiency on standardized tests, as shown in Figures 10–11 and 10–12. For instance, it can be helpful to know whether or not children reading level R in the fall of fourth grade are likely to pass their state test in the spring. You might also want to find out, if you investigate children who do pass the test, what levels most of them were reading. Knowing this data helps you not be surprised

Fifth Grade—March 2015

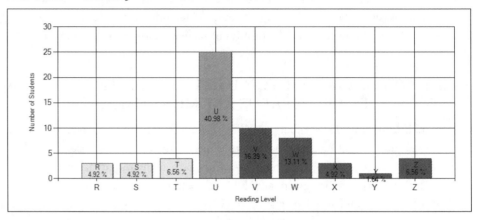

FIG. 10–7   Fifth grade 2015

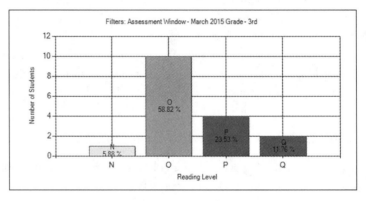

FIG. 10–8   Third grade, March 2015

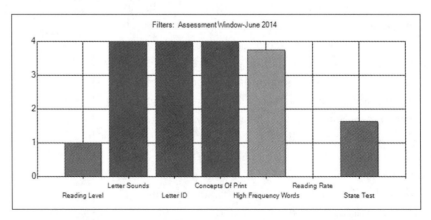

FIG. 10–9   Class chart with all assessments

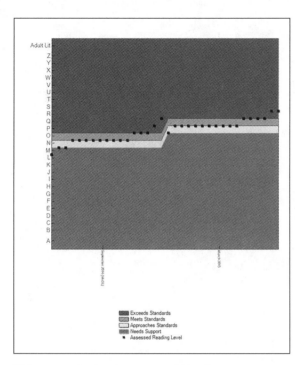

FIG. 10–10   September 2014 and March 2015

*Colors displayed reflect reading level benchmarks.

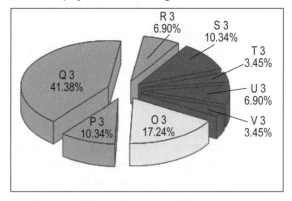

FIG. 10–11   A look at fourth-grade students who received a 3 on the state test for June 2014: What were their September reading levels?

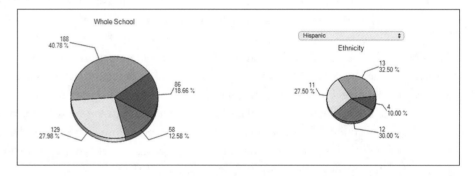

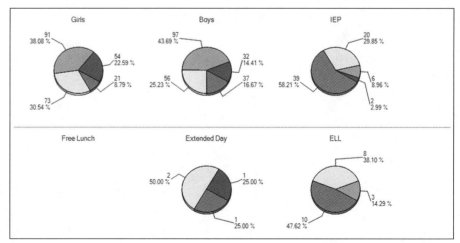

FIG. 10–12   Disaggregated data

by your tests. Instead, you can predict children's current status, take steps to give extra support, and be realistic about the challenges the test may pose to particular readers.

The charts let you get a bird's-eye view of how the school is doing in terms of testing data—looking at overall proficiency. If you examine two or more charts together, you can also see growth over time. You could, of course, create these same charts for a classroom or grade or to display other reading data. You'll notice that we color-code, using the same colors systematically so that the colors themselves alert teachers to signs of achievement and of trouble.

Finally, the report in Figure 10–14 is one of the most helpful things to get into a teacher's hands. This table lists the performance of each student on the prior year's state exam and allows teachers to track reading levels across time. It allows teachers to see, at a glance, whether or not students are progressing and how quick that progress is. It also helps teachers identify where there may be discrepancies between assessed reading levels and state tests, indicating a need to study a student's performance and reassess. This chart is also helpful for thinking about students who can be grouped together for small-group work. You might, perhaps, notice a group of students who have been stuck at level Q for some time and pull them together to scaffold their transition to level R together, introducing the new work at that level of text complexity and setting up the students to work together to tackle those new challenges.

This data gives us a great deal of information that can shape our instruction and policy. However, it's important to keep this information in perspective. David Berliner, a renowned educational psychologist, recently visited us at Teachers College and spoke to us about the wisdom of making data-*informed* decisions rather than data-*driven* decisions. The data doesn't make the decision for us—our professional judgment does. But the data informs our decisions, focusing our attention on the issues that need it most. Data launches questions that begin an investigation and conversation that can help us to hone our teaching and meet our students' needs in more targeted ways than ever before.

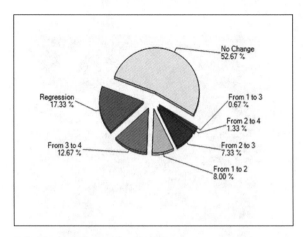

FIG. 10–13 Whole school

Student Name	ELA 2014			Sep 2014		Nov 2014		Jan 2015		Mar 2015		Jun 2015	
	Raw	Level	Perf	IRL	Bench	IRL	Bench	IRL	Bench	IRL	Bench	IRL	Bench
ALISA	369	4	Low	Q	3 *	R	3 *	S	3 *	T	4		
MATTHEW				O	2	O	2	P	2	R	3		
EARL	345	3	High	R	4	S	4	T	4	U	4		
ANGELIKA	307	2	Med			O	2	P	2	R	3 *		
ANDREW	304	2	Med	Q	3 *	R	3 *	S	3 *	T	4 *		
MARVIN	363	4	Low	R	4	S	4	T	4	T	4		
WENDY	341	3	Med	O	2 *	P	2 *	Q	2 *	R	3		
VINCENZO	286	1	High	O	2 *	P	2 *	P	2 *	Q	2 *		
DARIA	369	4	Low	P	3 *	R	3 *	R	3 *	S	3 *		
ELIZABETH	354	3	High	Q	3	R	3	Q	2 *	T	4		
GRACE	354	3	High	Q	3	R	3	S	3	T	4		
SEBASTIAN	324	3	Low	P	3	Q	3	R	3	S	3		
KYLA	327	3	Low	P	3	Q	3	R	3	S	3		
MARIA	307	2	Med	O	2	P	2	Q	2	S	3 *		
VINCENZO	376	4	Low	S	4	T	4	T	4	U	4		
JADEN	291	2	Low	R	4 *	R	3 *	S	3 *	T	4 *		
JANIECE	291	2	Low	O	2	O	2 *	P	2 *	R	3 *		
JOSEPH										R	3		
VALERIE	311	2	High	O	2	O	2	P	2	Q	2		
ALEXANDRA	304	2	Med	P	3 *	P	2	R	3 *	S	3 *		
VALERIYA	321	3	Low	O	2	O	2	P	2	R	3		

FIG. 10–14   At-a-glance class report

Narrative Reading Learning Progression

	Grade 2	Grade 3	Grade 4	Grade 5	Grade 6
	LITERAL COMPREHENSION				
Orienting	I preview a book's title, cover, back blurb, and chapter titles so I can figure out who is in the story and what might happen. I ask myself, "What big problem might the character face?"	I preview a book's title, cover, back blurb, and chapter titles so I can figure out the characters, the setting, and the main storyline (plot).	I preview to begin figuring out the characters, setting, and main storyline. I also use what I know about this kind of fiction to set me up to look for things that will probably be important (e.g., in historical fiction, I plan to learn about the time period; in mystery, I'm alert to clues).	I preview the book to begin figuring out not only the setting and characters, but also the possible themes. I am alert, early on, to clues about the themes and issues that will become significant. I also use what I know about this genre to set me up to look for things that will probably be important (e.g., in fantasy, I'm expecting to learn about the characters' quest).	I preview the book, paying attention to information from the cover and the first chapter/prologue to orient me to the story's characters, conflicts, and possible themes. I also use what I know about the genre and author to build expectations for the characters, the setting, the plot, and the theme.

	Grade 2	Grade 3	Grade 4	Grade 5	Grade 6
			LITERAL COMPREHENSION		
Envisioning/ Predicting	As I read, I make a movie in my mind, picturing what's happening. Sometimes the mental movie comes mostly from the words, and then I add in details that are from the pictures. Sometimes I start with the pictures and add in what I learn from the words. I predict what will happen next, drawing on earlier parts of the text.	I make a mental movie as I read. I imagine the setting, the characters, the events, and characters' reactions to them. I predict what the main character will do, say, and think (and how the character will react to things) based on earlier parts of the text. I can explain the reasons for my predictions.	I make a mental movie as I read, trying to experience the story as if it is real life. I draw on earlier parts of the text to add to the details in my mental movie. That is, I draw on what I know about characters' traits and motivations, the setting, and the events to envision and predict. I also use what I know from real life about what these places tend to look and feel like. I also base my predictions on my sense of how stories tend to go and can explain my reason for my predictions.	I make a mental movie as I read, trying to experience the story as if it is real life. I draw on earlier parts of the text to add to details in my mental movie of the characters, setting, and events. I look for clues to help me know the mood and the feel of the actions. I also use what I know from real life about what these places tend to look and feel like. I also base my predictions on what I know about this genre of fictional texts. I predict not just what will happen to the main character, but also to the secondary characters across multiple plotlines.	I realize that envisioning matters as a way to picture unfamiliar people and places in the books I read. As I read, I draw on films and television shows, real life, my knowledge of this genre, as well as scenes from other books to fill in the movie I'm making in my mind and to make sense of what happens. I base my predictions on what has happened in the text, my knowledge of the genre, and details I've gathered about story elements.

	Grade 2	Grade 3	Grade 4	Grade 5	Grade 6
		LITERAL COMPREHENSION			
Monitoring for Sense *Fitting the Pieces Together*	When I'm reading, I know to say "Huh?" when I'm not sure what the text is saying, and I go back to reread.	I expect the story to make sense, and when it does not, I use fix-up strategies such as rereading and asking questions, including the 5 Ws. To regain my grip on the storyline, I recall the sequence of events, often trying to sort through what the main character really wants, the problems he or she confronts, and ways the character rises to those challenges.	I read, expecting the parts of the story to fit together in such a way that I can understand why things are happening. When things don't seem to fit—if they feel as if they come out of nowhere—I check to see if I missed something important.	I realize that in more complicated stories, I sometimes have to wait longer for the parts to fit together or for things to become clear. If I'm unsure how a new chapter or part fits with the earlier story, I'm aware that my confusion may be caused by gaps in time or place or shifts in point of view. I may be reading a subplot that brings a minor character on stage. At these points, I may reread to figure out how the parts of the story fit together, but I may also read on with questions in mind.	I anticipate that a story may contain more than one plotline, timeline, and point of view. I am alert to moments when I begin to feel confused as I read, and I check to see if I'm keeping track of those plotlines and shifts in time or perspective. I use a repertoire of strategies to reorient myself, including going back to the beginning of the chapter and the end of the last chapter.

	Grade 2	Grade 3	Grade 4	Grade 5	Grade 6
	LITERAL COMPREHENSION				
Story Elements: Time, Plot, Setting	When I read, I think about how the part I'm reading now fits with what happened earlier.	I keep track of what is happening and how much time goes by in a story. Is it one day? One week? One year? I can tell where the story takes place.	As I read, I'm alert to the structure of a story, aware that it is not always told sequentially. I note sequence words (e.g., *Two weeks earlier . . . Thinking back, I remembered . . .* or *A week later . . .*) that clue me in to the presence of a backstory or gaps in time between scenes. I know that when the story goes backward, it is usually to give me important information. I can tell when the setting changes.	As I read, I'm alert to ways in which more complicated stories are not always told sequentially. I note backstory, gaps in time between scenes, flashback and flash-forward, and subplots. I'm aware that subordinate characters may support subplots. I can make sense of unfamiliar settings.	I expect time to be structured in challenging ways across a story, and I am alert to the small clues that time is changing, including verb tenses, white space, or changes in setting. I realize sometimes the reasons a character *says* he or she did something may not be the truth; readers are supposed to figure this out. I notice how the setting affects other story elements.

	Grade 2	Grade 3	Grade 4	Grade 5	Grade 6
	LITERAL COMPREHENSION				
Establishing Point of View	When I'm reading a story, I can keep track of who is talking.	If a character is telling the story (in the "I" voice), I ask, "Who is telling this story?" "Who is the narrator?" If this is not in the first person, I ask, "Who is the main character? Whose point of view am I hearing?"	If a character is telling the story (in the "I" voice), I ask, "Who is telling this story?" "Who is the narrator?" If this is not in the first person, I ask, "Who is the main character? Whose point of view am I hearing?"	I expect that no matter whose point of view the story is told from, many characters' perspectives will be important to understanding this story. I expect that characters' or narrators' accounts or opinions may be different, and I will have to figure out how to make sense of those different perspectives.	In third-person narratives, I pay attention to how closely the narrator is connected to one or more characters' inner thoughts. In first-person narratives, I'm on the lookout for ways the author has made the narrator unreliable or limited in his or her point of view. I also know I will have to do more work to read for others' perspectives, but I trust the author has left clues for me to do so.

	Grade 2	Grade 3	Grade 4	Grade 5	Grade 6
	LITERAL COMPREHENSION				
Fluency *The sound of my voice*	I aim to make my reading voice sound like I'm talking or storytelling. I can do that out loud or in my head. I scoop up a bunch of words at a time. I do this in ways that make the story easy to understand.	I can read in my head and aloud in ways that help my listeners and me understand the story (e.g., changing my voice to show dialogue or a character's feelings). The new work I'm doing now is that I can do this even when I'm reading longer sentences.	The way my voice sounds (whether in my head or out loud) is mostly based on what is going on in the story and on what each character is thinking, feeling, or experiencing. It might also be based on what I've learned about characters and the kind of people they are.	I pay attention to what's happening in the story and make sure my voice reflects the mood of the scene, the emotions of the characters, and the kind of people they are (slowing down when it gets scary, for example). I do this with both prose and poetry.	As I read aloud or in my head, I pay attention to what's happening in the story or poem and make sure my voice reflects the mood of the scene and the emotions of the characters (slowing down when it gets scary, for example). I'm also alert to changes in mood and pace and make some choices about the sound of my voice based on my ideas about the story and characters.

	Grade 2	Grade 3	Grade 4	Grade 5	Grade 6
	LITERAL COMPREHENSION				
Punctuation and Sentence Complexity	When I read dialogue, I can make it sound like a character is really talking. I use punctuation as a road signal that helps me know when to pause.	When I read dialogue, I can make it sound like a character is really talking. I use punctuation as a road signal that helps me know when to pause. I can do this with longer, more complex sentences now.	Punctuation steers my reading, but it is not something I have to think a lot about. However, when sentences are complex, the punctuation can help me figure out how to read them.	Usually punctuation just gives me subtle signals as to how to read, but sometimes it's used in unusual ways, in which case I ask, "How does the author probably want this part to sound?" Also, when reading complex sentences, I adjust my voice to show that some parts of the sentence (like this part) are meant as small additions. How does the author want this to sound?	As I read aloud, I use the punctuation to guide my voice, especially in dialogue. I also know that when I read longer sentences, the punctuation indicates ways I should change my voice (as when a sentence poses a question at the end or leads to an exclamation). I am also aware that an author might use punctuation to create mood and adjust my voice accordingly.

	Grade 2	Grade 3	Grade 4	Grade 5	Grade 6
	LITERAL COMPREHENSION				
Word Work *Word Solving*	When I don't know what a word means, I reread the words before and after and try to think of a substitute word that means the same thing. I make sure the word I try makes sense, sounds right, and looks right, before I keep reading. I use what I know about letters and sounds to read the beginning, middle, and end of a word.	When I try to figure out the meaning of a tricky word or phrase, I read around the word, looking for clues to what it might mean. I also look inside the word, relying on what I know about parts of words. I know that authors play with words. I ask, "Could this word or phrase mean something funny or special (e.g., 'The path snakes . . .' or 'His eyes were glued to the clock . . .')?"	When I try to figure out the meaning of an unknown word or phrase, I read around it. I use clues from the story to help me think about whether the word is positive or negative and to notice whether there is an example later that can help me figure it out. I use what I know about prefixes, suffixes, and root words. When the author has used language in unusual ways—maybe describing one thing by comparing it to another—I figure out what the phrase probably means.	When I try to figure out an unknown word or phrase, I continue to ask questions, such as "Is the word positive or negative? Moderate or extreme? An idiom? Is there an example? Might there be a secondary meaning for the word or one I'm not familiar with?" I use all I know about phonics, Greek/Latin root words, prefixes, and suffixes. I expect to see similes and metaphors, especially when the author compares the emotions of a character to something else or tries to establish the tone or mood of a setting.	When I try to figure out an unknown word or phrase, I continue to ask questions, such as "Is the word positive or negative? Moderate or extreme? An idiom? Is there an example? Might there be a secondary meaning for the word or one I'm not familiar with?" I use all I know about phonics, Greek/Latin root words, prefixes, and suffixes. I'm alert to the use of metaphor, simile, personification, and so on because I know these are ways authors show tone, emotion, nuance, and relationship.

LEARNING PROGRESSIONS, GRADES 2-6

	Grade 2	Grade 3	Grade 4	Grade 5	Grade 6
	LITERAL COMPREHENSION				
Building Vocabulary	I recognize a whole lot of words in a snap and am always learning more "snap" words. *"snap"= high frequency	When talking about a character, I reach for the more accurate word for a trait.	I not only use precise language to describe characters, I also use literary language—words like *genre*, *narrator*, *setting*, and so on—when talking about story elements.	I speak and write about books in academic ways (not only using words for story elements but also for craft moves, e.g., focus, perspective).	I use specific academic and literary terms when speaking and writing about books, such as point of view, symbolism, multiple plotlines, and so on.

	Grade 2	Grade 3	Grade 4	Grade 5	Grade 6
			LITERAL COMPREHENSION		
Retelling/ Summary/ Synthesis *Within Text*	As I read, I see that a story has parts and I can talk briefly about a part that I just read. After I read another part, I can put the parts together and talk about them. At the end of a story, I can retell it by saying something about the main character(s) and the big events, in order.	As I read a novel, I can think back over and briefly summarize the parts of the story that relate to what I'm reading. When I finish a book, I can briefly summarize it in a way that shows what I know about the story and its story elements. I talk about the characters— their traits and wants—and recap especially important events using sequence words. Alternatively, I may talk about the problem and solution. If the character learned a life lesson, I mention that, most likely at the end of my summary.	As I read a novel, I can think back over and briefly summarize the parts of the story that relate to what I'm reading. When I finish a book, I can briefly summarize it in a way that shows knowledge of the important aspects of the story, including the story elements. I talk about the characters—their traits and wants—and recap important events using sequence and cause-effect words or using a problem-solution structure. I talk about the big ideas/themes that the story teaches.	I make decisions about how to summarize a story. Sometimes I name a theme and then summarize the most important parts of the story that support that theme. Sometimes I trace the significant changes in a character. I stay focused on the parts of the story that are most important to the kind of summary I am giving, leaving out parts that are not.	I am able to summarize a story by looking at it from a bird's-eye view. When I do this, I see the pieces of the story as blocks that fit together. I can summarize by focusing on a character, a conflict, a theme, and so on. When I do this, I sort out moments of the story that support my idea about the character, conflict, theme, and so on. I explain why these parts matter. I angle and limit my summary to the parts of the text that support my idea.

LEARNING PROGRESSIONS, GRADES 2–6

	Grade 2	Grade 3	Grade 4	Grade 5	Grade 6
			INTERPRETIVE READING		
Inferring about Characters and Other Story Elements *Character Traits*	I notice big things that a character says, does, and thinks, and I think about what this might show about a character's feelings. I think about whether the main character meets with a problem, and if so, how the character solves it.	I can develop ideas (theories) about the kind of person a character is. I know this means talking about a character's traits (personality), and I'm careful not to confuse the way a character feels for a trait. When a character makes a decision and does something, I can usually figure out why, based on what I know of the character and what happened earlier.	I keep in mind that characters are complicated. For example, I might think about how the character is different on the outside than the inside or in one part of the story or in one relationship than another. I'm interested in what *really* drives a character to make the decisions or take the actions he or she takes. What does the character *really* want? I know that a character's action will sometimes seem small (closing a door) but will actually signal a deeper meaning.	I can see places in a story where the characters are not what they seem at first. For example, the character might say or act as if he or she doesn't care, but readers see signs that he or she really does. That is, I see hidden sides to characters. I know that what drives the character (his or her motivation) can be complicated. There may be several things that drive or pressure a character, and often he or she is pulled in conflicting ways.	I continue to develop theories about main and minor characters, thinking how they are affected by other story elements such as the plot, setting, issues, and conflicts.

	Grade 2	Grade 3	Grade 4	Grade 5	Grade 6
	INTERPRETIVE READING				
Character Response/ Change	I can talk about how a character changes and why.	I notice how a character changes across the story (for example, the character's feelings, traits, motivations, or behaviors might change). I think about what key moment(s) in the story caused the character to change.	I notice how a character changes across the story. I think about many possible causes of these changes, including other story elements (the problem, the setting, other characters, and so on). I know that what a character learns about life can often be the theme of a story.	I can notice small, subtle changes in characters in addition to more obvious ones. I know that the causes of these changes may also be subtle or complicated. I think about how a character's change is important to the whole story. I am aware that characters can represent ways that people can be—the bully who is insecure, the boy with feelings locked inside—and that when a character changes or learns something, this can teach readers about ways that people like that character deal with challenges or issues.	I can distinguish between temporary changes and changes in the character's perspective. I consider how inside and outside forces cause characters to change. I understand that a character's changes can be symbolic and can connect to bigger themes in the story.
Supporting Thinking with Text Evidence	When asked, I can point to the part of the text that gave me my ideas.	I support my ideas with details from the text.	I support my ideas with details from several parts of the text. I discuss how those details actually *do* support my ideas.	I support my ideas with specific details and quotes from several parts of the story. I select these because they are strong and they actually do match my points. I discuss how those details and citations support my ideas.	I support my ideas and claims with specific details from the story, and I can evaluate this evidence for which is strongest.

	Grade 2	Grade 3	Grade 4	Grade 5	Grade 6
	INTERPRETIVE READING				
Determining Themes/ Cohesion	At the end of a story, I can name the lesson the character learned. I might say this in a word or a phrase.	At the end of a story, I can say a few sentences about the big life lesson (the theme) that a character has learned.	I read, asking, "What's this story really about?" and I come up with tentative ideas that I test as I read on. I have an internalized checklist of what makes a good interpretation— that the theme applies to most of the story, that it suggests a life lesson. I know that often the theme becomes most clear at the end, but then I can look back and see the theme trace through other parts, such as times when a character makes a decision or realizes something big.	I read, asking, "What seem to be the big themes of this story?" I can figure out a couple of themes that are especially significant, noting which are best supported. To think about these, I tie together what several significant parts of the story seem to mean. I know themes are shown not only by the content of the text, but also in the way it is written.	As I read, I gather up parts of the story that support particular themes. I also actively look for themes that seem more hidden. As new parts of the story suggest new meanings, my understanding of a story's theme becomes more nuanced. When I am considering which themes are most important in a story, I weigh which are most strongly supported across the story. I note literary devices that support the theme, such as symbolism.
Supporting Thinking with Text Evidence	I can point to and read a part of the story to support my ideas. This is usually the ending.	I can talk and write about parts of the story that support my thinking.	After deciding on a theme that is important to a story, I can look back on the story, finding textual details from across the text that support that theme.	I can cite details that support each of several themes, keeping straight which details support which themes. I don't just summarize—I also sometimes quote. I know the exact words used can help convey the theme.	I notice where the author develops each of several themes. I can sort details to show which go with which theme, and I can rank which details seem most important and discuss why.

	Grade 2	Grade 3	Grade 4	Grade 5	Grade 6
	INTERPRETIVE READING				
Comparing and Contrasting Story Elements or Themes	When I read books that go together, I can think about how they're the same and how they're different. When one story is written in different versions, like when a fairy tale is written differently in different cultures, I can compare them.	When I read books in a text set or series, I can talk about how the major events across the two books are similar or different. I can also talk about how other story elements are partly the same and partly different—like the characters, setting, or the life lessons (the themes).	I can discuss similarities and differences in stories, noticing theme. For example, "Is the theme similar but different? How is it developed differently?" (E.g., in one, a girl saves her friend, in another, the boy saves a dog, but both show that friendship takes risk.) I can also compare other aspects of the stories. I ask myself, "Do characters from the texts react in similar ways to an issue?" I can compare and contrast two different versions of the same text (e.g., comparing the book and the movie version of a text).	When I'm shown several texts in the same genre that explore the same theme, I can explain how that theme is the same and different across the texts. I can also explain how the theme is developed differently in the two texts and discuss author's craft to do so. I think, "Does one use a symbolic object to show the theme? Does another show the internal thoughts of the villain to convey that villains aren't all bad?"	When I'm shown several texts in the same genre that explore the same theme, I can explain how that theme is the same and different across the texts. I can also explain how the theme is developed differently in the two texts and discuss author's craft to do so. I think, "Does one use a symbolic object to show the theme? Does another show the internal thoughts of the villain to convey that villains aren't all bad?" I can also compare and contrast different multimedia versions of texts and discuss the effects these versions have on the development of the theme.
Supporting Thinking with Text Evidence	I can point to and talk about parts from each book to explain my ideas.	I can give details from each book to explain my ideas.	I can support my thinking with exact details and examples from the text.	I can support my thinking with exact details and examples from the text, including specific quotes.	I continue to support my thinking with exact details and examples from the texts, including specific quotes.

	Grade 2	Grade 3	Grade 4	Grade 5	Grade 6
	ANALYTIC READING				
Analyzing Parts of a Story in Relation to the Whole	When asked to talk about the importance of a part in a story, I think about how that part fits into the sequence of events. I can talk about what came before and what comes after. When asked, I can talk about how a problem is introduced in the beginning of a story (if it is) and how it is resolved by the end.	When asked to talk about the importance of a part of a story to the whole, I use what I know about story structure to name what part of the story it is: the setting? The problem? I can also think about how the part is important to the whole story. If it is the setting, for example, I think "How is this particular setting important to the story?"	When asked, I can take one part or aspect of a story—an event, setting, minor character—and talk about the importance of it to the whole story. To do this, I use what I know about how one part of a story connects to another or to the whole story (e.g., a scene may explain a later choice a character makes or show that the character is changing; a setting creates a mood or explains the tension).	When asked, I can take one part or aspect of a story—an event, setting, minor character—and talk about the importance of it to the whole story. To do this, I use what I know about how one part of a story connects to another or to the whole story (e.g., a scene may explain a later choice a character makes or show that the character is changing; a setting may be symbolic). I can also discuss if this part supports a larger idea or theme in the text.	The new work that I am doing now is that I am able to take even a small part—a sentence, a stanza—and think about the role it plays in creating the whole. I can think about the part's importance structurally and also ask how it develops larger ideas. I ask, "Does this part help to develop a theme, a character, the mood?" I also ask, "How?"

	Grade 2	Grade 3	Grade 4	Grade 5	Grade 6
	ANALYTIC READING				
Analyzing Author's Craft	I know that authors use precise words to show (not tell) feelings and to show how characters are behaving. I use this to help me create a clear picture in my mind. I notice when the author uses special language, and I stop and think, "What does the author want to show?"	I know that just as I write different leads to a story, choosing the one that works best, authors do that, too. And just like I elaborate on the most important parts, authors also do that. I notice when the author has done something that stands out—elaborated on a part, used an image or line repeatedly, used figurative language, begun or ended a text in an unusual way—and I think, "Why did the author do that?" My answer shows that I think about how the author's choice supports something important to the story.	I know that just as I write different leads to a story, choosing the one that works best, authors do that, too. And just like I elaborate on the most important parts, authors also do that. I notice when the author has done something that stands out—elaborated on a part, used an image or line repeatedly, used figurative language, begun or ended a text in an unusual way—and I think, "Why did the author do that?" I might begin to think about what the author's words show (e.g., a character's traits or what a story is really about).	When parts of a text stand out, I think about the technique the author used and the goal that the author may have been aiming to achieve. I use literary language to name these techniques and goals, using phrases like *The author uses flashback to increase tension,* or *The author repeats a line to support the theme.* I can talk at length about techniques and goals. One way to do this is to discuss how the text would have been different had the author made different choices: "Had he or she written . . . the effect would have been different because . . ." and so on.	I bring my knowledge of writing craft to my reading, thinking not just about the characters, setting, and problem(s), but how the author introduces those, and noticing the choices/literary techniques/language an author uses across a story. I think about what tone, mood, and effect is created by the author using certain words. This also means thinking about the shades of meaning of a word and the way it is used or repeated.

LEARNING PROGRESSIONS, GRADES 2–6

	Grade 2	Grade 3	Grade 4	Grade 5	Grade 6
	ANALYTIC READING				
Analyzing Perspective	When asked about a character's perspective, I can talk about how a character feels in a scene.	When asked about a character's perspective, I can talk about how the character feels about something important to the story (another character, the setting, an event). I use what the character does, says, and thinks to support my ideas.	When asked about a character's perspective, I can talk about how the character feels about something important in the story (other characters, the setting, an event). I use everything I know about the character's life experience (where he or she is from, what groups he or she belongs to) to explain why the character feels this way.	When asked, I can talk about how different characters have different perspectives about events, characters, settings, and issues. I consider the characters' different life experiences as well as the roles they play in their lives (daughter, friend, student, and so on) to compare and explain their perspectives.	When asked, I can compare characters' perspectives about key story elements. I consider the characters' different experiences and roles in the story to compare and explain their perspectives. I also notice when characters may represent types of people and typical perspectives, or when characters develop perspectives that are surprising.

	Grade 2	Grade 3	Grade 4	Grade 5	Grade 6
	ANALYTIC READING				
Critical Reading *Growing Ideas*	I can read even just one picture or page and have a lot of ideas and questions. Sometimes I think up answers to those questions or find them in the story.	When I read fiction, I get ideas and information about the world. I might be learning about places, growing ideas about families, or thinking about my friendships.	I can choose to let the story I'm reading spark ideas as I read. Those ideas might be about the world, other people, a topic I read about, or the story itself. If appropriate, I develop my ideas by paying attention to the text. I use my ideas as a lens for rethinking or rereading.	Sometimes I read a story with the lens of my own interests. I might weigh the pros and cons of rural life, for example. I find the parts of the book that develop my inquiry and often end up reading other texts that relate, synthesizing information from more than one place.	As I read, I am in a constant conversation with the text, letting what I know shape how I think about the text and letting what the text says shape how I think and act. I am open to being changed by what I read, including how I judge myself and others, how I make decisions about my actions, and how I perceive things.

LEARNING PROGRESSIONS, GRADES 2–6

	Grade 2	Grade 3	Grade 4	Grade 5	Grade 6
	ANALYTIC READING				
Questioning the Text	I have opinions about the story. I notice when someone does something mean or unfair in a story.	I notice when characters' experiences don't match my own, and I think about how they are different. I notice when something happens in a text that is not fair, and I think about why it is not fair and what could have happened instead.	As characters come to terms with issues, I know that the author is helping the reader to come to terms with these issues also. I read what an author writes, asking, "What is it you want me to think/feel?" I also think about what an author wants me to think or feel, and I am willing to be critical. I ask myself, "Do I agree?"	I consider what a text is saying about an issue and what values the text seems to show as *good* ones. I think about whether I agree or disagree. I can talk back to texts, critiquing how characters are portrayed or what actions they take.	I question stories I read, thinking especially about social issues and stereotypes. I think about what a text might be getting me to think about these issues, and I ask myself if I agree. I can read against the text, considering other possibilities for characters and events.

Informational Reading Learning Progression

	Grade 2	Grade 3	Grade 4	Grade 5	Grade 6
			LITERAL COMPREHENSION		
Orienting	Before I read, I use the title, illustrations, back blurb, headings, and table of contents (if there is one) to predict what I will learn from reading this text. When asked to, I can show the parts of the text that led to my predictions.	Before I read, I preview the text(s). I also study the table of contents (if there is one), the title, introductions, headings and subheadings, and illustrations. I do this to decide what to read and also to predict the major subtopics I will learn about. I also notice if this is an expository or a narrative nonfiction (biography) text to organize myself to get started learning from the text (e.g., "First I'll probably learn . . . Then I think I'll learn . . .").	Before I read, I preview the text(s). I also study the table of contents (if there is one), headings, introductions, topic sentences, text features, and so on. I can recognize a common structure in the text (such as chronology or cause-effect or compare and contrast). I rely on all my previewing to help me predict how the text will go, and when doing research, to decide what to read and in what order. My previewing helps me decide how to organize my note-taking or thinking. I ask, "Will I organize what I am learning into subtopics? Cause and effect?"	I'm experienced enough with complicated texts to know the structure and main idea of a complex text may be revealed slowly. Before I read, I preview the text(s). I use transition words and phrases to cue me into how the text will be structured. I not only think about how the text is structured (compare-contrast, claim and supports), but also about whether this is a genre I know—a biography, a research article, an overview, or an argument. My knowledge of genre shapes my expectations. My previewing also helps me structure my note-taking and thinking. When I anticipate learning about several subtopics and main ideas, I ready myself to synthesize information on several bigger categories. I also know I'll probably incorporate information from several texts.	Before I read, I preview to see how the text(s) is organized and what challenges it will present. I also think about how *expert* it is—looking at things like the vocabulary and the diagrams. I make a plan for reading the text, including possibly reading something else first or alongside it. My previewing gives me tentative ideas for what the central idea might be or the author's point of view. My previewing also helps me plan for note-taking and thinking. I consider how much I should read before pausing to take notes. I'm experienced enough with complicated texts to know that the structure may change across the text, that the headings may not guide my understanding, and that the bigger ideas might be revealed slowly.

May be photocopied for classroom use. © 2015 by Lucy Calkins and Colleagues from the Teachers College Reading and Writing Project. *Reading Pathways, Performance Assessments and Learning Progressions: Grades 3–5* (Heinemann, Portsmouth, NH).

	Grade 2	Grade 3	Grade 4	Grade 5	Grade 6
	LITERAL COMPREHENSION				
Envisioning	As I read, I add what I am learning from the words in the text to what I see in the illustrations. The words I read help me say more about different parts of the illustrations on the page.	I read narrative and expository texts differently. As I read narrative nonfiction, I picture what I'm reading as a mental movie (like when reading fiction). When I read expository text, I create images/models in my mind (boxes and bullets, timelines, diagrams). I add on to these images as I get more information.	I continue to read expository and narrative texts differently, creating mental movies or images/models in my mind. As I read, I draw on details from the text and my prior knowledge to add to what I'm picturing. When reading expository texts, my mental models (boxes and bullets, timelines, diagrams) act as places to catch all of the new information I am getting.	I'm flexible as a reader of nonfiction. When reading narrative nonfiction, I can make a mental movie similar to the way I would as a fiction reader, drawing on details from the text and my prior knowledge. With expository text, I envision a combination of mental models to capture and organize what I am learning (outlines, boxes and bullets, diagrams). I revise and add to these models as I get new information.	As I read, know that I need to picture what I'm learning. Depending on the text, I might make mental movies of characters/ subjects in scenes or try to picture procedures or sequences (e.g., the process of photosynthesis) as a series of steps, perhaps picturing a flowchart, list, or diagram. As the concepts I read about become more complex, I sometimes seek out extra information from outside sources to clarify my models of the information.

	Grade 2	Grade 3	Grade 4	Grade 5	Grade 6
			LITERAL COMPREHENSION		
Monitoring for Sense	When I'm reading a nonfiction book and I have a hard time remembering what it is about, I know that means I have to DO something. I usually reread, use the pictures and headings to help, and try to teach what I'm learning to someone else or myself.	When I can't keep the main ideas straight or figure out how the information goes together, I reread, stopping after each chunk to review what I have read. I ask, "Is this a new subtopic or does it add onto what I have already learned?"	I read, expecting the parts of the text to fit together in such a way that I can understand the main ideas. To check my comprehension, I try to make sure that as I move from part to part, I ask, "How does that part fit with my overall picture of the topic?" When a part feels disconnected from the rest of the text, I reread to see if I missed something or I read on, carrying questions.	I realize that in more complicated nonfiction texts, I sometimes need to read on with questions in my mind. The texts I'm reading now will sometimes contain many different parts, and it can take work to figure out how those parts go together. I especially try to think about what is most important and how the parts fit into that.	I anticipate that nonfiction will make sense, and when it stops making a lot of sense (which I can tell because I can't retell it, remember it, or name the main ideas), I DO something. I might talk to a partner, I might reread, I might outline or diagram the parts of the text. I don't just read on, letting the words flow past me.

	Grade 2	Grade 3	Grade 4	Grade 5	Grade 6
	LITERAL COMPREHENSION				
Fluency *The sound of my voice*	I aim to make the reading voice inside my head smooth and to sound like I'm talking (or teaching someone). Sometimes I need to reread to make my voice sound that way.	I still aim to make the reading voice inside my head help me understand the text. The new work I'm doing now is that I can do this even when I'm reading longer sentences.	When I read, the voice inside my head (or my read-aloud voice) helps me understand the text. That voice highlights the big points that are important, tucks in things that are less important, shows when things are in a list, and shifts from an explaining voice to a storytelling voice as the text requires.	As I read nonfiction aloud or in my head, I try to use my voice to add meaning to the text. I read emphasizing the big points. Perhaps I have in mind what great science and history videos sound like to guide my reading.	As I read nonfiction aloud or in my head, I try to use my voice to add meaning to the text. I have in mind what great science and history videos sound like, and I try to read like that, emphasizing the big points, using my voice to link the supporting examples within the big points.

	Grade 2	Grade 3	Grade 4	Grade 5	Grade 6
			LITERAL COMPREHENSION		
Punctuation and Sentence Complexity	I use punctuation as a road signal, letting me know when to pause.	I use punctuation to know when to pause. Punctuation also tells me when the sentence is a question or is especially important.	Punctuation steers my reading, but it is not something I have to think a lot about. However, when sentences are complex, the punctuation can help me figure out how to read them.	Usually punctuation just gives me subtle signals as to how to read, but when it's used in unusual ways, I ask, "How does the author probably want this to sound?" When the sentences are complicated, I adjust my voice to show that some parts of the sentence (like this part) are meant to be subordinate.	I pay attention to punctuation as well as words to help figure out the mood, tone, and changing pace of a piece. I notice when punctuation is used to separate, and when it is used to connect.

	Grade 2	Grade 3	Grade 4	Grade 5	Grade 6
	LITERAL COMPREHENSION				
Word Work *Word Solving*	When I don't know what a word means, I check the illustrations, reread the words before and after, and try to think of a substitute word that means the same thing. I make sure the word I try makes sense, looks right, and sounds right before I keep reading. I read all the way across the word and use what I know about letters and sounds.	When I still don't recognize a word even after I have tried to say it, I look to see if the author has given a definition or an example to help me figure out the meaning. If not, I reread to remember what that part of the text is teaching me and to figure out what kind of word it seems to be. I ask, "Is it a thing? An action?" I substitute another word and reread to see if it makes sense. I also look inside the word, relying on what I know about prefixes and suffixes.	When I try to figure out the meaning of an unknown word or phrase, I look to see if the author has given a definition, an example, or a synonym. If not, I reread to remember what the text is teaching me and also to figure out what kind of word it is. I try to substitute another word that is similar and reread to check that it makes sense. I also use what I know about prefixes and suffixes and root words to solve the word as best I can.	When figuring out an unknown word or phrase, I continue to use context, looking for examples, synonyms, and definitions in the text and features. Sometimes the meaning I know doesn't work in the text. I think, "What else might this word or phrase mean?" I continue to try to substitute words or phrases that are similar and check that they make sense. I also use what I know about prefixes, suffixes, and root words to solve the word.	When I try to figure out an unknown word or phrase, I look first to see if there are examples or definitions in the text that will help me figure out the meaning. I continue to try to substitute words or phrases that are similar and check that they make sense. If needed, I look up the meaning outside the text. I also use all I know about root words, prefixes, and suffixes.

	Grade 2	Grade 3	Grade 4	Grade 5	Grade 6
	LITERAL COMPREHENSION				
Building Vocabulary	I know that learning about a topic involves learning some of the words that are used by experts in that topic. I use those words to teach others about the topic. I recognize a whole lot of words in a snap and am always learning more high-frequency words.	As I read about a topic, I keep track of the new words the text is teaching me (the ones that seem most important) and use them to teach others about the topic.	I know that learning about a topic means learning the vocabulary of the topic. I know there are words that represent concepts (e.g., *revolution, adaptation*). Those words require a lot of thinking to understand them. As I read, I keep learning more about each concept word. I also try to accumulate more technical vocabulary associated with the topic. I meanwhile take the risk of using this new vocabulary to talk and write about the topic.	I know that learning about a topic means learning the vocabulary of the topic. I know there are words that represent concepts (e.g., *revolution, adaptation*). Those words require a lot of thinking to understand them. As I read, I keep trying to learn more about each concept word. I also try to accumulate more technical vocabulary associated with the topic. I meanwhile take the risk of using this new vocabulary to talk and write about the topic.	As before, I expect to accumulate technical vocabulary from nonfiction, especially new science and historical terms. As I read, therefore, I keep glossaries or notes, and I actively incorporate new terms into my talk and writing. As I continue to develop and deepen my vocabulary of a topic, I particularly notice secondary meanings of words and connotations of words.

	Grade 2	Grade 3	Grade 4	Grade 5	Grade 6
			LITERAL COMPREHENSION		
Main Idea(s) and Supporting Details/ Summary	I can say the big topic a text (or part of a text) teaches me. I can name information about that topic, which I learn from parts of the text.	As I read, I ask myself what the text is mostly about. To figure out the main idea, I see if there is a pop-out sentence that captures it. I can say the main idea in more than just a word and am careful to name the main idea of most of the text. I can also choose important supporting details (or points) that go with the main idea. I summarize briefly, leaving out unimportant things.	As I read, I often pause to summarize as a way to hold onto what I'm learning, saying the main idea(s) of that part and linking it/them to related points. As I do this, I select points that are especially important to the idea. I can use the primary structure(s) in the text to help me grasp what it mostly teaches (e.g., if it is organized as a main idea or supporting points or a claim and reasons, I can use either structure to help me determine importance and select supporting details). I am careful to keep my own opinion separate from the ideas presented in the text.	I can figure out several important main ideas in a text, and I'm aware that sometimes those ideas thread through the whole text instead of being located in chunks of it. I can sort all the details in the text and weigh their importance so that I can also discuss important details that best support each of the main ideas. I am careful to keep my own opinion separate from the ideas presented in the text. I also avoid mentioning minor details.	I can figure out several important main ideas in a text and weigh and evaluate which of those ideas seems most significant in the text. I am careful to include in my summary only what the text says, and none of my own opinions, ideas or judgments.

	Grade 2	Grade 3	Grade 4	Grade 5	Grade 6
	INTERPRETIVE READING				
Inferring Within Text/ Cohesion	I can talk and write about how information goes together in a text, such as how one event leads to another or how doing each step in a "how-to" can create a result.	I can talk and write about information and ideas that hold parts of the text together. Usually this means I talk about the relationship between cause and effect or about the things that happened first and next or main ideas and examples. I might also talk about the reasons for something or the kinds of something. I use words that show connections to do this (*because of, as a result, a few years later, after*).	I can discuss relationships between things in scientific, historical, or technical texts. This usually means discussing examples, causes, parts, reasons, results, or kinds of a topic. I reach for specific and academic terms.	Not only can I discuss major relationships that occur across a discipline-based text, but I can also come up with my own ideas about relationships/ interactions between events, ideas, and key concepts. I can do this even when the author hasn't laid out these relationships. I use academic and domain-specific vocabulary to do this, especially terms that help me to be more logical (*nevertheless, however, in addition, similarly*).	Not only can I see how different threads in a text tie together, but I can also track one thread across a text. I can think and come up with my own ideas about these relationships, even when the author hasn't set them forth. I can do this in ways that link information from separate parts of the text. I'm careful to choose exactly the right terms to explain my ideas, considering both a word's dictionary meaning and its connotations.

	Grade 2	Grade 3	Grade 4	Grade 5	Grade 6
	INTERPRETIVE READING				
Cross Text(s) Synthesis	When I read several books (or parts of one book) on the same topic, I add what I learned from one text or part of text onto what I learned from the other text or part of text in no special order.	When I read two texts (or parts of a text) that teach about the same subtopic, I can find the information on a subtopic from both texts (or parts of one text) and put that information together.	As I read two or more texts (or parts of a long text) on a topic, I can collect and merge information and ideas from both texts (or parts of a long text) in a way that makes a new organization for the combined information. If there are ways to categorize the information on the subtopic, I sort information from both texts into a category.	As I read texts on a topic, I collect information and ideas by subtopic and form categories with my own headings. I sort what I am learning about the subtopic under those headings. This means the organization of my learning may not match the organization of the original texts. I am aware that sometimes one text contradicts another. When this happens, I think, "Which author is saying which points?" I wonder whether the differences come from the author's point of view (e.g., might differences come from one being firsthand and one secondhand?).	I organize what I'm learning about a topic into subtopics—categories, points, or main ideas. I can keep track of the major ideas each individual author contributes to my overall understanding of the topic/issue. I am aware that sometimes one text contradicts another. When this happens, I think, "Which author is saying which points?" I wonder whether the differences come from the author's point of view (e.g., might differences come from one being firsthand and one secondhand?). I also consider whether an author has vested interests that explain the differences.

	Grade 2	Grade 3	Grade 4	Grade 5	Grade 6
	INTERPRETIVE READING				
Comparing and Contrasting	When I'm given two books or pages on a topic, I can point out general ways they are the same and the ways they are different (e.g., "One has more information than the other." "They both talk about eating habits.").	I can identify when a text is structured as a compare-contrast. When asked to compare and contrast the information that two texts (or parts of a text) teach about a topic, I can point out and discuss similarities and differences in the specific information each text presents.	When asked to compare and contrast how several texts (or parts of a text) deal with one topic, I can talk about similarities and differences in the information and also in the treatment of the topic, including the craft techniques used, the focus, and the perspective. I can also notice if there are different perspectives (e.g., is one a primary firsthand account and the other, a secondary source?).	I can compare and contrast different texts or parts of texts, considering content, perspectives, and/or craft and structure.	I can compare and contrast different texts in more than one way. I can consider how the information overlaps, reinforces, or contradicts across texts, as well as what perspectives authors bring. I can also compare *how* authors present their ideas and information—especially how their craft and structure makes their meaning or message more powerful.

SAME?

DIFFERENT?

Similarities?
differences?

FOCUS?
PERSPECTIVE?

★ content
★ perspectives
★ craft & structure

AND...
ALSO...
BUT...
HOW?

LEARNING PROGRESSIONS, GRADES 2–6

	Grade 2	Grade 3	Grade 4	Grade 5	Grade 6
ANALYTIC READING					
Analyzing Parts of a Text in Relation to the Whole	I can talk about the order of the events or steps in a text. I can say how a part fits into an order or how it says more about the main topic. I can answer the question of what came before or after.	I can talk about how a part of a text I am reading fits with the content of the rest of the text. I can say, "This is more on the same topic or subtopic," or "This just turned to a new topic or subtopic," or "This shows what happens next." I can talk about the order of events or steps, answering questions about what comes before or after and about what caused an effect. In texts that have text boxes, graphs, charts, and illustrations I think about the ways these parts fit with the whole. When I write about these connections, I rely on the way the content of the part goes with the content of the whole.	I can talk about why an author included one part of a text (a text box, a chart, an anecdote). To do this, I draw on some predictable ways that parts tend to be important to the main idea, such as a paragraph may be an example of a main idea or a different perspective on that idea. Sometimes the part is important to the structure: a solution to a problem, an effect of a cause, an answer to a question. When thinking about how one part is important in an argument, I'm aware of how an author uses reasons and details to support claims/points.	When thinking about why a part is important to the text, I think not only structurally about how the part goes with other parts, but I also think about how the part advances the author's main ideas/claims. I check whether the part in question illustrates an idea/claim, raises a new perspective, or shows an implication of an idea. I can use academic terms to talk about this. When a part of the text feels extraneous, I can talk about its relationship to the main ideas/claims (background, implications, another perspective). When I am reading an argument, I can explain which details go with which points.	I am able to take even a small part of a text—a sentence, a few lines, a text feature—and think about the role that the part plays in the whole text. I ask myself, "What does this part contribute? How is it connected? Does this part engage the reader, or does it help to develop a central idea? How?" I use my knowledge of authors' techniques to talk about this. I can also study one aspect of a text (an event, an individual) and discuss how this part of the text was introduced and developed (e.g., through anecdotes). When I am reading an argument, I can explain which claims are most strongly supported and which details are most convincing.

	Grade 2	Grade 3	Grade 4	Grade 5	Grade 6
			ANALYTIC READING		
Analyzing Author's Craft	I notice when the author has done something obvious in the text (bold words or graphics).	I know that authors of informational texts make craft decisions with readers in mind. I especially notice when the author has done something that stands out—a repeating line, an illustration, and I think, "Why did the author do this?"	I know that authors of informational texts make craft decisions with readers in mind. I can elaborate on why the author used these techniques. One way I do this is to ask, "How would the text be different without this?" I can note the craft techniques that have been used and can say, "The author has used (this technique) to accomplish (this goal)." For example, "The author has made a comparison to help readers grasp an idea."	I know that authors of informational texts make craft decisions with readers in mind. I use academic language to name these goals and techniques, using terms like *surprising statistics* and *suggests the significance of a point*. I can talk at length about these. I ask myself, "How would the text have been different had the author made different choices? Had she instead . . . , the effect would have been different. For example . . ."	I bring my knowledge of writing craft to my reading, thinking not just about the ideas in the text, but about how the author introduces these ideas, noticing the choices/techniques an author uses across a text, and describing these using academic language. I think about what tone, mood, and effect is created by authors using certain words. This means thinking about the different meanings of a word or the surprising uses of words or phrases to stir up emotions in the reader.

	Grade 2	Grade 3	Grade 4	Grade 5	Grade 6
			ANALYTIC READING		
Analyzing Perspective	I notice who the author of a text is and who the subject of the text is (if there is one).	I notice if there is an obvious point of view in a text—like if the text is being told from the point of view of an animal or of a specific person.	I can recognize if the author is writing as if he or she was present at an event (a firsthand source) or if he or she was not present (a secondhand source). I am aware that the difference in those points of view will result in differences in the accounts.	I can notice when two texts on the same topic are written from different points of view, and notice ways in which the content (or the way the texts are written) will be different because of those different points of view. I think specifically about why the narrator thinks and feels as he or she does. Might the person's perspective come from life experiences, group membership, role, time period? For example, I notice if one text is a diary in the voice of a general and another is a diary from a foot soldier, and I think about how their roles led them to want different things.	I am aware that the author brings out his or her perspective by choosing to highlight particular incidents, voices, issues, and stories. I think about how this might relate to the author's vested interests and roles.
					I am also aware of multiple points of view in the text and can separate them from the author's point of view.
					I can also point to places in the text where the different points of view and perspectives have led to particular word choices.

AUTHOR

SUBJECT

ME

FIRST HAND

SECOND HAND

GENERAL

vs.

SOLDIER

A vs. B

How do I know?
How is it shown?

tasty ✓
nutrition

flavored
sugar ✗

	Grade 2	Grade 3	Grade 4	Grade 5	Grade 6
	ANALYTIC READING				
Critical Reading *Growing Ideas*	When I read even just one picture or page, I have a lot of ideas and questions. For example, "How does that bug get food?" Sometimes I think up answers to those questions or find them in the book.	When I talk or write about a text (or a text set) I not only summarize it, I also grow my own ideas. For example, I might ask a question and try to answer it.	I develop my own ideas about what I have read. Those ideas might be about values, the world, or the book. My ideas are grounded in text-based information and ideas, and I draw on several parts of the text(s). I raise questions and larger theories about the topic or the world. I read and reread with those questions in mind, and this leads to new insights.	I can synthesize several texts in ways that support an idea of my own. I select the points that do the best job of supporting my idea(s). For example, "How will this author add to or challenge my argument?"	I can synthesize several texts in ways that support ideas of my own. I select the points from different texts that do the best job of supporting my points.
		When I am asked to apply what I have learned to a real-world problem or situation, I can do so.	My reading helps me to develop my ideas. I think and sometimes write things like "Is this always the case?" or "Could it be . . . ?" I am not afraid to think in new ways.	I think and sometimes write things like "Is this always the case?" or "Could it be . . . ?"	I develop my own theories and claims as I research. Some of these may be debatable questions. I sometimes agree or disagree with authors completely or partially. I don't reject a text because an author disagrees with my ideas, but instead let it affect my thinking.
		I notice when what I'm learning doesn't match my prior knowledge/ experience, and I think about what to make of that.		I can apply what I have learned and my own ideas to solve a problem, make an argument, or design an application.	I can apply what I have learned and my own ideas to solve a problem, make an argument, or design an application.

LEARNING PROGRESSIONS, GRADES 2–6

LEARNING PROGRESSIONS, GRADES 2–6

	Grade 2	Grade 3	Grade 4	Grade 5	Grade 6
	ANALYTIC READING				
Questioning the Text	I have opinions and reactions about what I am learning.	When I disagree with an idea in a text, I still try to think about it, and I also talk back to it. I also notice if something is described positively or negatively, and I think about how it could have been described.	I think about what implications my theories and what I have learned might have for real-world situations. I can apply what I have learned. I'm aware that texts can be written to get readers to think and feel something about an issue or topic, and I can say, "I see what you want me to think/feel, but I disagree."	I consider what a text is saying about an issue, idea, or argument and whether I agree or disagree. I weigh and evaluate a text for how convincing and reliable it is. I consider who wrote the text and what the author might gain from the text. I can talk back to texts.	I question nonfiction I read, thinking especially about other texts on the topic. I weigh and evaluate how logical, convincing, and reliable a text is. I take into account who wrote the text as part of this judgment, thinking about how reliable and unbiased this author might be. I consider how this relates to issues of power.

Reading to Learn: Grasping Main Ideas and Text Structures
Grade 3: Nonfiction, Unit 2

Readers, today you will read three texts to learn more about motor racing. Read texts 1 and 2, then answer questions 1 and 2 on a separate sheet of paper. Then read the rest and finish up.

1. Summarize the article, "Start Your Engines."

   When summarizing, remember to:
   * write about the main idea
   * include supporting details
   * keep your summary ½ page or less
   * leave out what's not important.

   Main Idea(s) and Supporting Details/Summary

2. Both "Start Your Engines" and "Cars with Wings" include information about an important subtopic—the design of Formula One cars. Explain briefly what these texts teach about the design of Formula One cars.

   When synthesizing (fitting together information from both texts), remember to:
   * focus on the subtopic
   * include information from each text that fits with this subtopic.

   Cross-Text(s) Synthesis

3. Summarize the story, "Racer Danica Patrick."

   When summarizing a story, remember to:
   * include important story elements (for example, character, setting, problem)
   * include important details from across the story
   * leave out unimportant parts.

   Retelling/Summary/Synthesis (Narrative)

4. Write briefly about one idea you have grown from these texts.

   When writing about your idea, remember to:
   * grow an idea about information or ideas in the text
   * explain your idea and include details from the text to support it.

   Critical Reading: Growing Ideas/Questioning the Text

Please remember that including the bullets after the question is a teacher's option. As students become more familiar with these performance assessments, you delete this scaffold. A version without bullets is available on the online resources.

SELECTED ASSESSMENT EXAMPLES

Text 1

Start Your Engines: All about Motor Racing

Ready, Set, RACE!

1   Imagine a stadium filled with cheering people. In the middle of the stadium is a giant track. Cars race around the track, going so fast you can hardly see them. This is car racing, one of the most popular sports in the United States today.

5   There are three main kinds of car racing: stock car racing, Formula One racing, and drag racing. They are different in the way the cars race and in the design of the cars. But all race cars are built to support racing!

Stock Car Racing

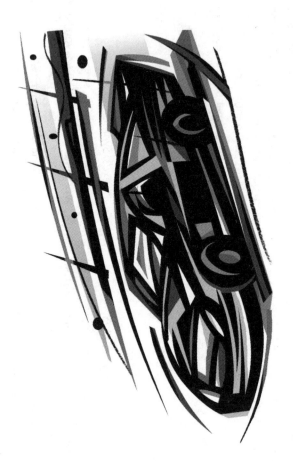

Stock car racing is the most popular kind of car racing in the United States. Stock cars race on oval tracks. Cars often circle the track hundreds of times in a single race.

10   Stock cars are designed like everyday cars you see on the street. They have doors that open like street cars, and the driver sits on one side. But, stock cars are much faster than street cars. Some stock cars can drive as fast

Text 1: Start Your Engines: All about Motor Racing ◆ PAGE 1

as 200 miles per hour. That's about four times faster than street cars usually go!

15

Formula One Racing

Formula One (F1) cars, like stock cars, race on tracks, but the tracks are longer and irregularly shaped. F1 cars race around a track dozens of times before a winner crosses the finish line. These cars can drive faster than 220 mph.

20

F1 cars look a bit different from stock cars. They look a little like small planes. The driver sits in the middle of the car to keep the weight in the center. That keeps the car stable. The driver gets into the car through the top, not through a side door. The seats are made to fit the driver's body exactly. When the cars are going full speed around turns, the drivers use a lot of energy to keep the car from flipping.

25

Text 1: Start Your Engines: All about Motor Racing ◆ PAGE **2**

May be photocopied for classroom use. © 2015 by Lucy Calkins and Colleagues from the Teachers College Reading and Writing Project from Units of Study for Teaching Reading (Heinemann: Portsmouth, NH).

SELECTED ASSESSMENT EXAMPLES

May be photocopied for classroom use. © 2015 by Lucy Calkins and Colleagues from the Teachers College Reading and Writing Project. *Reading Pathways, Performance Assessments and Learning Progressions: Grades 3–5* (Heinemann, Portsmouth, NH).

Drag Racing

The way that cars race in drag racing is different from stock car and F1 racing. Drag cars race in a straight line. The fastest drag race is the Top Fuel race. In the Top Fuel race, cars can drive as fast as 330 mph. They use a special kind of fuel, or gas. Top Fuel races are louder than a jet plane. People cover their ears as a Top Fuel car drives by. Top Fuel races are also very short. Tracks are only 1,000 feet long. Races are over in four seconds!

Any kind of car can race in a drag race, but most drag racing cars are long and narrow. Just before a drag race, drivers do a burnout. The driver spins the back wheels. The wheels spin so fast that the tires melt on the track. The melted tires help the car start fast when the race begins.

30

35

Crossing the Finish Line

Even though these kinds of car racing are different, they have one thing in common. The fans! Car racing is a very popular sport. Millions of people watch car racing each year. With the excitement and danger of car racing, it's easy to see why so many people love to watch.

40

Photo credit: Formula One Racing car © mevans/iStockphoto.com, drag racing car © jacomstephens/iStockphoto.com

Text 1: Start Your Engines: All about Motor Racing ◆ PAGE 3

Text 2

Cars with Wings

1   Formula One (F1) cars have large "wings" on the front and back of the car. The wings on the front of the car are small and low to the ground. The wings on the back of the car are larger and higher up on the car. These "wings" aren't actually wings. In fact, they work the opposite way that wings do. They help keep the car on the ground instead of in the air.

5   At high speeds, wind pushes down on the wings and keeps the car from flipping.

Photo credit: Natursports/Shutterstock.com

Text 2: Cars with Wings ◆ PAGE 1

Text 3

Racer Danica Patrick

When Danica Patrick was ten years old, she and her sister drove gokarts around a track their their dad put together. They swerved around cans and bottles their dad placed as obstacles for them. Although her sister soon lost interest, Danica kept practicing. Some people told her to stop because gokarts were for boys. People got angry at her father for letting her enter gokart races. She had other troubles, too. Once, she crashed into a wall, flipped the go-kart over, and set her coat on fire.

1

5

Text 3: Racer Danica Patrick ◆ PAGE 1

By the time she was in high school, it was clear that racing was more than just a childhood dream. There was no place near her home to get the training she needed, so her parents agreed that she could go to England to train. At age sixteen, it's not easy to study halfway around the world from your home, but Danica wasn't afraid.

In England, Danica came in second in a very tough event called the Formula Ford Festival. This was the best that any woman had ever done in that race. In 2008, Danica became the first woman to win an IndyCar race.

Photo credit: Daniel Huerlimann/Shutterstock.com

Text 3: Racer Danica Patrick ◆ PAGE 2

SELECTED ASSESSMENT EXAMPLES

Informational Reading Self-Assessment Rubric

	Level 2	Level 3
Main Idea(s) and Supporting Details/ Summary	☐ I named the topic (but not the idea) that the text tells about. ☐ I told information I learned from different parts. MAIN TOPIC *Animal Families*	☐ I wrote about the main idea(s). ☐ I wrote about the important details. ☐ I wrote a brief summary (½ page or less). ☐ I left out any unimportant information. *Mothers do a lot to care for their young.* MAIN IDEA
Cross Text(s) Synthesis	☐ I added what I learned from one part of text onto what I learned from another part of text. ANTS BUGS *This tells MORE about...*	☐ I put together information on a subtopic from different texts or parts of a longer text. AND... BUT...

(continues)

Informational Reading Self-Assessment Rubric (continued)

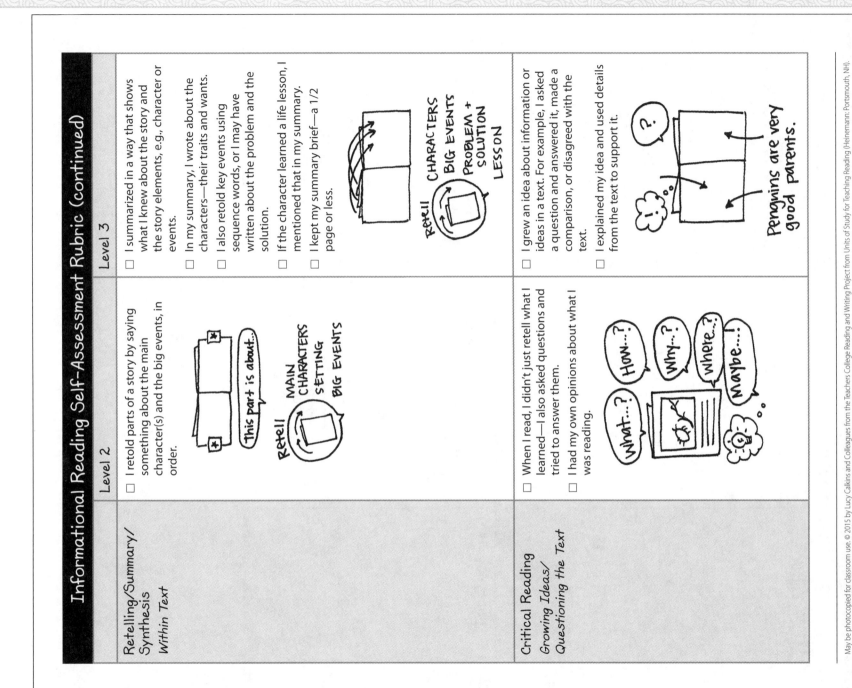

Retelling/Summary/Synthesis
Within Text

Level 2

☐ I retold parts of a story by saying something about the main character(s) and the big events, in order.

RETELL
MAIN
CHARACTERS
SETTING
BIG EVENTS

This part is about...

Level 3

☐ I summarized in a way that shows what I knew about the story and the story elements, e.g., character or events.

☐ In my summary, I wrote about the characters—their traits and wants.

☐ I also retold key events using sequence words, or I may have written about the problem and the solution.

☐ If the character learned a life lesson, I mentioned that in my summary.

☐ I kept my summary brief—a 1/2 page or less.

RETELL
CHARACTERS
BIG EVENTS
PROBLEM + SOLUTION
LESSON

Critical Reading
Growing Ideas/Questioning the Text

☐ When I read, I didn't just retell what I learned—I also asked questions and tried to answer them.

☐ I had my own opinions about what I was reading.

what...? How...? Why...? where...? maybe...!

☐ I grew an idea about information or ideas in a text. For example, I asked a question and answered it, made a comparison, or disagreed with the text.

☐ I explained my idea and used details from the text to support it.

Penguins are very good parents.

?

SELECTED ASSESSMENT EXAMPLES

Learning Progression

	Grade 2	Grade 3
Main Idea(s) and Supporting Details/ Summary	I can say the big topic a text (or part of a text) teaches me. I can name information about that topic, which I learn from parts of the text. *MAIN TOPIC (Animal Families)*	As I read, I ask myself what the text is mostly about. To figure out the main idea, I see if there is a pop-out sentence that captures it. I can say the main idea in more than just a word and am careful to name the main idea of most of the text. I can also choose important supporting details (or points) that go with the main idea. I summarize briefly, leaving out unimportant things. *MAIN IDEA (Mothers do a lot to care for their young.)*
Cross Text(s) Synthesis	When I read several books (or parts of one book) on the same topic, I add what I learned from one text or part of text onto what I learned from the other text or part of text in no special order. *BUGS / ANTS (This tells MORE about...)*	When I read two texts (or parts of a text) that teach about the same subtopic, I can find the information on a subtopic from both texts (or parts of one text) and put that information together. *AND... BUT....*

	Grade 2	Grade 3
Retelling/Summary/Synthesis *Within Text*	As I read, I see that a story has parts and I can talk briefly about a part that I just read. After I read another part, I can put the parts together and talk about them. At the end of a story, I can retell it by saying something about the main character(s) and the big events, in order. RETELL → MAIN CHARACTERS, SETTING, BIG EVENTS "This part is about..."	As I read a novel, I can think back over and briefly summarize the parts of the story that relate to what I'm reading. When I finish a book, I can briefly summarize it in a way that shows what I know about the story and its story elements. I talk about the characters—their traits and wants—and recap especially important events using sequence words. Alternatively, I may talk about the problem and solution. If the character learned a life lesson, I mention that, most likely at the end of my summary. RETELL → CHARACTERS, BIG EVENTS, PROBLEM + SOLUTION, LESSON
Critical Reading *Growing Ideas*	When I read even just one picture or page, I have a lot of ideas and questions. For example, "How does that bug get food?" Sometimes I think up answers to those questions or find them in the book. What...? How...? Why...? Where...? Maybe...!	When I talk or write about a text (or a text set) I not only summarize it, I also grow my own ideas. For example, I might ask a question and try to answer it. When I am asked to apply what I have learned to a real-world problem or situation, I can do so. I notice when what I'm learning doesn't match my prior knowledge/ experience, and I think about what to make of that. ? Penguins are very good parents.

May be photocopied for classroom use. © 2015 by Lucy Calkins and Colleagues from the Teachers College Reading and Writing Project. *Reading Pathways, Performance Assessments and Learning Progressions: Grades 3–5* (Heinemann, Portsmouth, NH).

GRADE 3 UNIT 2 PREASSESSMENT SAMPLE RESPONSES

Following are sample responses for each question, at a range of levels. These samples will help students notice if they have done similar work in their responses, and thus will be a helpful part of their self-assessment. These can also serve as mentor texts to help your students identify specific ways they can lift their work to the next level.

Question	Approaching Level 2	Level 2	Level 3
1. Summarize the article, "Start Your Engines." *Main Idea(s) and Supporting Details/ Summary*	**NOTE to teacher:** *Compare your students' work to level 2. If it does not meet level 2 work, then consider it to be "approaching level 2."*	This teaches about car racing. Race cars can go 330 miles per hour! Formula One cars have wings that keep them from flipping. *Responses at this level tend to name just the topic of the text. Sometimes students just list facts that might be unimportant.*	"Start Your Engines" is about the ways that different kinds of cars are built and the different ways that they race. Stock cars and F1 cars race around tracks many times, but drag cars race in a straight line. *Responses at this level name the main idea of the text and also provide details to support the main idea.*
2. Both "Start Your Engines" and "Cars with Wings" include information about an important subtopic—the design of Formula One cars. Explain briefly what these texts teach about the design of Formula One cars. *Cross-Text(s) Synthesis*	**NOTE to teacher:** *Compare your students' work to level 2. If it does not meet level 2 work, then consider it to be "approaching level 2."*	F1 cars race on tracks, they can go more than 220 mph, and they have wings on the front and back of the car. *Responses at this level often combine two related details or may add information learned from one part to another.*	The F1 cars look like small planes because they have wings. The wings on the front and the back of the car help keep the car from flipping. In F1 cars the driver sits in the middle of the car. *Responses at this level tend to compile information across sources—often in a listlike fashion.*
3. Summarize the article "Racer Danica Patrick." *Retelling/Summary/Synthesis (Narrative)*	**NOTE to teacher:** *Compare your students' work to level 2. If it does not meet level 2 work, then consider it to be "approaching level 2."*	Danica's Dad helped her race go-karts. She moved away from home to train and won a big race and won an IndyCar race. *Responses in this level tend to include the main character(s) and major events in order of the text.*	As a kid, Danica Patrick learned to race go-karts. People thought she shouldn't do it, but she was so determined she didn't give up even when she crashed. In high school, she moved to England to train. She won a big race. Her hard work paid off. *Responses in this level tend to include story elements—characters and their traits, important events in sequence, setting, and problems and solutions.*

SELECTED ASSESSMENT EXAMPLES

Question	Approaching Level 2	Level 2	Level 3
4. Write briefly about one idea you have grown from these texts. *Critical Reading: Growing Ideas/ Questioning the Text*	**NOTE to teacher:** *Compare your students' work to level 2. If it does not meet level 2 work, then consider it to be "approaching level 2."*	I wonder how much race cars cost? I bet they are way more expensive than regular cars. *Responses in this level tend to show students asking and answering questions and tend to include students' own opinions about what they are reading.*	I think that the drivers need to know how to drive differently for the different kinds of cars. Some go faster and some go around a track, not straight. When Danica was learning to race, she had to go to England to get special training. I'm not sure why England teaches more than the USA. *Responses in this level tend to show students have grown an idea, explained it, and used details from the text to support it.*

Argument and Advocacy: Researching Debatable Issues
Grade 5: Nonfiction, Unit 3

Readers, today you will read three texts about cellphones in schools. Read text 1, then answer questions 1 and 2 on a separate sheet of paper. Then read the rest and finish up.

---

1. Summarize text 1, "Cell Phones Raise Security Concerns at Schools."

When summarizing, remember to:

- write about more than one main idea
- include carefully selected details to support each main idea
- keep your summary brief
- write about the ideas in the text, not your own opinions.

Main Idea(s) and Supporting Details/Summary

---

2. Read lines 6–8 from text 1, "Cell Phones Raise Security Concerns at Schools."

An undercover investigation by police found that at least 24 devices had been stolen over two months at the school, according to nbcphiladelphia.com.

Why is this line important to the text?

When writing about how one part of the text fits in with another, remember to:

- explain how the part in question fits into the whole structure of the text and with the main ideas
- use academic language: This part explains/describes/supports/introduces . . .
- include evidence or details from the text to support your explanation
- write just a few sentences.

Analyzing Parts of a Text in Relation to the Whole

---

3. What is the author's point of view in text 3, "Cell Phones Should Be in Schools"? How does your knowledge of the point of view help you think about the text's content?

When analyzing point of view, remember to:

- name who the author is, as well as his role/age or the group he belongs to
- discuss how the author's points are influenced by the above
- write about why the narrator probably thinks or feels the way he does.

Analyzing Perspective

---

4. Based on this packet of texts, decide whether cellphones should be banned or allowed in schools. Imagine you are going to write a letter to your mayor and convince him or her that your position makes the most sense. Map out a plan for your persuasive letter to the mayor, making sure you reference the texts. (You do not need to write the actual letter, just your plan.)

When synthesizing among texts, remember to:

- pull together relevant and important information from different texts (or different parts of a longer text)
- organize that information.

Cross-Text(s) Synthesis

Please remember that including the bullets is a teacher's option. As students become more familiar with these performance assessments, you delete this scaffold. A version without bullets is available on the online resources.

Text 1

Cell Phones Raise Security Concerns at Schools

Many people think that students having cell phones in school is a great idea. However, cell phones in school can lead to problems.

One problem is theft. Cell phones can be stolen. In January 2012, police arrested 13 high school students in Bucks County, Pennsylvania. People accused them of stealing more than $4,000 worth of cell phones and tablets from their classmates. An undercover investigation by police found that at least 24 devices had been stolen over two months at the school, according to nbcphiladelphia.com. Theft is a real concern when cell phones are allowed in schools.

Another problem is cell phone use during emergencies. Many people want students to have cell phones in emergencies. But this might not be safe. The National School Safety and Security Services (NSSSS) says that people in charge should have cell phones during emergencies. But it may cause harm if *students* use their phones in emergencies. If thousands of students make calls at the same time during an emergency, that could slow down the phone system. The NSSSS website says, "The use of cell phones by students could . . . decrease, not increase, school safety during a crisis."

When students use their cell phones during emergencies, another problem can be caused. Students' calls may cause their parents to rush to the school during an emergency. Emergency workers might not want to have tons of parents running to the school. All those parents might get in the way during an emergency. They might make things less safe.

Schools must think about these concerns. They must think carefully about security. Only then should they decide what to do about cell phones.

C. J. Perkins
School safety officer in Walmouth County

1
5
10
15
20
25

Text 1: Cell Phones Raise Security Concerns at Schools ◆ PAGE 1

SELECTED ASSESSMENT EXAMPLES

Text 2

New York City Mayor Changes Cell Phone Policy in Schools

Mayor reverses a ban on cell phones that has existed since 1988

In January 2015, students in New York City received some happy news. Mayor DeBlasio changed the policy about cell phones in schools. Now, students could bring their phones to school. Now, school principals could decide the rules for using cell phones in their schools. Some of the options that principals can consider are:

- ask students to store their phones in backpacks or another place during the day

- say that cell phones can be used during lunch time or in special areas of the school

- allow cell phones to be used in classrooms for instructional purposes

"Parents should be able to call or text their kids," the Mayor said when he announced his reform. "Lifting the ban respects families."

Prior to this change, some had claimed that the "no cell phones in school" policy was not enforced fairly. Some schools enforced the ban strictly. Some schools with metal detectors could easily find out if students had cell phones. In those schools, which were mostly in low-income areas, students were having their phones taken away or having to pay each day to store their phones in vans parked outside of the schools. But other schools ignored the ban. As long as teachers did not see the phones, they were okay with students having them.

Many students are happy to be allowed to bring their phones to school. But not everyone agrees with this ruling. Many argue that phones are a major distraction in class. In an op-ed piece for *The New York Post*, Naomi Schaefer Riley argues it is a "terrible idea to allow cell phones in school." She claims that students already spend too much time staring at screens. She says students will now spend their class time looking at their phones. They should be paying attention in class instead. Teachers could make cell

1

5

10

15

20

25

Text 2: New York City Mayor Changes Cell Phone Policy in Schools ◆ PAGE 1 phones part of the lessons for student. But Riley says they will have to check kids' phones. They will need to make sure kids are doing educational work and not texting or visiting social media sites. Riley says, "Where once kids might have been using their phones to do some texting or even calling each other, now they can spend hours on social-networking sites, ignoring their [math] lessons."

Cell phones can be a distraction in class in another way. A phone ringing during a lesson can distract the other students and the teacher. Students report that when this occurs, the ringing is very distracting. In addition, some teachers argue that when mobile phones are banned in their classrooms, bullying decreases.

But other people say this change is a good thing. Yin Cherd, a parent from Jamaica, Queens, talked to *The Wall Street Journal*. She said, "When my daughter gets off of school I want to text her and she texts me." Cherd said she would worry about her children if they didn't have phones.

And some teachers are excited to bring cell phones into learning. Many apps can help students learn. There are apps that let students work on collaborative projects. There are apps that let teachers poll their students. Teachers can quiz students using their phones or let the class play games related to the lesson. There are even apps to support study skills and resources for history. Still, not all students have cell phones and that could be a problem.

Schools will have to think very carefully about how to make good rules for cell phone use. Schools will need more training on how to identify and prevent cyber bullying. And all schools will require that no phones can be out during tests.

Whatever rules are made about cell phones, though, some students might still find ways to break them. Lucia Paz, a 14-year-old from Brooklyn, told *The Wall Street Journal*, "At lunch I'll just play music," she said. "It's like a relaxer for me sometimes."

What do you think? Should your town allow cell phones in schools?

Article from NYBeat

Text 2: New York City Mayor Changes Cell Phone Policy in Schools ◆ PAGE 2

SELECTED ASSESSMENT EXAMPLES

Text 3

Cell Phones Should Be in Schools

Every day when kids go to school and they have to leave their cell phones behind them at home, that is a huge problem. Everyone has cell phones today (well, everyone over the age of 8). And telling kids that just because they are kids and in school that they can't bring their cell phones is not fair. Kids need their cell phones for the same reasons that adults need their cell phones. They want to keep in touch with their friends and check the Internet, too.

Sometimes after school we have play dates. That means we might need to use our phones and check with our parents that it's okay. If we don't have our phones in school, what are we supposed to do? They don't let you use the office to call home just for any reason. You have to have an emergency and they don't think a playmate is an emergency. But what if you forgot you had a playmate and you really needed to call home? You need your cell phone.

Also, if we could have our cell phones in school, we'd probably do a lot better in school. Like you could use your phone to look up how to spell words and to look up information like if you didn't know the capital of a country.

In addition, sometimes parents have to text or call their kids. For example, I had a dentist appointment two weeks ago and my mom forgot to tell me. She didn't have any way to let me know about it until the end of the day so I didn't know I had to go until school was over. If I could have had my cell phone in school, then she could have texted me so I would have been prepared.

This is why it is very important for schools to change the rules and let students bring their cell phones to school. Right now, in my school, if you bring your cell phone to school and your teacher sees it he or she has to take it away from you and your parent has to go to school to get it back. This is a very unfair policy which should be changed. Students should be able to have their cell phones in school.

A blog post entry, from Jeremy, age 11

Informational Reading Self-Assessment Rubric

	Level 4	Level 5	Level 6
Main Idea(s) and Supporting Details/ Summary	☐ I wrote about the main idea(s). ☐ I included a few carefully selected details that link to the main idea. ☐ I used the text structure in my response. ☐ I wrote a brief summary. ☐ I kept my own opinions separate from the ideas in the text.	☐ I wrote about more than one main idea. ☐ I included carefully selected details that support each main idea. ☐ I wrote a brief summary. ☐ I kept my own opinions separate from the ideas in the text.	☐ I wrote about several main ideas or a central idea. ☐ I identified the idea that seems the strongest. ☐ I supported my ideas/ claims with specific details or quotes, and chose evidence that is the strongest. ☐ I kept my own opinions separate from the ideas in the text.

(continues)

SELECTED ASSESSMENT EXAMPLES

Informational Reading Self-Assessment Rubric (continued)

	Level 4	Level 5	Level 6
Analyzing Parts of a Text in Relation to the Whole	☐ I wrote about why the author seems to have included one part of the text. What does it add? ☐ I explained how that one part is important to the whole text (e.g., it's an example of a main idea or it provides reasons to support the author's argument).	☐ I wrote about how one part fits with the whole structure and with the main idea(s). ☐ I used academic language to explain how one part is important to the whole text (e.g., it illustrates an idea/claim, it shows the implication of an idea). ☐ If the text was an argument, I explained which details went with which points.	☐ I wrote about how a part contributes to the development of the author's central idea or contributes in other ways to the text (for example, it engages the reader by . . .). ☐ I used academic language to discuss authors' techniques. ☐ If the text was an argument, I explained which claims were more strongly supported and which details were most convincing.

CAUSE & EFFECT
Q? A

Advances a main idea...

Raises a new perspective...

Suggests the significance of a point...

How is it connected?

This detail is convincing

Informational Reading Self-Assessment Rubric (continued)

Analyzing Perspective	Level 4	Level 5	Level 6
	☐ I named the point of view of the writer—firsthand or secondhand.	☐ I named the point of view and discussed how the author's point of view probably affected the slant in which the information was presented or the choice of information.	☐ I noted the details that reveal the author's perspective, and I wrote about how these details do so.
	☐ I wrote about how the author's point of view probably affected the information that was/ wasn't revealed in the text.	☐ I noted when the texts showed different points of view.	☐ I identified how the author's perspective was related to his or her vested interests or roles.
		☐ I wrote reasons why the narrator probably thought/felt as s/he did (when possible).	☐ I noted when two texts showed different points of view and/or when there were different points of view in one text.

FIRST HAND

SECOND HAND

GENERAL vs. SOLDIER

A vs. B

How do I know?
How is it shown.

tasty
nutrition   flavored
sugar X

SELECTED ASSESSMENT EXAMPLES

Informational Reading Self-Assessment Rubric (continued)

Cross Text(s) Synthesis	Level 4	Level 5	Level 6
	☐ I put together information and ideas about a topic from different texts or parts of a longer text.	☐ I put together information and ideas about a subtopic.	☐ I sorted information/ideas into subtopics or categories.
	☐ I organized the information into categories (if possible).	☐ I included information from several sources.	☐ I included information from several sources.
		☐ I formed categories (my own headings) and sorted the information that way.	☐ I explained which information came from which source.
		☐ When one author said one thing and another, something different, I could notice this. I tried to explain the differences. Was one text a firsthand account and the other, secondhand?	☐ I noted when one author says one thing and another, something different, and I try to understand and explain the differences in their information or ideas.

Learning Progression

	Grade 5	Grade 6
Main Idea(s) and Supporting Details/ Summary	I can figure out several important main ideas in a text, and I'm aware that sometimes those ideas thread through the whole text instead of being located in chunks of it. I can sort all the details in the text and weigh their importance so that I can also discuss important details that best support each of the main ideas. I am careful to keep my own opinion separate from the ideas presented in the text. I also avoid mentioning minor details. MAIN IDEAS	I can figure out several important main ideas in a text and weigh and evaluate which of those ideas seems most significant in the text. I am careful to include in my summary only what the text says, and none of my own opinions, ideas or judgments. MOST SIGNIFICANT / minor detail
Analyzing Parts of a Text in Relation to the Whole	When thinking about why a part is important to the text, I think not only structurally about how the part goes with other parts, but I also think about how the part advances the author's main ideas/claims. I check whether the part in question illustrates an idea/ claim, raises a new perspective, or shows an implication of an idea. I can use academic terms to talk about this. When a part of the text feels extraneous, I can talk about its relationship to the main ideas/ claims (background, implications, another perspective). When I am reading an argument, I can explain which details go with which points. Suggests the significance of a point... Advances a main idea... Raises a new perspective	I am able to take even a small part of a text—a sentence, a few lines, a text feature—and think about the role that the part plays in the whole text. I ask myself, "What does this part contribute? How is it connected? Does this part engage the reader, or does it help to develop a central idea? How?" I use my knowledge of authors' techniques to talk about this. I can also study one aspect of a text (an event, an individual) and discuss how this part of the text was introduced and developed (e.g., through anecdotes). When I am reading an argument, I can explain which claims are most strongly supported and which details are most convincing. How is it connected? This detail is convincing

SELECTED ASSESSMENT EXAMPLES

	Grade 5	Grade 6
Analyzing Perspective	I can notice when two texts on the same topic are written from different points of view, and notice ways in which the content (or the way the texts are written) will be different because of those different points of view. I think specifically about why the narrator thinks and feels as he or she does. Might the person's perspective come from life experiences, group membership, role, time period? For example, I notice if one text is a diary in the voice of a general and another is a diary from a foot soldier, and I think about how their roles led them to want different things.	I am aware that the author brings out his or her perspective by choosing to highlight particular incidents, voices, issues, and stories. I think about how this might relate to the author's vested interests and roles. I am also aware of multiple points of view in the text and can separate them from the author's point of view. I can also point to places in the text where the different points of view and perspectives have led to particular word choices.
Cross Text(s) Synthesis	As I read texts on a topic, I collect information and ideas by subtopic and form categories with my own headings. I sort what I am learning about the subtopic under those headings. This means the organization of my learning may not match the organization of the original texts. I am aware that sometimes one text contradicts another. When this happens, I think, "Which author is saying which points?" I wonder whether the differences come from the author's point of view (e.g., might differences come from one being firsthand and one secondhand?).	I organize what I'm learning about a topic into subtopics—categories, points, or main ideas. I can keep track of the major ideas each individual author contributes to my overall understanding of the topic/issue. I am aware that sometimes one text contradicts another. When this happens, I think, "Which author is saying which points?" I wonder whether the differences come from the author's point of view (e.g., might differences come from one being firsthand and one secondhand?). I also consider whether an author has vested interests that explain the differences.

GRADE 5 UNIT 3 PREASSESSMENT SAMPLE RESPONSES

Following are sample responses for each question, at a range of levels. These samples will help students to notice if they have done similar work in their responses, and thus will be a helpful part of their self-assessment. These can also serve as mentor texts to help your students identify specific ways they can lift their work to the next level.

Question	Level 4	Level 5	Level 6
1. Summarize "Cell Phones Raise Security Concerns at Schools."	This is about how cell phones in school are bad. One reason is because they could get stolen. Another reason is students using their phones during emergencies. You wouldn't want a ton of parents to come to the school in an emergency.	The author argues that cell phones in schools can cause problems. One problem is theft. Another problem is that if too many students call during emergencies that can slow down the phone system. Also, students can all call their parents and their parents would come to the school, which might be unsafe.	The author, a school safety officer, explains why he thinks that cell phones in schools are a security problem. He argues that having cell phones in schools can lead to theft. In addition, he also argues that during emergencies students using cell phones can slow down phone systems and also bring parents to the school, which might not be safe. He ends up by advising schools to consider safety concerns before deciding to allow cell phones or not.
			Responses at this level will identify a second main idea or a central idea from the text and show how ideas are supported. Responses will include specific details or quotes, and students will weigh evidence, considering which evidence is strongest. At this level, the writer is expected to weigh the importance of details so as to discuss particularly important ones. In this case, the writer could have included minor details such as the cost of the theft of cell phones in the example given in the article or the number of devices stolen but did not. The writer did not come out and explicitly discuss the choice of what parts of the text to include but the details chosen suggest that the writer made the decision to weave in parts that are the most important.
Main Idea(s) and Supporting Details/ Summary	*Responses in this level name the main idea of the text and also provide details to support the main idea. If the text being summarized is structured in a clear way, the summary often reflects the structure.*	*Responses at this level will refer to multiple main ideas and will give specific details from across several parts of the text as support. Although students at this level often quote the text, they need not.*	

SELECTED ASSESSMENT EXAMPLES

Question	Level 4	Level 5	Level 6
2. Read lines 6–8 from text 1, "Cell Phones Raise Security Concerns at Schools." An undercover investigation by police found that at least 24 devices had been stolen over two months at the school, according to nbcphiladelphia.com. Why is this line important to the text? *Analyzing Parts of a Text in Relation to the Whole*	I think they put this line in to show a reason why cell phones are bad. *Responses at this level explain not just connections in content across parts but how one part fits with the rest of the text structurally. The writer is apt to also discuss how the part relates to the main idea of the text. If the text is an argument, the writer will point out how the author uses reasons and evidence to support points.*	This line is important because it helps support the point that cell phones in school can lead to the theft. *Responses at this level point out how one part fits with the text structurally and with the author's main ideas. This may involve discussing how the part in question connects to a main idea of that section of the text. Additionally, the writer will use more academic language. If the text is an argument, the writer will point out which reasons and evidence support which points.*	This line is important because it supports one of the author's major points—that cell phones in schools can lead to theft. This point supports the author's overall idea that cell phones in school can cause security concerns. *Responses at this level point out how the part helps to develop the main idea(s) of the text and how those main idea(s) help to develop the central idea. The writer may alternatively discuss another way that the part contributes to the text (engaging the reader). If the text is an argument, the writer will comment on whether or not the point in question is well supported. In this response the reader did not comment on how well supported the point was, but otherwise it fits level 6.*
A second set of possible responses to question 2	This part is important because it shows a reason why cell phones should not be in schools.	The author is making an argument that cell phones should not be in schools and this line is important because it supports one of the author's reasons. It shows that cell phones can be stolen.	This line is important because it supports one of the author's major points—that cell phones in schools can lead to theft. This point is supported but there is only one example of theft. That's not a lot. This point supports the author's overall idea that cell phones in school can cause security concerns.
3. What is the author's point of view in text 3, "Cell Phones Should Be in Schools"? How does your knowledge of the point of view help you think about the text's content? *Analyzing Perspective*	The author is writing a first-person blog post. He wants cell phones in schools so he is saying good things about them. *Responses at this level tell whether the account is firsthand or secondhand (or whether the account is written in first person), and discuss how the author's point of view affects the way the information is presented.*	The author is an 11-year-old boy writing a blog post. This is important because since he wants cell phones in schools he is only saying good things about them like that they can help you arrange play dates. *Responses at this level discuss how the author's point of view affects the way the information is presented and also includes reasons the author or narrator might think or feel a certain way.*	The author is an 11-year-old boy named Jeremy. It seems like he is talking to other kids about things that kids think are important like play dates and going to the dentist. He doesn't think about what reasons he could give that would be most convincing to adults who might be against kids having cell phones in school. *Responses at this level note how the author's point of view is affected by his vested interests, and explain different points of view found in the text.*

May be photocopied for classroom use. © 2015 by Lucy Calkins and Colleagues from the Teachers College Reading and Writing Project. *Reading Pathways, Performance Assessments and Learning Progressions: Grades 3–5* (Heinemann, Portsmouth, NH).

Question	Level 4	Level 5	Level 6
4. Based on this packet of texts, decide whether cellphones should be banned or allowed in schools. Imagine you are going to write a letter to your mayor and convince him or her that your position makes the most sense. Map out a plan for your persuasive letter to the mayor, making sure you reference the texts. (You do not need to write the actual letter, just your plan.) *Cross-Text(s) Synthesis*	Cell Phones Should Be in Schools • They help you make play dates. • Parents won't worry about their kids if the kids have cell phones. • Teachers can use the phones to help kids learn more. *Responses at this level tend to include ideas that are sparked by information from several parts of the text(s). When possible, readers do not just repeat the information, but they do something with it (compare, connect, wonder, reorganize.).*	Cell Phones Should Be in School • You need them in emergencies • play dates • dentist. You need them to help you to succeed in school. • Apps can help students work on group projects, take quizzes and play games. • You can look up how to spell words and capitals of countries. *Responses at this level tend to organize information about the subtopic by putting information into larger categories. They often create their own headings for the categories. Responses at this level might include more text detail than other levels and may highlight different perspectives, when applicable. In this response, the reader did not note where texts disagreed, but otherwise this fits level 5.*	Cell Phones Should Be in School • You need them in emergencies • play dates (text 3) • dentist (#3). You need them to help you to succeed in school. • Apps can help students work on group projects, take quizzes and play games (#2). • You can look up how to spell words and capitals of countries (#3). But some say they are a distraction in class (#2) and a security problem (#1). If students use them properly, this won't be a problem. *Responses at this level track information across texts and reorganize the information into new subcategories. Readers indicate the source of the information and the different information and perspectives provided across texts.*

SELECTED ASSESSMENT EXAMPLES

Question	Level 4	Level 5	Level 6
A second set of possible responses to question 4	Cell Phones Should Be In Schools • They help you make play dates. • They help you with schoolwork. • They help you if you have an emergency.	Cell Phones Should Be in School • You need them in emergencies • play dates • dentist. • You need them to help you succeed in school. • Apps can help students work on group projects, take quizzes, and play games. • You can look up how to spell words. • C. J. Perkins says they are a problem because of theft. He just cares about security because he's a security guard.	Cell Phones Should be In School You need them in emergencies • play dates (text 3) • dentist (#3). • C. J. Perkins says they are harmful in emergencies (#1) but if there are rules, then it won't be a problem. He may want to scare schools away from using cell phones because he's a security guard. You need them to help you to succeed in school. • Apps can help students work on group projects, take quizzes, and play games (#2). • You can look up how to spell words and capitals of countries (#3). • Naomi (#2) says kids will be playing on social media and not doing work but she doesn't know that for sure.